COMING INTO COMMUNION

SUNY series in Feminist Criticism and Theory
Michelle A. Massé, editor

Coming into Communion

Pastoral Dialogues in Colonial New England

Laura Henigman

STATE UNIVERSITY OF NEW YORK PRESS

Published by
State University of New York Press, Albany

© 1999 State University of New York

For information, address State University of New York Press,
State University Plaza, Albany, N.Y., 12246

Production by Cathleen Collins
Marketing by Patrick Durocher

Library of Congress Cataloging in Publication Data

Henigman, Laura, 1960–
      Coming into communion : pastoral dialogues in colonial New England
/ Laura Henigman.
            p.   cm. — (SUNY series in feminist criticism and theory)
      Includes bibliographical references and index.
      ISBN 0-7914-4337-X (alk. paper). — ISBN 0-7914-4338-8 (alk.
paper)
            1. Women in Christianity—New England—History—18th century.
2. New England—Church history—18th century.   I. Title.
II. Series.
      BR530.H46   1999
      277.4'07'082—dc21   98-56189
                                                                                                          CIP

10 9 8 7 6 5 4 3 2 1

For Bill.

Contents

Acknowledgments

Writing a book is an isolating process, but finishing one is a pleasurable occasion for mentioning all those friends and colleagues who have been a part of it for these many years. A Charlotte Newcomb Fellowship and Columbia University President's Fellowship supported the research in its earliest stages. I benefited from the expert guidance of the librarians and staff members at the Massachusetts Historical Society, the Massachusetts Archives, the Beinecke Library, Columbia University's Butler Library, the New York Public Library, Union Theological Seminary, Essex Historical Institute, Ipswich Historical Society, and Newbury Historical Society. I owe more than they can know to Emory Elliott and Andrew Delbanco, who in their different ways have always been my best readers and professional models. Meryl Altman, Jeannie Van Asselt, and Beth Harrison, through their friendship and incisive conversation, helped me understand, at a very early stage of its conception, what this book was really about. Stacey Olster read the entire manuscript at a critical point in its development and generously contributed her time and powerful editorial intelligence to keep it in a reasonable shape. The readers for the State University of New York Press saw past the flaws in the initial manuscript version and provided generous encouragement and advice on how to bring out what was most valuable in it. The steadfast friendship of Alice Robertson and Ursula Appelt helped me keep my sense of humor and humanity during the writing process. I must pay tribute as well to my students, with whom I have learned so much about writing. Finally, I would also like to thank my parents, in the face of whose relentless cheerfulness it is all but impossible to descend too far into a writer's dark night of the soul; my sister, whose serenity and determination I resolve every day to emulate; and last, my husband, Bill, who has been nothing less than the best gift of my life.

Abbreviations

DCWS	John Rogers, *Death the Certain Wages of Sin*, (Boston, 1701).
FN	Patience Boston, *A Faithful Narrative of the Wicked Life and the Remarkable Conversion of Patience Boston* (Boston, 1738).
JER	*A Jonathan Edwards Reader*, ed. John E. Smith, Harry S. Stout, and Kenneth P. Minkema (New Haven: Yale University Press, 1995).
LC	Thomas Foxcroft, *Lessons of Caution to Young Sinners* (Boston, 1733).
M	Benjamin Colman, *The Government and Improvement of Mirth, According to the Laws of Christianity* (Boston, 1707).
PV	Benjamin Colman, *Practical Discourses upon the Parable of the Ten Virgins* (1707); Boston, 1747.
RT	Benjamin Colman, *Reliquiae Turellae, et Lachrymae Paternae. The Father's Tears over His Daughter's Remains . . . To Which Are Added, Some large Memoirs of Her Life and Death* (Boston, 1735).
SG	Benjamin Colman, *Some of the Glories of Our Lord and Saviour Jesus Christ, Exhibited in Twenty Sacramental Discourses Preached at Boston in New-England* (London, 1728).
SP	Eliphalet Adams, *A Sermon, Preached on the Occasion of the Execution of Katherine Garret* (New London, 1738).

Introduction

"My thoughts are my own when they are in, but when they are out they are another's." Thus Susanna Martin, accused Salem witch, tartly answered her judges when they inquired into her alleged witchcraft. People accused of witchcraft at Salem could avoid execution by confessing, but Martin refused to do so, and was hanged in June 1692.[1] Her remark testifies to the peculiar dilemma that a "witch" faced: keeping silent would give her no chance to affect her destiny, but speaking would involve self-betrayal or lying. Forced to speak and yet de-authorized as speaker, Martin risked losing control over her language, thus playing no more than a ritualized role in someone else's drama if she exchanged words with the court, and we can admire her choice not to play. Her remark, in fact, nicely illustrates one way of looking at all Puritan women's discourse in the seventeenth century: that their speech was dangerous to themselves and others, that any dialogue in which they engaged would be highly coercive, that in any event they were silenced either through exacted conformity or banishment, excommunication or, as in Martin's case, execution.

Certainly, all linguistic exchanges are inflected by the type of power relations Martin worried about. Not all encounters between colonial New England women and powerful men, however, were so overtly confrontational. Not all pushed at the margins of community, functioning to define and expel difference, as did the court examinations at Salem. Some encounters, on the contrary, occurred safely within the boundaries of community, functioning to establish shared values and a shared language. Pastoral dialogues, exchanges between ministers and their parishioners, were supposed to function in this way: laywomen (or laymen) would testify to or worry aloud about their spiritual identities, and ministers would listen, counsel,

1

admonish, and direct them. The genre of pastoral dialogue testifies, therefore, to the persistence of two competing values within the reformed congregationalist tradition: the necessity that each person work out his or her own salvation, and respect for the authority of the clerical calling.

This book takes the pastoral relationship as a central focus for New England religious culture, and examines the way in which power was exercised in those relationships. I have chosen texts that represent dialogues in which women's voices are not brutally suppressed, that is, dialogues that represent less stark confrontations than do the witchcraft or excommunication trials, in which women's voices had more staying power than Susanna Martin imagined. What happens in such dialogues, whether they are preserved in recorded conversations, in the exchange of written letters, or in other records of clerical preaching and lay response, is that, as Martin feared, meanings get destabilized. In the course of conversational exchange, thoughts get "out" and become "another's" to repeat and revise, decontextualize and recontextualize.

While for Martin, this meant that her own words could be used against her, the cases I have chosen for this study suggest other possibilities for such destabilization, possibilities that women's voices might be, not silenced, but incorporated into religious discourse; that ministerial language, not laywomen's language, might, once "out," be revised or co-opted, quoted back with a difference by "another." In the pastoral dialogues I describe, women who did let their thoughts get "out," were able to use the authorized discourse of their culture to give expression to their own concerns and in fact to reinfluence their clerical partners. I want these readings to demonstrate that it is through the study of dialogue that we can understand how religious communities negotiate coherence despite variations in the way their members read the Bible, conduct their spiritual lives, and imagine their communities; it is through the study of dialogue that we can understand, that is, how much diversity religious communities can incorporate. In addition, it is through the study of dialogue, I believe, that we can understand one avenue through which theological change takes place.

By focusing on pastoral relationships, I am arguing that the laity played a constitutive role in early New England religious culture. Much of colonial New England scholarship since the 1970s has been at pains to argue that the intellectual history of the type practiced by Perry Miller, the founder of modern Puritan studies, is severely limited in its ability to help us understand culture beyond the functioning of a small group of admittedly prolific clergymen. New England religion, historians have wanted to show, was not simply handed down from Harvard and Yale to lay New Englanders; church history does not consist solely in pamphlet wars between clerics. While following Miller in my conviction that religious discourse remains crucial to understanding early New England history, I have been influenced by work by European and American historians in "collective mentalities" that attempts to extend the study of the history of ideas to include wider populations, and to document, as far as it is possible, how nonclerical New Englanders lived with the religious ideas that were articulated by their pastors.[2]

The historian engaged in such a project must walk a line, though, between on the one hand, assuming that lay people simply followed the theological teachings articulated in the formal treatises that are the provenance of the intellectual historian, and on the other, exaggerating the divergence and indeed hostility of interests between laity and clerical elite. By taking pastoral interchanges as my focus, I develop a way of talking about religious communities that is sensitive to the diversity of voices and interests within them but that avoids, when appropriate, an overly simplistic story of oppression and resistance within a community. It is certainly true that the women I discuss here had nowhere near the freedom to speak and write that the men did. Clergy with social status, education, access to the press, and the authority of the church behind them certainly had more access to discourse and more power to deploy it, power to out-talk the women here. These dialogues testify, therefore, to unequal power relationships. But I believe that the words "unequal" and "relationship" must be given equal force in that descriptive phrase. An unequal distribution of power is still a distribution. As David Hall has written, the imperative within Protestant culture that even lay people read the Bible placed an important check on clerical power.[3] My study rests on the proposition that under most conditions the exercise of power in human affairs is multivalent; that exercise is most fascinating, I find, when it is understated and subtle rather than overtly repressive or resistant. The book builds into its methodology, therefore, a way of bringing into focus the various ways in which laywomen exercised the limited power they had within their clergy-dominated culture.

Trying to do justice to a vision of religious community that goes beyond the pronouncements of its clergy requires a different kind of reading. It means re-understanding even clergy-authored texts as pastoral documents, recreating their pastoral context and showing how they imagine an audience and respond to that audience's perceived needs. It means paying great attention to what scraps of lay writing we do have, and using them and clergy-authored texts as evidence of devotional practice ("lived religion") rather than the history of ideas. And especially, it means reading attentively within single texts so as to bring into focus traces of multivocalic, rather than monolithic, aspects of culture. Mitchell Breitwieser has applied this method of reading to Mary Rowlandson's captivity narrative, showing how moments of disruption within the text betray the conflicting impulses within Puritanism. William J. Scheick reads a variety of colonial woman-authored texts as "sites of logo-nomic conflict," or moments when authorized meanings and resistant mean-ings come into conflict.[4] My study shares the ambition of these scholars to deepen our understanding of the way texts actually function within culture, processing competing interests and values. To see individual texts as parts of a series of exchanges, to see them interacting in dialogue, is a strategy for read-ing that brings to the surface points of tension within a culture, tensions that play themselves out within literary texts themselves and as dramatic interac-tions between different speakers.

By definition, though, most pastoral dialogue takes place not within public ritual ceremonies but in the private space of religious devotionalism, crisis, and doubt. Direct records of such dialogues, therefore, don't always exist; moreover, the interchange between laity and clergy consists not only in conversations that may have on rare occasions been transcribed, or in exchanges of letters that survive, but also in lay people's listening, note-taking, and collating clerical pronouncements with their own scripture readings, past and present. I have selected a series of pastoral relationships that are docu-mented in some way and have reconstructed them, triangulating documents so as to recreate, as vividly as I could, the dynamic pastoral situation of which they were a part. In doing so, I make the most of a limited sample of lay docu-ments, for, as will become clear, more meanings emerge from the dialogic con-text than do by considering writers (especially women writers) in isolation.

In chapter 1, I show how women condemned for the crime of infanticide—murdering their own newborns—gave spiritual confessions that responded to or distanced themselves from the execution sermons they had heard preached for them, how that sermon was received by other elements of the community, and how those sermons themselves responded to the genre as it had been developed in previous examples, adapting as well to the specific pastoral situa-tion. Next, I examine the exchange of letters between Benjamin Colman and Jane Colman Turell, a poet active in the 1720s and 1730s, and place her devo-tional acts, including the poems for which she is remembered today, in the context of that dialogue. And finally, I consider a Great Awakening text, Sarah Edwards's narrative of her spiritual experience, as a document most revealing if considered not as a heroic composure by a woman unaccustomed to writ-ing religious treatises but as a text generated as part of a continued pastoral relationship with her famous husband, Jonathan, and standing in significant dialogue—not just relationship, but dialogue—with his own Great Awakening writings. In each case, common concerns and a common vocabulary unite all dialogue participants from the start—but it is in the interchange of voices that we can see extra meanings.

I believe that attentiveness to the multivocalic nature of religious discourse proves particularly helpful in illuminating the transition between seventeenth- and eighteenth-century New England culture, and all my examples are chosen from the years 1690 to 1750. In fact, it is Miller himself who directs me to this period, by arguing that the exquisite rigor of Puritan theology declined over the course of the seventeenth century, so that by the 1690s, "real Puritanism" was dead. As an index of this decline Miller comments that "For more than a generation after 1689, no New England writer except Stoddard produced anything worth remarking in the way of a purely theological treatise."[5]

It is precisely this refocusing of clerical energies on their pastoral rather than theological roles, that I am interested in examining, not only as a matter of methodology, but as an enterprise that is particularly appropriate to the several decades following that period of final "decline," as Miller would put it. Although these decades, referred to by one historian as the "glacial age,"[6] have traditionally been viewed as a period of dullness between two spectacular events—the Salem witchcraft trials and the Great Awakening—in fact the relationship between laity and clergy came into serious, if quiet, contention during these years. The Salem witchcraft outbreak itself (1692), which Miller described as a "peripheral episode" in New England history, signals the beginning of such a period. Historians of witchcraft have developed the argument that witchcraft accusations tend to correlate with social conflict, or, as John Demos puts it, with "felt levels of distress." Salem had experienced, as Boyer and Nissenbaum showed, economic changes that were leaving behind some segments of the Salem community and advancing others; as Demos reminds us, the entire region had experienced long years of Indian wars and epidemics. But perhaps the most significant cause of "felt distress" or "sense of crisis" was the constitutional issue raised by the revocation of the Massachusetts Charter in 1684, a maneuver by the Crown to exert more control over its sometimes too-independent colony by reorganizing colonial government and imposing, by 1692, a royal governor.[7] The years and decades that followed saw a shifting of the accustomed forms of local control and in the status of all colonial authorities. And as colonial identity was being renegotiated, lay-clerical relationships were being renegotiated as well.

The responses within the clergy itself to its changing status are well understood. With the loss of the charter, Puritan hegemony came to an end. Dissenting sects had more rights. In the wake of an overall loss of influence and prestige, congregational ministers had to reexamine their roles as leaders, at once forming protective professional structures and experimenting with different techniques of outreach to lay people—changing their preaching styles, and allowing, in some cases, a proto-Arminian theology to creep into their sermons. Some members of the clerical establishment became interested in an international, ecumenical Protestantism, again rethinking traditional assumptions about the boundaries of significant religious community. At the same time, factional disputes within churches rent apart congregations, forcing lay people as well as clergy to confront, in very practical, immediate ways, the meaning of religious community.[8]

All the examples of pastoral dialogue I have chosen, therefore, took place in a cultural context in which religious affiliation was a vexed and thorny issue, raising questions that were quite real: What are the bases for unity and division? When can we say we belong together in spiritual fellowship, and when must we say we do not? How much diversity can we tolerate within a community that remains meaningful, and what differences must force us to dissolve? The variations in idiom and inflection to which I point below are subtle enough so that they were not heard as discordant by the participants themselves. But it is precisely those dialogues that took place well within the boundaries of community, I would argue, that are most important in understanding theological and social change. While more dramatic confrontational encounters can lead to the hardening of positions and excluding of variations, more gentle exchanges, in contrast, allow variations to flourish and persist within a discourse, and so to be available in time of more overt and dramatic change.[9]

It is one of the implicit ideas in this book that the lay voice gradually becomes more important in published discourse during the decades leading up to those revivals, when, it is usually thought, converted lay people were viewed as having potentially more religious credibility than an "unconverted ministry." Daniel A. Cohen's recent book on execution literature, which examines some of the same texts that I do in chapter 1, makes the argument that that literature introduced the lay voice into public discourse with considerable authoritativeness, so that the authority of the lay voice was not a new phenomenon by the time of the revivals.[10]

I turn to texts by women because they made up an increasingly important constituency for ministers in these decades. As early as 1692, Cotton

Mather remarked that the churches had "three Maries to one John." The pattern of significant alliance between clergy and women that Ann Douglas argued characterizes nineteenth-century New England, begins here, for as ministers renegotiated their relationships with their congregations, women, now dominating the church rolls, became crucial to their professional identities. And yet, historians are divided over how to interpret this fact. Does the increase in women's prominence in the churches signal simply a loss of prestige in that institution (Dunn)? After the crescendo of misogyny expressed at Salem, does female-centered imagery drop out of mainline congregationalist discourse (Porterfield) or does the female saint become a more prominent figure than ever within clerical discourse as a "type of the regenerate" (Masson, Ulrich)? What is the significance, anyway, of the appearance within homiletic literature of such imagery? Can we assume that by using gender-linked images of maternity or the Holy Spouse, that clergy were in fact making direct appeals to their special constituency of women, or that women responded to this imagery in a predictable way?[11]

For all these questions, it is the quality and meaning of clergy-laywomen relationships that is at issue. And yet the intimacy of that relationship is itself in some way the problem for scholars. The relationship is difficult to interpret because documentation of it is often controlled by one side alone. Most writings of colonial American women survive because they were solicited by ministers and shepherded through the press by those men to fit their agendas, edited and shaped, we may assume, to an undetermined extent by their pens. Once "out," women's words were "another's."

Each woman's text I describe in this book was solicited or otherwise taken up by a minister with access to the press who had his own reasons for revising and presenting it. For example, the only surviving text of Sarah Edwards's manuscript account of her religious experience, which is the focus of my chapter 3, is buried in a nineteenth-century biography of her husband, Jonathan Edwards. Her original manuscript has been lost. Edwards used her narrative as a source for his *Some Thoughts Concerning the Revival,* in which he describes the experiences of an unidentified saint—his wife—to defend the authenticity of the Great Awakening. When Jonathan did incorporate it into *Some Thoughts,* he not only summarized it, but concealed the identity and even the gender of "the person," as he refers to her, whose spiritual experience he was offering as a model.[12] While the textual history of Sarah Edwards's narrative may be read to illustrate the story of the erasure of women in New England discourse and culture, I propose that we turn these circumstances of publication (or perhaps I should say, survival) to our advantage.

If we look at women's documents as compromised texts, and evidence of women's suppressed textuality, we embrace a rather romantic model of the writer struggling for writerly autonomy. But by choosing instead to foreground each text's interrelatedness and interdependence, reflecting the pastoral relationship that generated it in the first place, we recognize that discursive power can be exercised in multiple directions. Such an approach is consonant with the movement within American women's history, as articulated by Susan Juster, to "[identify] relations of power, rather than the boundaries between men's and women's 'spheres', as the primary object of study."[13]

So, Jonathan's editings of Sarah show us, for one thing, how he read her, bringing his own agenda into sharper focus; a close comparison between his texts and hers underscores nuanced differences that exist between them; and, I will argue, the interactions of these two texts show how each shaped the other, in a mutual exercise of power and influence. All three chapters below, containing case studies in this dialogic way of reading, illustrate a way of reading our limited archive, turning textual liabilities into strengths.

Although my texts are arranged roughly chronologically, no one text that I discuss acts as a precursor or necessary condition or turning point. My interest is in plumbing the depths of local pastoral interactions, and my focus is therefore deep not wide. Rather than describing a specific historical change or development, as do Bushman's *Puritan to Yankee* or Miller's *Colony to Province* (to choose just two classics whose very titles indicate their developmental arguments), this book is more similar in its structure to Natalie Zemon Davis's *Women on the Margins*, containing loosely related case studies of the lives of colonial women. Its major burden is to demonstrate a model for reading, rather than to make a developmental argument. I have chosen texts that allow me to model that method of reading.[14]

Because women had less professional occasion to write than the ministers whose writings make up so much of our archive, because they had less access to print than did men, women's texts, when they did come into being, and especially, when they did get into the press or otherwise into the public record, did so under extraordinary circumstances. Typically, colonial women whose words got "out" occupied liminal positions (or were undergoing significant life transitions). The seventeenth-century New England women best known to posterity certainly occupied such positions: they were on trial for their lives, like Susanna Martin; or on the brink of excommunication, like Anne Hutchinson, who like Martin courageously argued with her judges during her trial; less dramatically, they were undergoing a conversion experience; or they were dying. Perhaps the best known Puritan women writers, Mary

Rowlandson and Anne Bradstreet, write from liminal positions: Rowlandson describes her captivity among the Narragansett Indians, which profoundly alienates her from her home community, recapitulating a ritual of conversion in many ways; and interestingly, Bradstreet adopts the persona of a dead or dying person both in her short essay "To Her Children," and in her poem "Lines before Childbirth," in which she speaks to her husband as if from beyond the grave, imagining her death in childbed. The women who figure in this book are women on trial for a capital crime, women who have had a significant religious experience, women who are dying (and dead by the time of publication)—or some combination of these. It is at such moments of liminality that women's voices, usually deauthorized, speak with most authority; it is also at these moments that women's voices tend to get preserved; and these are moments as well of the most intense pastoral interaction. The particular text selections here, therefore, reflect the idiosyncrasies, but also the logic of the archive.[15]

"Coming into Communion"

In each of the examples I discuss, a woman is undergoing an arduous process of trying to articulate her relationship to the church community—a process, that is, of coming into communion. It is appropriate to meditate a little on the meaning of these two terms.

The seventeenth-century New England Puritans were infamously intolerant—excommunicating Anne Hutchinson, banishing Roger Williams, persecuting Quakers and accused witches, preaching endless accusatory jeremiads. Commenting from the provinces on the controversy over whether to grant Parliamentary status to Presbyterians and Independents, Nathaniel Ward, writing in the persona of the "simple cobler of Aggawam [Ipswich]" cautioned the Revolutionary Puritans in England against a policy of toleration, urging them "rather to compose than to tolerate differences in religion."[16] Ward's comment is worth pausing over if we direct equal attention to the other part of his prescription: "to compose differences." The word implies, of course, not a willingness to live with diversity, but a desire to create communion by striving toward consensus; it suggests as well that achieving unity is a process, and that crucially, it is a linguistic process—it takes place through conversation that looks for a common language, that composes. Clearly such "composing" can have its coercive aspects, and clearly when such conversation takes place among unequals, it might very well represent the coming into conformity of the less powerful speaker. Frequently, the genre of the dialogue, when it appears in New England literature, represents unequal relationships, functioning as a teaching tool in such texts as catechisms (such as John Cotton's *Spiritual Milk for Babes*) or missionary texts (such as Roger Williams's *Key into the Language* or John Eliot's *Indian Dialogues*), to bring the reader into theological knowledge, with an authorized voice who speaks the truth and an unauthorized interlocutor who listens and learns. Nevertheless, Ward's remark reminds us that, as a practical matter, consensus is after all the goal even for those who won't tolerate dissent and is achieved not just by expelling dissenters but by a process of linguistic exchange.

And this community, for all its well-known intolerance and misogyny, valued, indeed demanded, the dialogue process as part of its religious life, as it recognized that spiritual experience takes place not in utter isolation but in interaction with an environment; it constitutes, therefore, a narrative that unfolds in time. Edward Taylor, the poet and minister whose long career overlapped significantly with the decades of this study, gives us in his long poem sequence "Gods Determinations Touching His Elect," a vivid illustration of the importance within New England culture not just of theological orthodoxy, but of the process of coming into communion. Taylor, one of the more conservative New England ministers with respect to ecclesiology, structured his poem partly as a dialogue. It tells the story of an individual, "Soul," coming into communion, struggling to achieve the right amount of assurance of salvation so as to conscientiously become a full member of the church and take the Lord's Supper, or, as Taylor's conceit has it, enter into the "coach" riding to Heaven. What is at stake is not merely working out the right relationship with God, but working out one's relationship to a human community, the church. Therefore, getting into that coach is a matter of preparing oneself not only through introspection and prayer, but also through conversation with others.

Significantly, those conversations take place not only between Soul and the stock figures of Satan and Christ, but also between Soul and "Saint," a church member and perhaps a minister. In an extended section of "Gods Determinations," Saint labors to convince Soul that he or she is eligible for church membership. Typically, in their dialogues Soul expresses some confidence in his or her salvation status, which then disintegrates; he or she then has to be reintegrated by further dialogue with Saint. Dramatizing clerical commitment to the process of dialogue, Taylor's poem shows us that such congregational conversation could be a long and drawn out process, as Soul and Saint alternate for stanzas and stanzas:

Soul

> Methinks my heart is harder than a flint,
> My Will is Wilfull, frowardness is in't,
> And mine Affections do my Soule betray,
> Sedaning of it from the blessed way.

Saint

> Loe, Satan hath thy thoughts inchanted quite,
> And Carries them a pickpack fro the right.
> Thou art too Credulous: For Satan lies.
> It is not as you deem; deem otherwise.

Soul

> But I allow of sin: I like it Well.
> And chiefly grieve, because it goes to hell.
> And Were it ever so with you, I see
> Grace hath prevented you which doth not mee.

Saint

> I thought as you: but now I clearly spy,
> These Satans brats will like their Curst Sire ly.
> He squibd these thoughts in you, you know not how.
> And tempts you then to deem you them allow.[17]

The sequence emphasizes the role of the church community, represented by Saint, in stabilizing the individual Soul. Thus Taylor's poem (unlike his better known "Sacramental Meditations") testifies to the importance of pastoral dialogue to communal self-definition in the congregational tradition in which the New England churches partook, as part of everyday religious life. As in the pedagogical dialogues that appear in catechisms, Saint is clearly the more authoritative speaker here. But it is important to notice that it is Soul's worries that dictate the course of the conversation. Sometimes it is appropriate for Saint simply to deny Soul's fears: "It is not as you deem; deem otherwise." In other exchanges, Saint takes Soul's own images and recasts them in a more hopeful light. In the following passage, which may be read as witty repartee, both Saint and Soul pick up the other's words and turn them back with a twist:

Soul

> Such as are Gracious grow in Grace therefore
> Such as have Grace, are gracious evermore.

> Who sin Commit are sinfull: and thereby
> They grow Ungodly. So I feare do I.

Saint

> Such as are Gracious, Graces have therefore
> They evermore desire to have more.
> But such as never knew this dainty fare
> Do never wish them 'cause they dainties are.

Soul

> Alas! alas! this still doth me benight.
> I've no desire, or no Desire aright.
> And this is Clear: my Hopes do witherd ly,
> Before their buds breake out, their blossoms dy.

Saint

> When fruits do thrive, the blossom falls off quite.
> No need of blossoms when the seed is ripe.
> The Apple plainly prooves the blossoms were.
> Thy withred Hopes hold out Desires as Cleare.[18]

As stanza moves to stanza, first "grace," then "desire," and then "blossoms"
are recast with different inflections. Taylor thus depicts through his poetic
and pastoral sensitivity to language the mutuality of the pastoral relationship,
showing that the lay voice does not merely echo the cleric's, but gives audibil-
ity to its own concerns and its own idiom, which Saint follows. This segment
of dialogue, in fact, with its rewriting of poetic images, nicely introduces my
own readings of pastoral dialogues, for we will be concerned there too with
the ways in which specific images and terms are exchanged between speakers,
taking on varying and expanding meanings.

Of course the less stylized, "real life" dialogues that I examine below do
not resolve themselves so neatly as they do in Taylor's poem, where Soul,
coming into communion, embarks on the coach and participates in the harmonious music of the spheres. On the contrary, examining these dialogues to
underscore the *process* of coming into community must complicate our
understanding of community itself. Community, as I use the term, need not
mean unity or agreement, but instead constantly negotiated relationship. I
have found David Sabean's comment on his own study of early modern
Germany illuminating in this regard. "Community," he argues, need not be
understood in an idealized, utopian way. Rather, the study of community
must include the study of conflict and hostility. "By emphasizing relation-

ships, it can be seen that community includes both negative and positive elements, both sharing and conflict. From the theologian's or psychologist's point of view, then, community exists, where not just love but also frustration and anger exist. . . . What is common in community is not shared values or common understanding so much as the fact that members of a community are engaged in the same argument, the same *raisonnement*, the same *Rede*, the same discourse, in which alternate strategies, misunderstandings, conflicting goals and values are threshed out. . . . What makes community is the discourse."[19] His remark reminds us that discourse is by definition multivocalic, and that the history of early modern communities, even religious communities that have a great stake in "composing differences," will reveal dynamic interactions of variations within their respective discourses; turning our attention to dialogues helps us understand that community is precisely an amalgam of "alternate strategies, misunderstandings, and conflicting goals."

Part of my intention is simply to show that variations occur within a community without forcing it to a breaking point. Sometimes, alternative idioms can serve a subversive function, existing "underneath" the "official" language and practice. It is also the case, though, that different idioms can exist side by side in a discourse community without overtly registering conflict.[20] Specifically, these case studies will demonstrate that the "glacial age" decades leading up to the Great Awakening contain evidence of evangelical energies of the kind we associate with religious revivals. Revivals, with their emphasis on direct spiritual experience, the levelling of social distinctions, and consequent disregard for duly constituted religious authority, may be described as outbreaks of what Victor Turner calls *communitas* in the midst of rigidified society.[21] People undergoing periods of transition (liminality), which can include religious conversion, or who are otherwise marginal within society tend to perceive their own communities as united in the charismatic spiritual experience of an intimate God or closely held ideal. Such a phenomenon can be profoundly threatening to those who are unaffected by those liminal conditions (or conversions) and perceive themselves, as is the norm, as living within a society made up of complex, differentiated, and hierarchical relationships and institutions (a model that Turner calls "structure"), and certainly some of the reactions to the Great Awakening itself can be described as recoil at the disorderly *communitas* provoked by charismatic spiritual experiences.[22] My interest, however, lies not so much in identifying which "party" articulates which vision of religious community, but rather in showing that the two versions talk to each other continuously. I am most interested in Turner's terms, that is, insofar as they exist within a culture in dialectic with one another. To be sure, positions might be polarized at particular moments, but in general, especially in periods of relative calm, like the "glacial age" decades, I believe that people felt the legitimacy of both impulses: the security and logic of an orderly society and the seductions of a utopian *communitas*. In early New England culture, images of an orderly, hierarchical cosmos governed by a distant deity or of an inclusionary *communitas* with an intimate relationship with God are both heard as orthodox enough to get into print; even dialogues between two parties, say a minister articulating structure and a laywoman articulating *communitas*, will easily remind each of the alternative version that makes significant claims on both of them.

Partly, this kind of dialogue between significantly contrasting theological ideals was possible because the conversation was conducted in a biblical vocabulary, that is, a language that all agreed was authorized and sanctioned. Therefore, the speakers who articulated conflicting models did so in ways that were heard as friendly, not foreign. The gently polarized conversations described here served not to further alienate, but to remind of the other alternative, an alternative that makes powerful claims on the loyalties of the hearer.

The two recurring images that are most important to my analysis are the traditional and biblical images of the human relationship with God: the marital relationship and the mother/child relationship. Participants in these dialogues used one or the other of these images to describe spiritual experience; it is not surprising that that fundamental experience would be imaged in terms of a profound bodily experience, such as sexuality or pregnancy. Both bodily images, of course, in suggesting human relationships, also imply relationships to God.

And since, in Mary Douglas's words, "the cosmos is seen through the medium of the body," these images reveal as well how the speaker imagines his or her community. As Douglas explains, the "two bodies"—the human corporeal body and the social body—tend to be symbolized in terms of each other in religious symbol systems.[23] Therefore, images of intimate body experience— sexuality, pregnancy, or maternity—indicate not only the speakers' striving toward articulating his or her relationship with God, but also his or her understanding of how the whole community—a church community—is shaped. In general, images of polarized sexuality help describe a community with fixed hierarchies and structure, while the images of maternity, I will argue, tend to be associated more frequently with the idea of *communitas*.

I will argue that these images, though both typed "female," function during these decades in very different ways, competing with rather than complementing each other. Neither, I believe, has an inherent appeal to women just because it has some relationship to women's biographical experience. They help us understand, therefore, not only how the individual is working out her salvation, but also how she is coming into communion.

The Stories

In addition to the abstract issues that have engaged me, one of my desires in writing *Coming into Communion* has been to tell the stories of these mostly obscure women, stories that deserve to be retold and remembered. I have schooled myself in their idiom, trying to hear in their language the associations that they heard, assuming always that those associations had to be specific to the area in which they lived, the historical experience of their particular communities. But I have also given myself some latitude to use my historical imagination. Any historian must—especially a historian of women, who must ask new questions of the historical record, adopting different epistemologies. Sometimes, I have made an imaginative, though still historically informed step in interpretation, to push the limits of what our intractable sources tell us. Since I believe that we give the dead new life again mostly through narrative, I have allowed myself to contruct the stories of these women in narrative form, a form that humanizes and dramatizes their lives.

Chapter 1

To Love and Make a Lie

Narratives of Infanticide

"November 22 [1700]. A poor wretch at Newberry, called Hester Rogers, murdered her bastard child (had by a Negro)."[1]

A thin layer of snow had already coated the ground when Esther Rogers, trying to be as inconspicuous as her full-term pregnancy and periodic labor pains would allow, slipped out of the public house where she lived as a servant and walked hurriedly past the meetinghouse down to the pond. Soon afterward, the lifeless body of a newborn baby girl was found half buried in the dirt and snow. Thus began the first capital murder case in colonial Essex County. Esther, confronted with the evidence, was taken in to the Newbury jail for a month before being sent the ten miles south to the County seat of Ipswich to await trial. During the legal proceeding against her, Esther confessed to being responsible for the death not only of this child but also of one born four years previously, successfully concealed until now; and on July 16, 1701, a jury found her guilty of murder. The court directed that the sheriff "erect a Gibbet within the town of Ipswich at a place called Pyngrass Plain," and she was hanged there on July 31.[2]

Esther Rogers had begun her life in obscurity, by her class and gender counted among the least esteemed of New Englanders. She ended it, though, surrounded by an impressive array of prominent people. Judge Samuel Sewall had heard her case and recorded in his diary the pronouncing of her sentence; four Ipswich-area ministers had in one way or another attended her in the months before her death; her execution at Ipswich attracted thousands of spectators; and soon afterwards, local clergy arranged for a lengthy publication in

17

the Boston press containing an account of her crime and her last days, which they called *Death the Certain Wages of Sin*.[3]

Esther Rogers was not the only condemned criminal to be thus memorialized in early New England. Executions often became occasions for publication, not only of sermons by ministers but increasingly of other types of gallows-side material: criminal narratives taken from court papers, accounts of prisoners' conversations on the way to the scaffold, "last dying warnings" addressed to the spectators there, and possibly statements of religious conversion. At the turn of the century a number of New England women became the subjects of such books—always, like Rogers, after their executions for infanticide.[4] What made her case unique were its sensational details and equally sensational outcome, for during her imprisonment she experienced a religious conversion, the authenticity of which was not doubted by witnesses. This young woman, then, was the most successful convert among all the infanticides in the group, in two senses: first, she satisfied many people that she did achieve spiritual conversion; and second, that very success guaranteed that she was not consigned to silence and obscurity after her death but instead was allowed to record her story in her own words, inspiring as well the literary production of others. Esther Rogers was allowed to be a speaking celebrity and a heroine of her own story, and we know many details about her of the kind that have been lost for others in her situation.

Historians of early modern Europe and colonial America have remarked on the ceremonial aspect of staged executions, which were often described in books such as *Death the Certain Wages of Sin*, interpreting them as rituals asserting the power of the early modern state.[5] And certainly this execution fits that paradigm. As is important in these stagings, the criminal in this case accepts her punishment and the community's definition of sin through her religious conversion. My interest in the documents printed in *Death the Certain Wages of Sin*, however, comes less from their ritual character than from the fact that they are also representations of a pastoral encounter—in this case, a very complex one, involving many elements of the community. Three sermons by the Ipswich minister, by coincidence named John Rogers, form the center of the book and give it its title, but there are supplementary writings as well by five other ministers, by Esther herself, and by at least one other lay person, an Ipswich woman who was her confidante. The diverse material in the book lets us know that Esther Rogers became a community project of sorts in the months before her execution. In a note to the reader, Samuel Belcher, a local minister, says that the whole town (or, as he puts it, the

"Nation" of Ipswich), both clergy and laity, prayed for her and with her during her imprisonment. She received visitors in the Ipswich jail and evidently was allowed to visit people in their own houses for prayer and counseling as well. The contributions of all these persons to her book help us understand the complex process by which Esther Rogers came to believe she was saved as well as the pastoral values that guided the community of ministers and lay people as they helped her come to that realization.

   Death the Certain Wages of Sin represents, then, a complex pastoral dialogue, with a number of ministers and lay people "working" on a laywoman in spiritual crisis. Since Esther Rogers was memorialized after her death by people whose motives we may justly suspect, it may seem counterintuitive to hope to recover her voice from *Death the Certain Wages of Sin*: she is clearly playing a role, in the most coercive, highly ritualized situation imaginable. But, as Daniel Cohen has argued, part of the function of execution literature in eighteenth-century New England was precisely to foreground lay testimony and lay experience, "boldly privileg[ing] the spiritual insights and subjective experiences of . . . disadvantaged groups" and paving the way, in fact, for the crucial role these voices would play in the Great Awakening revivals.[6] There are indeed many of Esther Rogers's own words represented in *Death the Certain Wages of Sin*: a criminal narrative, a conversion story "taken from her own mouth," accounts of conversation that claim to be verbatim, her "last dying warning." It is precisely the strategy of *Death the Certain Wages of Sin* to represent her words as part of a multivocal conversation taking place within the community, to dramatize the cultural process of coming into communion. The book, then, illustrates the stake the community has in the lay voice, and in the process of dialogue. But the final editor of *Death the Certain Wages of Sin* seems surprisingly uninterested in weaving the distinct voices that participate in that dialogue together to present a coherent vision of community. The dynamic interchange of voices represented in execution literature reveal competing symbols for sin and community, a competition that predicts, interestingly enough, the more dramatically realized conflicts that will be revealed in the Great Awakening. *Death the Certain Wages of Sin* is unique among the literature of New England infanticide that appeared at the turn of the eighteenth century in that it exposes a greater than usual variety of pastoral agendas and techniques at play. The various ministers involved, and Esther Rogers herself, deploy subtle but significant variations in the way they discuss sexuality, variations that play significant roles in their theorizing about communal integration or alienation of an individual.

Clerical Anxiety and the Execution Sermon

By the time *Death the Certain Wages of Sin* was published, the execution sermon had become a recognizable ministerial genre, albeit a profoundly ambiguous one. Its most active author was Cotton Mather, whose very first publication, *The Call of the Gospel*, was a collection of sermons and accounts of pastoral encounters concerning James Morgan, executed in 1686 for murder. Mather, always a shrewd participant in the literary marketplace, returned periodically to the genre throughout his career, and just two years before Rogers's execution, published *Pillars of Salt*, a volume that included sermons addressed to a condemned Boston infanticide, Sarah Threeneedles, and the stories of twelve other convicted and executed criminals.[7] As its name suggests, *Pillars of Salt* is notable in containing no examples of repentant criminals, much less converted ones. While these examples may establish the minister as an authority on sin and provide stark warnings of its dangers, they do not speak well for the pastoral efforts of the ministry. On the contrary, execution literature most often presents portraits of a recalcitrant sinner and a very frustrated minister, a minister who must perforce do nothing but decry the sinner's resistance to him, documenting his own ineffectiveness while dwelling on the details of the crime. It is not a flattering professional self-portrait.

By its very hybrid form, *Pillars of Salt* illustrates well the professional pressures on the ministry. A collection of sermons like any other that might find its way into the press, it claimed a religious, teaching function. But it also made use of the sensationalist—and book-selling—appeal of a "true crime" story. Standard ministerial pronouncements compete with the details of lay infamy, as Mather literally interrupts the application section of his printed sermon to insert those twelve stories. While the application had always been the part of the sermon appropriate for comment on current events and conditions, surely *Pillars of Salt* stretches those boundaries to their limits. In other execution publications, including *The Call of the Gospel* and *Death the Certain Wages of Sin*, lay material is included after the sermons themselves, in an extensive appendix. Thus those works set up a dialogue between clerical and lay voices. And as this appended material becomes longer and more varied, as it is in Esther Rogers's book, it is less and less the case that it simply illustrates the minister's chosen sermon text. It exists, rather, in counterpoint and sometimes in contradiction to that sermon.

This is so even in those cases involving successful conversions, which presumably testify to clerical success rather than failure. In effect, two forms compete within the book: lay conversion narrative and clerical sermon. We are accustomed to granting sermons a privileged place in New England letters, but what we see here is evidence of generic bleed. David Hall has pointed out, rightly, that by inserting himself into the conversion story, the minister claims an essential ritualized role in what had always been construed as a highly personal, internal process.[8] While such a gesture looks like an attempt at professional aggrandizement, in *Death the Certain Wages of Sin*, which has six ministers lending their pens to the telling of Esther Rogers's story, surely it is more a case of clerical overkill. The spectacle of six Harvard graduates clamoring to attach themselves to the day's celebrity, a twenty-one-year-old servant girl condemned for killing her illegitimate, mixed-race child, suggests that we are entitled to wonder which Rogers, John or Esther, would sell the most books.

It was perhaps with Cotton Mather's example in mind that John Rogers's Ipswich colleagues urged him to choose for his publishing debut the three sermons he had prepared during his work with Esther Rogers. A number of his neighbors did all they could to squire it through the press. Five ministers contributed supplementary material. His uncle and senior colleague at Ipswich, the venerable William Hubbard, who had himself preached a sermon for Esther, wrote an introductory note. Nicholas Noyes and Joseph Gerrish, both with Newbury roots and Boston connections, collaborated on a second. Samuel Belcher, an area minister, seems to have collected the documents that make up the appendix to the sermons' supplementary material. John Wise, of neighboring Chebacco parish, who had himself paid a visit to Esther Rogers, contributed notes from that encounter. All are eager to take credit for the ministry for Esther's conversion, and all work strenuously to deflect attention from one Rogers to another, to give John's sermons rather than Esther's conversion story primacy in the book. Wise notes particularly that "the special instrumental cause of her Awakening and Comfort, was an Ambassador of Jesus Christ,"[9] and the other contributors also shower compliments on John Rogers for his work. In their introductory note, "To the Christian Reader," Noyes and Gerrish claim in praising him that even the work of conversion has become a ministerial function: "God hath Crowned his Ministerial Labours with good success, and hath owned and honoured his Ministry . . . with the convincing, humbling, comforting, and [as is generally believed] converting [so] leud, and rude, and wretched a Sinner." Significantly, though, while condemning Esther Rogers with such harsh language, they also rely on her own words to credential her clerical namesake, in a move that reflects the uneasy textual relationship between lay and ministerial authority within the volume. Three separate times in the book—in this section, in

Hubbard's, and in Wise's—Esther's own words on the night before her death are quoted to affirm John Rogers's central role: "O Blessed Rogers, O happy prison."

Even as they advance John Rogers with their laudatory comments, however, these elder ministers betray as well some frustration with their rising young star. Noyes and Gerrish more than once mention his modesty, especially his reluctance to publish his sermons, being "averse even to a fault, and very hardly perswaded to suffer it to be done." Their remark is, in one sense, a standard invocation of the modesty topos, similar to Anne Bradstreet's brother-in-law claiming to have stolen her manuscript across the ocean to be published without her consent. But these senior Harvard graduates, well accustomed to public discourse, seem to harbor something less than approbation for their younger colleague, who, as they so pointedly say, is not well known outside the Ipswich area.[10]

Most precisely, they appear to disapprove of John Rogers's homiletical commitments, his interest, that is, in addressing his congregation rather than his clerical colleagues. The purported reason for his reluctance to publish is that these occasional sermons—one preached at the trial, one at the condemnation, and one at the execution—are pastoral efforts directed at his community and at Esther Rogers herself, not theological disputations meant to engage a professional audience; he intended them, they say, as pastoral efforts, not as theological works, and he fears they would not stand up to the "cavelling" of an "adversary." They, however, are not impressed by the distinction that John Rogers makes between pastoral homily and theological treatise, and they are impatient with his idea that he is a mere shepherd of souls. While the young Ipswich minister is most concerned with his local audience, his professional colleagues see in the execution not only a plum publishing opportunity but also a chance for him to make a broader statement on public policy. And they are disappointed that he has not done so. Specifically, they seem uncomfortable with John Rogers's apparent willingness to pass up an opportunity to lecture the young on their besetting sin.

They say explicitly, in a defense of Rogers that is really an expression of their own reservations, that he "might have been more particular on this occasion, in setting forth the danger and mischief of the Sin of Fornication, for the warning of the Rising Generation." Curiously, the principal lesson they draw from the case of Esther Rogers is the danger of sexual activity, rather than the severity of the crime of murder, although the latter is the capital offense; it is "a Warning to such, as indulge themselves in the breach of the Seventh Commandment, least thereby they lead themselves into temptation, and so God leave them to break the Sixth." They hope that the lesson will be particularly potent for a very narrowly defined audience, young people, and that it "may be a means to startle the Rising Generation." They try to correct John Rogers's broader congregational emphasis by directing the reader's attention to his third sermon, which is the only place that he addresses youth in particular. And they note with some satisfaction that his uncle and colleague at Ipswich, William Hubbard, did preach at the time of Esther Rogers's trial more directly on the issue of youthful sexuality, taking as his scripture text 1 Cor. 6.9, "Know ye not that the unrighteous shall not inherit the Kingdom of God? Be not deceived; neither fornicators, nor idolaters, nor adulterers, nor effeminate, nor abusers of themselves with mankind."

Whether the contrast between Hubbard and John Rogers represents a generation gap, a real pastoral difference, or simply a division of labor between co-ministers in the Ipswich pulpit, it, together with Noyes's and Gerrish's comment, points to a peculiarity of New England infanticide literature generally. Although the capital crime for which the woman is condemned to die is murder, the focus of most of those turn-of-the-century sermons—John Rogers is a conspicuous exception—is not on murder but on "uncleanness," their most common word for the sexual transgression that led to the pregnancy. Generally speaking, this literature is a sampler of ideas about sexuality, presenting a theory of sexual sin and its etiology as well as a profile of those most vulnerable to it. What John Rogers doesn't do—and what clearly is Noyes and Gerrish's expectation that he *should* do—is provide a sociological analysis of uncleanness, one that links it most particularly with young people.

Rogers's omission is especially glaring when set against the emphasis on sexuality that characterized the execution sermons preached by others. When the infanticide Margaret Gallaucher was executed in 1715, Cotton Mather looked back over his own career and commented, "I cannot but think, that there is a *Voice of God* unto the Country in this Thing: That there should be so many Instances of Women Executed for Murder of their *Bastard-Children.* There are now Six or Seven such unhappy Instances, that are upon Record, and made *Pillars of Salt* in Printed Memorials. *Lo, God sends out his Voice, and that a mighty Voice,* in those Things. *Lord, help us to understand the Meaning in them.*"[11] His own *Warnings from the Dead* and *Pillars of Salt,* as well as John Rogers's *Death the Certain Wages of Sin,* were among those "Six or Seven" instances to which Mather refers, and his question here reflects the impulse that Noyes and Gerrish urge Rogers to follow: the impulse to make a large public pronouncement on this phenomenon, interpreting "the Voice of God unto the Country." Moreover, Cotton Mather's own answer to his question in the 1715 sermon is likewise one that Noyes and Gerrish would have liked to hear from John Rogers in 1701: the voice of God, Mather would say there, is giving New England a warning about "the sins of Unchastity."

"One Word": Sexuality and Separation

Women were executed in colonial New England most frequently for two crimes, witchcraft and infanticide. Historians have noted the connection between the outbreak of witchcraft accusations and prosecutions in Salem in the early 1690s and the loss of the Massachusetts Charter in 1684.[12] Prosecutions for infanticide spiked in the 1690s as well, as did the number of execution sermons that appeared in the press in that decade. The coincidence of infanticide and witchcraft prosecutions in the 1690s might suggest that outcast women functioned to help New England communities, whose Puritan roots were being loosened, sustain a sense of communal definition in a time of stress.[13] However, I will argue below that the rhetoric of sexuality in these sermons is remarkably gender-neutral, functioning not to exaggerate, but to mute the role of women in regulating community norms.

Not surprisingly, infanticide sermons tended to dwell on the role the execution has in maintaining communal identity by casting out a transgressor, protecting it from any threat. Modelling New England on the covenant community of the Hebrews, the ministers argue that sinners must be cast out for the spiritual health of the whole. Increase Mather tells Sarah Threeneedles, for example, "You have defiled the Land where you live. It should be an humbling Consideration to you, that all this Province of *New-England* must fare the worse, and be exposed to the wrath of Heaven if you should be suffered to live any longer in it."[14]

While the implicit threat to the community here is clear enough, these sermons go further in defining just what warrants that separation: consistently, they define that "uncleanness" more narrowly, as illicit sexuality. For example, the following passage, from a sermon included in a 1693 execution publication by Cotton Mather, illustrates well how two concepts, sexuality and separation, converge in the discussion of uncleanness.

> There is *One Word*, wherewith I am to acquaint you after all, 'tis in Zech 13.1, *There shall be a Fountain Opened* for *sin*, and *for Uncleanness*. Your *Sin* has been *Uncleanness*, Repeated *Uncleanness*, Impudent *Uncleanness*, Murderous *Uncleanness*: You must, like the *Leper*, cry

> out *Unclean! Unclean!* But behold, there is a *Fountain* set *Open* for
> you. Only be it known unto thee, that all thy known Sins must be
> *Vomited* out by thy Penitent *confession* of them, when thou comest
> unto that *Open Fountain.*[15]

The "one word" that Mather repeats over and over again signals his main
concern. The cry of the leper, perhaps the most dramatic feature of execution
sermons, establishes the levitical context and signals both sexuality and separation. The levitical mandate to which Mather refers here is that a leper, who
is not only ill but ritually impure, must live apart from the settlement and
identify himself to others so they may avoid ritual defilement through contact
with him: "And the leper in whom the plague is, his clothes shall be rent, and
his head bare, and he shall put a covering upon his upper lip and shall cry,
'unclean, unclean.' All the days wherein the plague shall be in him he shall be
defiled; he is unclean: he shall dwell alone; without the camp shall his habita-
tion be" (Leviticus 13.45–46). As is illustrated here, the Mosaic laws that provide the vocabulary of uncleanness to the New England ministry refer in their
original contexts to any sort of ritual impurity warranting separation from the
community, and more particularly disqualification from entering the temple.
The passage from Zechariah to which Mather refers clearly is talking specifically about religious idolatry as a form of uncleanness; however, in his usage,
here and in the sermon as a whole, it clearly means sexual sins. In this sermon, called "An Holy Rebuke to the Unclean Spirit," Mather scarcely mentions the sin of murder, which was after all the capital crime for which the
auditor, Elizabeth Emerson, had been condemned. In this passage, the fact of
the murder gets in only as an adjective to the more fundamental (sexual)
transgression ("murderous uncleanness").[16]

Many execution sermons for infanticides build on the levitical context
in their analysis of sex, typically using levitical categories to present a typology
of sexual misbehavior: lengthy and precise definitions, based on Leviticus, of
"uncleanness." Both Samuel Danforth the elder and Cotton Mather presented almost identical typologies of sexual sins, in ascending order of seriousness: self-pollution; fornication; (here Mather adds excessive enjoyment
of the marriage bed, which was perhaps his particular failing); adultery;
incest; sodomy (homosexuality); and buggery (bestiality). By increasing in
esoterica and sensationalism, these discussions may insulate the other listeners from the situation of the convict. Samuel Danforth's sermon for Benjamin
Goad, a young man condemned for bestiality, has this effect. More often,
though, these accounts imply as well a domino theory of sin: the ministers

warn that a sexual sin of lesser seriousness may lead to the next, more serious form.[17]

The "domino theory" of sin implies, in fact, that even the most severely condemned criminal stands in intimate connection to the community. Mather's sermon, for example, adds a twist to the standard progression: in the last, culminating position, he adds, quoting scripture, "looking upon a Woman to lust after her," and "filthiness" and "foolish talking"; that is, thoughts and words are given the same name as overt acts, "uncleanness," and are also culpable. The surprise value Mather finds in the rhetorical tactic only underscores how precisely the word "uncleannesss" usually denoted specific and outward sexual acts, but here the audience abruptly widens: if "foolish talking" and "looking after a woman to lust after her" are "uncleannesses," then many in the community, even those not facing capital punishment, are implicated in the sin of the condemned. The cry of the outcast leper, "Unclean! unclean!" warns others away but also accuses them of the same sin. The word "uncleanness" thus establishes a variable and ambiguous relation between the community and the convict, whether cautionary exemplar or castaway. However, that very widening of the audience actually works to strengthen the very narrow definition of "uncleanness" as a special category of sin, a complex of interrelated sexual behaviors.

The cry of the leper, so frequently invoked in these sermons, converts that entire transaction to a linguistic one. What does it mean for an infanticide to cry "Unclean! unclean"? Unlike in the Salem witchcraft prosecutions, a confession would not spare an infanticide from the gallows; that speech would simply seal her excommunication. But speech may also establish communion. In this passage, Mather is inviting Elizabeth Emerson to echo his speech with her own, to name her own sin and confess as a first stage in a process of being cleansed. She is invited to join the community by participating in its language even as she is being cast out of communion irrevocably by execution.

The paradox does not reside simply in the distinction between human law, which must mete out justice, and divine election, which is unpredictable, between communion in the body politic and communion in the body of Christ, but instead in the ambivalent pastoral situation. By foregrounding confession and speech, these sermons define communion and excommunicating uncleanness as linguistic phenomena. The many representations of Esther Rogers's speech in *Death the Certain Wages of Sin* suggest the importance of dialogue to the community's self-definition. The infanticide literature concerning nonconverted criminals, on the other hand, is filled with scriptural references depicting the criminal's estrangement, and more particularly, her nonparticipation in dialogue. Again and again, ministers fault the condemned woman for her silence, her lying, or her use of inappropriate language, all of which were seen as signs of estrangement from community. That fornication and secrecy—"loving and making a lie"—are more damning, more separating than murder, is a peculiar feature of the infanticide literature, reflected in the recurrence in that literature of the theme of linguistic trespass. Cotton Mather sounds quite affronted in *Pillars of Salt* when he comments that Sarah Smith reportedly fell asleep during John Williams's execution sermon, "the most unconcerned of any in the Assembly."[18] Even though Mather was probably not even in Springfield for Sarah Smith's execution, relying instead for his account on Williams's published text of that sermon, *Warnings to the Unclean*, Smith's silence, her "unconcern," her disengagedness, provoke his fury, perhaps even more than does her capital crime. He takes his cue from Williams, who had written that she had "contracted a fearful stupidity and sottishness" and was "stupefied by sin," commenting on her impassiveness even as she neared execution.

Williams had found in Smith's silence a homiletic problem. Obviously, her words don't contribute to *Warnings to the Unclean* in the way Esther Rogers's would in *Death the Certain Wages of Sin*, but Williams must draw her in, imputing language to her to construct dialogue even as she remained stubbornly silent. In the final pages of his application section, he sets up his numbered points as the excuses of sinners for their sins: "You say you are not convinced that such and such things are Sins. . . . You say your sins are Secret from the eyes of the world, and you were never left above once to be actually and grossly Unclean. . . . You say you have many good things as well as evil."[19] Each of these excuses is answered by his own theologically sounder reasoning. In effect, he rhetorically provides a question and answer format, constructing the pastoral dialogue in which Smith refused to cooperate. Soon afterwards, he turns his attention to Smith alone, and addresses her in the second person singular to recite the details of her biography: her community ties, her two marriages, her frontier life and its dangers. Sarah Smith slept through this recitation, and her silence echoes eerily through Williams's text as he angrily rehearses her life story and engages in imputed dialogue. Mather's outrage in *Pillars of Salt* is on behalf of his slighted professional colleague and on behalf of the identity of community itself, since Smith's "unconcern" has deprived it of its definition, consensus through dialogue. It is dialogue, more than conversion, that Williams must supply in *Warnings to the Unclean*.

Eighteen years later, Mather himself admonished the condemned Margaret Gallaucher in much the same language. "It *breaks* the *Hearts* of the Good People in this Place . . . to see that thou art thyself no more concerned for it" (39). In that sermon, called *A Sorrowful Spectacle*, he laments her "hardness of heart," a commonly used scriptural image, and spins out that trope to depict her impenetrability. A stone neither hears God's (or Mather's) words, nor speaks back, but remains silent: "As Good *Speak to a Stone!*" (11). Although Gallaucher did dictate a short confession that Mather reprints with his sermon, he notes that as the time for her execution neared, she lapsed back into silence again, refusing all comment. Like Esther Rogers, she had numerous visitors, including especially one woman who went often to read the Bible to her, but she remained unresponsive. Echoing Williams's language to Sarah Smith, Mather notes her "stupidity" and regrets "discovering [her] total Estrangement." As with Sarah Smith, the woman's estrangement is measured by her linguistic inadequacy. She is silent.[20]

Or, if she has made a statement, as did both Margaret Gallaucher and Elizabeth Emerson, her language itself is suspect. In "An Holy Rebuke to the Unclean Spirit," Mather reprints Emerson's long and detailed first-person autobiography, but worries that she is still concealing the whole truth (though we can hardly imagine that anything could be left out!): "I Fear I Fear! This is not *All* that she should have acknowledged." Even her repudiation of her sin might be untrustworthy, he warns her: "She dyes with a lye in her Right Hand." Moreover, the capital crime itself is a species of lying. As we have already seen, Mather's main concern in this sermon is uncleanness, and only at the end of his direct address to Elizabeth Emerson does he mention the killing, in what is perhaps the clearest statement in all the infanticide literature of its secondary status: "You shed the Blood of your own Children *to cover* your Uncleanness" (71, 73, emphasis added). What Elizabeth has done, more than murder her two infants, is "love and make a lie."

Lying. Silence. The affront to the community Mather describes in 1693 and 1715 is linguistic nonparticipation. "As good speak to a stone!"[21] But lying and silence—linguistic isolation—don't cover all the linguistic threats to the commmunity. A more aggressive one lies in the possibility of alternative conversations. Sinners, says Mather in his first sermon to Elizabeth Emerson, "call things by wrong names," using an alternative vocabulary. "They call darkness light, and light darkness." The name in Mather's sermon for this reversal is Madness, and conversion, in this vocabulary, is a "growing wise again." Madness is Mather's variation on a topos developed as well in other 1690s sermons: sin as folly. Samuel Willard echoes Mather five years later, with "they call evil good, and good evil"; Increase Mather devotes his 1698 sermon about Sarah Threeneedles to the proposition "That Sinners are Fools."

All these sermons describe an alternative valuation and language as a direct reversal of truth, a familiar theological idea, perhaps most strikingly expressed in Hooker's *Application of Redemption*: "sin is only opposite to God." To say that sinners are fools is to say for one thing that they make bad choices. "How unreasonable a thing it is to *chuse* Sin before Holiness," Willard observes.[22] Cotton Mather tells a story of a "chast Person sollicited unto folly" by a young man. This "chast person" responds to the young man's solicitation by asking him if he would first put his hand in the fire. "He refused this, as a very unreasonable thing; but she then Replied, *And how then can you ask me, for your sake, to throw my self Body and Soul, into the Fire of Hell; to Ly and Burn and Broil in that Fire throughout Eternal Ages: Is not that more unreasonable?*"[23] Increase Mather invokes one of the most vivid passages from Job, a description of an ostrich, to convey the idea that sin is incomprehensible folly: "*She is hardned against her young ones as though they were not hers, because God has deprived her of wisdom, neither has he imparted to her understanding.* Such an ostrich has the Condemned Prisoner (who was here the last Lord's Day) been. She has been hardned against her young one, as if it had not been hers. Yea, though it was crushed to death she regarded it not."[24]

This solitary and stupefied bird, unable to recognize her own kind, or by extension any community, is yet another figure for the estranged sinner. Mather does not supply the next line, however, which begins to suggest another dimension of that linguistic estrangement. The Hebrew here is difficult, but the King James Version reads, "What time she lifteth up herself on high, she scorneth the horse and his rider." Increase, who of course knew Hebrew, might also have appreciated the Revised Standard Version translation: "When she rouses herself to flee, she laughs at the horse and his rider." The ostrich is one of those creatures, like the horse, behemoth, and leviathan, whose existence baffles mankind, for they are evil or ugly or terrible; yet they have some awesome powers. The ostrich runs around the desert unconcernedly, disregarding norms of behavior; but in her very swiftness she has an alternative value beyond the ken of Job and human society.

Mather, echoing the biblical language, calls such alternative values the ostrich's lack of "wisdom" and "understanding." The idea that the ostrich is a mother who betrays her offspring is thus overshadowed by the notion that she outrages community by being outside its conventional wisdom. This discussion of sin, therefore, implies that more is at stake than the spiritual fate of an individual who may make good or bad choices. It implicates the sinner not only in theological or behavioral error but also in linguistic reversal, in a kind of "anti"-language. "What thinks he of Christ?" Cotton Mather asks in *Warnings from the Dead.* "He *madly* thinks, *Christ is a Stumbling-block and Foolishness.* What will he think of Religion? He *madly* thinks, *What is the Almighty, that I should serve Him, and what profit shall I have, if I pray unto Him?* He hath *mad* Thoughts about *Sin,* as if, *The Stolen Waters of it were sweet.* He hath *mad* Thoughts about the *World,* as if *Here were his Resting place.*"[25]

Since language is social, an anti-language is not only "opposite to truth," but implies as well the presence of an alternative community, one in which anti-conventions are shared. By calling sin "folly" or "madness," by assigning to it an entire mad vocabulary, then, ministers construct not just a single isolated sinner who is being cast out, but an entire anti-community. As Williams did with Sarah Smith, Increase Mather ascribes defiant speech to this anti-communion, recasting behavior as language and thereby casting sin as linguistic trespass, anti-conversation among an anti-community. The anti-community says, "[God] has threatened us a long time, but why does he not do what he threatens? Let him come and do his worst, the sooner the better, we fear him not. We must not suppose," Mather concludes, "that they did in words thus express themselves, but this was the language of their sinful practices. They lived as if they had been really of that opinion, as if they thought they could be too hard for the Almighty."[26] The emphasis on linguistic trepass is the vehicle through which ministers are able to imagine an alternative, competing community to their own.

Competing Communities and the Erasure of Maternity

The clearest illustration of the process of creating an anti-community can be found in execution literature concerning another class of criminals that increasingly claimed the attention of ministers: pirates. These captured pirates were most often privateers who had had the misfortune of raiding the ships of some European power with whom Britain had recently concluded a treaty. As Daniel Williams has shown, executions of pirates typically turned into theatrical contestations, for these criminals were anything but silent and cooperative, and whatever exasperation Cotton Mather may have felt with Elizabeth Emerson or Margaret Gallaucher was insignificant compared to his frustration with pirates like William Fly or John Quelch. Williams has written that Fly showed his contempt for the proceedings by smiling at the crowd and helping the hangman with his noose. Quelch's 1704 execution had been little different: he had bowed and doffed his hat to the assembled crowd like an actor.[27]

At first glance, these pirate sermons would seem to present a clear contrast to those on the infanticides. Mather's sermon preached on the occasion of the execution of Quelch and five of Quelch's colleagues, *Faithful Warnings to Prevent Fearful Judgments*, all but concedes that there is no possibility to recast Quelch's story as one of conversion, for Quelch and his company are completely outside communion from beginning to end. Mather develops no references to the notion that the community must protect itself spiritually by casting out the criminal: these criminals' actions have no implication for the province of New England. As a result, the depiction of sin in this sermon and in pirate sermons in general is very narrow indeed. Even in Mather's application section, where he details the sins that should be avoided, he describes a set of behaviors—swearing and cursing, gaming, extortion—that seem peculiar to that group of rough seafaring men, illustrating them with anecdotes about pirates and other sailors. He sets these criminals, that is, apart from the rest of his audience, defining a rather specific kind of lifestyle, so it is hard to see what his pastoral purpose is.

For the most part the sermon is less an analysis of the etiology of sin than a literary tour de force, an extended meditation on sin using crime on the high seas as a vehicle. Mather's sermon text, "Evil pursueth sinners," provides him not so much with a theological premise as with an image to amplify it. Sinners will be judged and punished, Mather argues, supplying an unusual depiction of the physical torments of hell: as pirates do their victims, the tormenters have "racked" and "booted" them, "burned" and "broke them on the wheel," and "Bastinado'd them to death." More important, though, these punishments will *pursue* them: "Hell follows."[28] It is the idea of pursuit that Mather develops most vividly, using a vocabulary suggestive of sea piracy and fugitive criminality to create a sense of terror and desperation.

Only at the very end of the sermon does Mather's pastoral agenda become clear. Having depicted a thoroughly alien world, one as different from his New England audience's as the spirit-world, hell, is from earth, the sermon's message to those New Englanders is that, as alien as that life is, some of them may be in danger of crossing over into it. It is that crossing over, even more than the vivid depictions of hell and mayhem, that is threatening. (Only a few years later, a young Ben Franklin growing up in Boston would daydream about running away to sea; the elder Mr. Franklin evidently was not the only father who worried about the pull the seafaring life exerted on his son.) Here, Mather tells the anecdote, "well known to all the People," of "a Person [formerly] in our Prison, who was the son of a Reverend" who had died under religious persecution. "This graceless Fellow said unto some in this place, while he was following his Lewd way of Living, *That he would never be such a Fool, as to be Hanged for Religion, as his Father was.* He was as bad as his word! He was not *Hanged for Religion;* he was *Hanged* for *Piracy,* and for *Murder!* He was *Twice Hanged,* before his Execution could be accomplished; and he was *Hanged a Third time,* in *Chains,* where Thousands daily beheld the Spectacle."[29]

Despite the anecdote, which individualizes the problem in a familiar way—filial impiety, an outraged clergy—Mather's analysis, fundamentally, is not about individuals but about competing communities. In the midst of this discussion of the ungodly behavior of pirates and other sailors, he sounds one familiar theme, the dangers of disorders in families. The problem is that the breakdown of one community allows the success of another, anti-community, and the alternative to a godly, well-ordered family is all too often "wicked company." "Alas," he says of condemned sinners, "they have *Ruined one another*": sin takes place in a group and as part of a group dynamic. "Sinners enticed one another; they said, *come with us, Let us lurk privily for the Innocent without a cause, we shall find all precious Substances.*"[30] The quotation from Proverbs, considered traditionally to be the collected wisdom of King Solomon addressed to his son or a young man, signals Mather's main pastoral concern: his audience, those most at risk for leaving one community for another, are young people. "*My Son,*" he writes, quoting Proverbs again, "*walk not thou in the way with them.*" Such alternative communities themselves, in New England as well as in Proverbs, are an active lure. "Some have come," he writes, "and Seduced and Enchanted our Young Men, to *Piratical Courses,*" noting with satisfaction the newly severe legal measures that should deter "such dangerous Criminals" in the future.[31] While Mather takes care to warn "our young men" of the danger of joining such communities, he is ultimately more interested in forestalling their temptation by keeping the "Enchanters" out in the first place. The language of seduction comes from Proverbs as well, for that book presents its audience of "young men" with opposing female figures, Wisdom and the adulteress (or harlot), adding a sexual cast to those competing communities between which they must choose: "Say unto Wisdom, Thou art my sister; and call understanding thy kinswoman: That they may keep thee from the strange woman, from the stranger which flattereth with her words" (Proverbs 7.4–5).

Significantly, all of the features of the pirate sermons—binary opposed communities, the special vulnerability of youth to the group dynamics of sin, and a metaphor of sexual seduction—show up as well in infanticide sermons of the '90s, in which well-ordered families and wicked company vie for the loyalties of young people. Samuel Willard, for example, in an introductory note to his 1699 sermon about an unnamed infanticide, invokes that binary opposition between well-ordered families and wicked company, referring, in fact, to Proverbs to do so: "Let all Children, and such as are under the Command of Parents and Family Government, beware of disobedience to their Parents, and those that have the Authority over them; let them be warned to take heed to themselves of being linked in vain company, and take the wise man's counsel, Prov. 1.10, *My Son, if Sinners entice thee consent thou not.*"[32] The anti-community in this case is not an exotic band of fearsome pirates, however, but a group much closer to home. Although all the sermons, like Willard's, note the danger of "wicked company," the real anti-community that emerges in these sermons is that of young people themselves. Willard's caution to parents to "use more prudence in maintaining that Authority over their Children, which God hath vested them withal, and beware of an over-fond indulgence, in giving them an unrestrained liberty," castigates them as heads of failed families; moreover, "Unrestrained liberty" and "a fond indulgence" allow a whole youth subculture, with its own practices and its own mores, to flourish, not in an alien, distant watery world, where pirates come from, but within the folds of the community itself. It is one thing to describe as an anti-community a group of swearing, blaspheming, thieving pirates; it is quite another to identify as an anti-community your own children. When these sermons identify young people as the unstable element, as not just individual members of families but as a distinct cohort liable to "cross over" from community to anti-community, they disrupt the very binary structure on which they depend. Installing the family as the basic social unit to whose authority all must submit, the sermons nevertheless testify also to disruptive centrifugal forces that strain against that structure.[33]

When it came to identifying the anti-communal enemy against which they were preaching, the infanticide sermons of the '90s employed a rhetoric of sexuality drawn from Proverbs and Leviticus to identify youth as a distinct cohort. "*Foolish Youth! Who hath Bewitched* thee?" asks Cotton Mather in 1693, targeting this segment of his community. Acknowledging again that all may be implicated in the sin of uncleanness, he nevertheless reminds them that "it is the Young people that are this way the most Extravagant." His sermon set not only names young people as its special audience throughout, but also lists those details describing a distinct youth culture, one very much marked by illicit sexuality and separated from urban family government by outdoor frolicking. "And there are especially two of the most ungrateful seasons, that *Young People* take to multiply their Diabolical Pollutions. There is the Close of the *Sabbath*, and there is the Joy of the *Harvest*; these instead of being improved in *Thankfulness* to God, are Employ'd in spreading of *uncleanness* through the Land."[34]

Mather, preaching to an urban audience, locates the threat to family government in outdoor frolicking and the rhythms of the agricultural year. John Williams, on the other hand, preaching to the frontier town of Springfield, paints a vivid picture of the same youthful anti-community disporting itself in secret indoor places: "They are to blame that suffer and allow their Children and servants in the black and dark night, to be absent from the Religious Orders of their Families, to be going the way to such houses. . . . Heads of Families are to be reproved, that see Young Ones, Children or Servants wantonly toying or dallying one with another, foolishly sporting on beds before their eyes, unreproved . . . they are to blame that know their Children make themselves vile, and restrain them not" (29–30). For these ministers, the threat to the household comes from both rural rituals and the urban milieu, both of which provide young people with communal alternatives, drawing them out of the household. Mather exemplifies his depiction of youth culture with reference again to Proverbs 7, which describes the perils of the urban streets to a young man. "You have been like that *mad* Young man of whom *Scripture* says, 11 Prov. 7.7, *He was a young man Void of Understanding*, and hence you have gone to the House of the Harlot, as an *Ox* to the *Slaughter & a Fool to the Correction of the Stocks*. I beseech you, to leave a *Mark* upon the Hellish *Baud-houses*, and upon all the other *Scandals* that have Ruined you."[35]

Insofar as these sermons depict an "othered" youth culture, with its own habits and practices that fly in the face of the principles of family government, they do *not* tend to single out female sexuality as a particularly dangerous, hard-to-control force. When Williams and Mather interweave language from Proverbs 7 with their discussion of youth culture, they do not choose those phrases that would allow them to vilify female sexuality.[36] Nor do they compare the condemned infanticide in the audience to the "harlot." While the language of Proverbs reinforces the theme of youth teetering between community and anti-community, it does so by ascribing these sexual activities to the youth cohort itself of both genders—to "Young ones wantonly toying or dallying one with another" as Williams says—not to an alien female. "Uncleanness" does not inhere in the female body specifically. Rather, the harlot of Proverbs is inflected with the leper of Leviticus.

This sinfully sexualized, though nongendered body, does appear in the sermons as thoroughly contaminated, both visibly and internally—contaminated and leprous, and therefore deserving of separation. Willard warns that the young people in his audience have "taken their fill of their mad mirth, and glutted themselves with sensual pleasures." With heavy sarcasm, John Williams quotes the most sensual parts of the harlot's tempting speech, underscoring the sensually punishing results of illicit sexuality. "They say they shall sollace themselves with love, and take their fill of love, But in these words you see what God appoints them to, not to a bed deckt with coverings of tapistry, with carved works, with the Linnen of *Egypt*, perfumed with myrrh, aloes and cinnamon; but to a lake burning with fire and brimstone." Cotton Mather makes a similar point about the humiliations of the sinful body in hell. The fires of hell are appropriate because the "*Unclean* have cherished an Internal *Fire* in their own Bowels." And he threatens his young audience with an eternal punishment that may be particularly distressing to those who have "glutted themselves with bodily pleasures": "The Unclean have done Brutish things with their *Bodies* in this World; they shall therefore be Raised with *Ugly Bodies* in the World to come."[37]

According to the rhetoric of sinful sexuality in these sermons, fornication is the important cultural and social problem, more important than neonaticide, and threatens the communal fabric more profoundly. Ministers certainly had at their disposal language to attack "unnatural mothers"; this language, then, and its connection to murder, is all the more conspicuous for its relative absence from most of these sermons. In his remark to Elizabeth Emerson already quoted, "You shed the Blood of your own Children to cover your uncleanness," Cotton Mather transforms Elizabeth's potential reproductive (dis)connection from community into a linguistic one: she has loved and made a lie. It is not betrayed motherhood that is at issue here, but fornication and secrecy.

That is, although sexuality and maternity are, of course, logically related, they *compete* in this discourse. Moreover, that substitution—fornication for neonaticide—redirects the focus of these inquiries into sin *away* from women, making the sermons more gender-neutral. Through this maneuver, the ministers combat, perhaps, a double standard of sexual morality, reintroducing, even into their discussions of illicit pregnancies, the notion that men as well as women may be sexually culpable. (An alternative view, suggested by Carol Karlsen, is that in such maneuvers ministers collaborate with a misogynist legal trend, masking the ways in which law enforcement targeted women's sexual behavior.[38]) In any event, the discourse of sexuality allows the ministers to stigmatize and isolate the youth cohort more thoroughly, I would suggest, than a discourse of maternal murder might have stigmatized women. In substituting youth for women as the targeted anti-community, these ministers make an important and curious move that in some ways proves more disruptive to the communal fabric. To reassert established gender hierarchies by declaring women sinful and weak and subordinate would be merely to restate the hierarchical binaries that theoretically structured all of Puritan, and indeed early modern society. To stigmatize young people as a class, though, is to disrupt that society's genealogy, its expectation of biological and spiritual continuity and wholeness, and to atomize that basic unit of Puritan society, the family. It is to create, rhetorically, an entire anti-community within.

The Pastoral Encounter: Maternity and Community in the Sermons of John Rogers

This was the homiletical situation when John Rogers took the Ipswich pulpit in the summer of 1701 to preach to Esther Rogers. The infanticide sermons published in neighboring Boston up till then had been about sex not murder, sexuality not maternity, youth not women. It was in this context that Noyes and Gerrish expressed their surprise and disappointment in John Rogers's analysis of sin. "For the warning of the Rising Generation," they would write, he should have explained "the danger and mischief of the sin of Fornication." Their comment illustrates their willingness to identify youth as a distinct cohort, and to mark illicit sexuality with the levitical jargon that establishes it as a distinct category of sin, and signals, again, that John Rogers's sermons will depart from those conventions.

We don't have any direct records of John Rogers's pastoral conversations with Esther. But *Death the Certain Wages of Sin* contains three sermons he preached during that ongoing drama in which "the nation" of Ipswich was so closely involved over the month or so before Esther Rogers's execution: one at the trial, one at the sentencing, and one at the execution itself. These three sermons suggest Rogers's homiletic practice was one that deviated from that of his contemporaries, but one as well that might have made Esther's conversion more possible. It explains how John Rogers's ministry in Ipswich may have brought Esther Rogers into communion, while his contemporaries report only failures.

Esther Rogers's trial was one of a number of cases heard during the travelling Superior Court's Ipswich visit that July. By the time of the court's arrival for that group of trials, she had been in the Ipswich jail for eight months and had been the object of great attention from the town's minister. Judge Sewall, a member of the Superior Court, had roots in the Newbury/Ipswich area, and had visited the previous January and "got time enough to hear Mr. Rogers preach" there, noting in his diary that "Mr. Rogers prai'd for the prisoner of death, the Newbury woman who was there in chains."[39] During that winter and spring, in fact, Esther had many visits from John Rogers and others, who left a detailed record of her progress toward conversion. When he came back to town for the trial the following July, Judge Sewall doubtless was pleased with the opportunity to hear John Rogers preach again and doubtless remembered that "prisoner in chains." As for the people of Ipswich, the whole month of July was taken up with the case of Esther Rogers.

As the court settled in to hear the Rogers case, John Rogers preached the three sermons that would appear in *Death the Certain Wages of Sin*. On the day of the trial the details of the crime were fresh in the minds of all those assembled at Ipswich who heard him preach the first of these. The sermon, however, mentioned her not at all, nor her specific sins, nor did John Rogers address her directly, as did many ministers preaching sermons about criminals. For his sermon text he chose a New Testament verse, Rom. 6.23, "For the wages of sin is death, but the gift of God is eternal life, through Jesus Christ our Lord." This first sermon, called "Death the Certain Wages of Sin to the Impenitent," develops the first clause, but with a relatively mild treatment of the subjects of death and judgment. Partly this is because of John Rogers's consistent use of the third person, which makes the sermon feel like a treatise rather than, as in some sermons by his contemporaries, a second-person indictment. Partly it is because the scope of his discussion is cosmic, the source of the current sad case being nothing less than the sin of Adam, which disordered the universe and human society.

Like his contemporaries, Rogers notes that original sin has disordered the body: "since the Fall, [man] is punisht with Deformity, Blindness, Lameness, Weakness and Imbecility in all parts, powers, and faculties, with an utter decay of all at Death" (*DCWS*, 5). Like them, he uses a metaphor of sensuous experience to describe that decay: "Our very Honey is mixed with Gall" (*DCWS*, 7). Yet, while they had dwelt on the pollution that invades the sinful body, Rogers prefers to describe sin as an absence.[40] "There is the loss or privation of the Internal Good of the Body" (*DCWS*, 5); "Sin only is an Enemy to good" (*DCWS*, 25). Along with this weakness, original sin makes humankind vulnerable, having turned the very earth into a threat to it. "The very Heavens, the Stars which seem to promise nothing but light & comfort, they infect his person and good by their malevolent influences and aspects. The Air proves contagious to him, and scatters its plagues throughout the world. Waters from above pour down upon him; the Waters beneath they swallow him up, and Earth is continually gaping and opening its mouth, devours the Inhabitants thereof. The Beasts of the Wood are ravenous and venomous" (*DCWS*, 7). "Yea further," Rogers continues, this sin has left a legacy of disorderly violence to human society, exemplified by the biblical story of the first murder by Cain, as well as all the other killings throughout history, implicitly including, though he does not mention it here, Esther Rogers's of her newborn child: "He suffers from his own kind" (*DCWS*, 7). In John Rogers's analysis, the sin of murder, while seemingly the most sensational of crimes, is an integral part of the world in which everyone lives. It is not set off from other sins in a special category, as the sexual sins of uncleanness are by those complex etiologies in the Boston sermons. On the contrary, "God makes every breach of his Law to be Capital" (*DCWS*, 21). Despite its threatening title, Rogers's sermon has a welcoming tone. His emphasis on "bloodguiltiness" actually brings Esther into the community rather than thrusting her out of it. Murder is a sin that reflects the way in which members of a community turn against each other. It is the ultimate anti-communal act, but it does not, in John Rogers's analysis, establish an anti-community. It is not the individual sinful body that is "unclean" and therefore set apart, but the entire created—and fallen—world.

Having heard the evidence against Esther Rogers, on July 15, the jury returned a verdict of guilty the next day; her capital sentence was to be pronounced July 17. John Rogers's second sermon, delivered on sentencing day, is called "LIFE the Sure Reward of Grace to the Penitent;" it continued the conciliatory tone he had struck in "Death the Certain Wages of Sin to the Impenitent." With the "prisoner of death" in the audience, Rogers developed the second clause of the text from Romans, "But the gift of God is Eternal Life." It is that "but," of course, that is the crux of the theological paradox. Though the law may require condemnation—"God makes every breach of His Law to be capital"—yet "every sin is venial upon repentance." John Rogers chose imagery of imprisonment to challenge his audience to see the pariah in front of them in a new light. While Esther Rogers may have been visibly in chains, apparently an emblem of condemnation, her hopeful conversion made it likely that she is really something far different. "The Pit indeed is deep, but there is an Infinite Arm of Grace that can fathom and reach to the bottom of it, and bring us out of it. A Sinners Chains and Fetters may be broken, and made to fall from them: the Prison doors are set open for man to come out." Further, he says, "The Gospel preaches Deliverance to these Captives, there is Release from Bondage of Corruption, for the Tyranny of Sin. Satan in part begun here, and opening the Prison Door to them that are bound. Then, as to the Evil of Suffering, and Consequents of Sin, there is a perfect freedom to be obtained." Not only may her chains be loosened, but the sentence she has heard this day may be reversed. "*Death, where is thy sting?*" (*DCWS*, 45–46, 50).

On the day John Rogers preached this sermon, Judge Sewall made a note in his diary of his final involvement in the case: "July 17. Mr. Cooke pronounc'd the sentence. She hardly said a word. I told her God had put two Children to her to nurse: Her Mother did not serve her so. Esther was a great saviour; she, a great destroyer. Said did not do this to insult over her, but to make her sensible."[41] The harsh tone that Sewall took with Esther Rogers contrasts notably with John Rogers's more conciliatory one. Never able to resist an opportunity to supply a biblical commentary, Sewall admonished her with a parallel to her biblical namesake, a parallel that neither John Rogers nor any of the other ministers make but one that is quite neatly damning by the contrast. His comments at the sentencing reflect the fact that he had been absent for the months of her imprisonment. He had had the chance in January to see that John Rogers was very involved in counseling Esther, but perhaps he did not know, as most of the pastor's audience did, that she had experienced a hopeful conversion. He did not know, perhaps, that the townspeople had been talking to her all winter, writing down her words and preparing them for an exemplary publication in *Death the Certain Wages of Sin*. Not aware of all the conversation in which she had already engaged, used, perhaps, to the Boston-style infanticides who sat like stones or fell asleep, on this day Sewall saw her not as in communion but as silent and sullen: "she hardly said a word" and he must admonish her "to make her sensible."

In other ways, however, Sewall was in step with what was happening in Ipswich. In Boston, he had heard many sermons by Cotton and Increase Mather, by Samuel Willard, perhaps had even heard those preached at the execution of the Boston infanticides. He might have heard them using the execution of a wretched young woman as an occasion to talk about sex and not murder, youth and not women, sexuality and not maternity. But on this day his legal interest pointed him in another direction. His concern, like John Rogers's, was with neonaticide, not fornication. From his legal standpoint, Esther Rogers had violated her biological and social connections to community through violating her maternity. "Her mother did not serve her so." Esther as mothered and Esther as mother: these are the two relationships that bind her indelibly to community and which she has violated. It is in this emphasis, if not the tone, that Sewall's remark resonates with John Rogers's sermon and serves, therefore, to underscore for us the themes that Esther Rogers and other auditors heard driven home that day, by both judge and pastor. For John Rogers's gentler sentencing day sermon, "Life the Sure Reward," dwells with great specificity on Esther Rogers's crime, which for him is maternal killing, not, as it was so frequently for his colleagues, illicit sexuality. Paradoxically, his stress on murder not sex produced a welcoming sermon, while the Boston sermons tended to be more exclusionary. In fact, John Rogers reconnects Esther to community through her potential maternity, however much she has sinned against it. It is as a mother that he draws her back into communion.

Being a pastor did not mean mincing words. The direct address to Esther calls attention to her legal crime, neonaticide: You "standest here guilty of a repeated Murder, and that attended with many heinous aggravations, in destroying the fruit of thine own Body: Thou hast not only been so unhappy as to bring forth Children for the Murtherer, but hast been so ungodly, as to be the Mother and Murtherer of them thy self" (*DCWS*, 68). "Mother and Murtherer": he does not spare her the truth, but speaks in most severe tones. "O cruel monster in Nature! Who shall deliver thee from such Uncleanness and Blood-guiltiness?" (*DCWS*, 69). It is not just in mentioning neonaticide and giving it center stage that John Rogers differs from his colleagues to the south; in naming the crime of which Esther is guilty, he also names the maternal relationship that had bound her. Throughout the sermon, the concept of maternity hovers over his description of salvation and communion. He makes several references to Mary Magdalen, a biblical figure associated with sexual transgression, but only to show "the conversion of some of extraordinary Guilt" (*DCWS*, 72). In addition, unlike his Boston colleagues, he connects illicit sexuality directly to the possibility of maternity, affirming that even sinful sexuality belongs in the wider community. "If we examine our Saviours Geneology as recorded in Scripture, we shall find a company of loose and lewd women." But these loose and lewd women are redefined, reconnected to community through their childbearing, for they are all ancestresses of Christ: "Tamar, who played the Harlot with *Judah* her Father in Law, *Rahab* the Harlot of *Jericho*, *Ruth* a Moabitess, the root of the whole generation was *Lots* son by incest with his own Daughters, *Bathsheba*, David's adulteress" (*DCWS*, 70). "Christs own Stock being thus tainted", Rogers acknowledges, community and church are nevertheless established and continued, in spite of sinful sexuality. No wonder, then, that he can say to Esther,

"*Thou* standest as fair for [salvation] as any Sinner on this side the Pit" (*DCWS*, 74). It is not only that he is invoking that standard theological reversal, but that he has defined Esther's sexuality in terms of the way it might have connected her to community. Although the effect is very different from Sewall's comment, structurally it proceeds from the same presumption: Esther Rogers is part of a genealogy, having had a mother and having been one. These two relationships connect her indelibly to a community, and while in violating those roles she must face the human law, those violations do not push her into an anti-community.

On July 31, execution day, John Rogers preached his final sermon for Esther Rogers, and had, presumably, his largest audience. It appears as well that for this sermon John Rogers had given in to the pressure he might have felt from Hubbard, his senior colleague at Ipswich, or other visitors who shared Noyes's and Gerrish's view that an infanticide execution was an opportunity too good to pass up to talk about young people and fornication. Accordingly, Rogers took as his text for that day, Ps. 99.9, "Wherewithal shall a young man cleanse his way: by taking heed thereto according to thy word."

Even here, however, John Rogers's treatment of this group differs substantially from that suggested by the other sermons published in Boston. His sermon seems to fulfill the demands of those around him in naming youth as his special audience, yet his tendency is always to pull back, to avoid stigmatizing that cohort unduly. A young man, he says, should "cleanse his way" not because he is especially prone to sin, but because "none are ever exempted from this Care" (*DCWS*, 85). Rather than ascribe to them a distinct sinful subculture, he allows that young people perhaps are vulnerable to sinfulness because they lack judgment. "Young men are all forward enough, but little in Reflection, much in activity, but little in study: hot and confident in their own way, but little inquisitory, deliberative and advisory. Youth are apt to try, rather than trust" (*DCWS*, 89). "Being of small experience," youth is "simple and easy to be deceived" (*DCWS*, 87). This is the context for the list of youthful sins he does provide a few minutes later, a list that includes but is not limited to fornication, a list that includes Esther Rogers's sin, bloodguiltiness (*DCWS*, 97–98). But even here, he returns to the context of the first sermon, the original sin of Adam: "a Foundation for this was laid by our First Parents" (98), which again broadens the discussion of sin beyond youth while of course making it universal.

Pivotal to this idea of universality is the idea of sin as a physical taint rather than an exclusively sexual one. To signal this shared sinfulness in church and community, rather than separation, to point to communion, not excommunication, John Rogers uses the familiar imagery of the leper. "Every child of Adam," he says, "is born a leper." All must, like the leper, cry "Unclean! Unclean!", not so much to name the sin of fornication, or to warn others away, but to name themselves and the fallen human condition. In effect, Rogers takes back the word uncleanness, which usually means sexual impurity, and rescues its more broad meaning. "Though there is one Sin which by peculiar use bears the name of Uncleanness, yet all Sin is so" (*DCWS*, 98). The result is that the imagery of the unclean body that appears in these sermons is of a different type from that which we found in other infanticide sermons. Sin has caused "a foul deformity," to be sure. But in picturing that tainted, deformed body's defilement, Rogers chooses images of filth that coats the body but does not invade it. "Both we defile our ways, and our ways us; or we by that which is in us defile our Actions, and then these reflect a Spot of Guilt and Filth upon us again; even as the Sow wallowing in the mire, then tumbleth in the Grass, and being washed returns to wallowing again: So the Scripture sets it forth; therefore man must needs be unclean" (*DCWS*, 97–98). "There is a Turpitude in [sin] it self, and staineth the person guilty of it. *Can a man touch Pitch, and not be defiled therewith?* . . . [S]in is filth and uncleanness. Hence so many legal institutions for purification, washing, rinsing, cleansing, etc." (*DCWS*, 98).

This imagery places the defilement outside the body, on its surfaces, so that, consistent with the biblical fountain imagery (invoked also by Cotton Mather), it may be washed off. Therefore, even when John Rogers's language seems to point to the most thorough corruption through original sin, that defiled body still retains its integrity: "Every child of Adam is born a Leper, all are defiled, from the Crown of the Head to the sole of the Foot; he is as it were one engrained spot, a lump of uncleanness" (*DCWS*, 95). Even when he figures sin as being inside the body, that body remains intact somehow; the corrupt heart, for example, is like a "Cage of Unclean Birds," or, more interestingly, the sinful body is "pregnant with the seeds of all sins."

The effect of such images, as Rogers uses them, is to keep the defiled body separate from the cause of its defilement. Rogers's imagery of blood-guiltiness coats the body with filth, or occupies its internal spaces, without breaking its boundaries. The sinful body retains its integrity—just as the audience that John Rogers constructs maintains its wholeness, allowing, in fact, Esther Rogers to be a part of it, to be brought into communion rather than cast out of it.

That is, the exact logic of John Rogers's images of the sinful body is important because it points to the conception of community that is operating in his sermon as well. Definitions of alienation reflect definitions of integration; or, to draw on the anthropological concept that, in Mary Douglas's words, "the human body is always treated as an image of society," images of endangerment of the body reflect theories about how a community is constituted and what endangers it.[42] It is significant, therefore, that images of sexuality and maternity *compete* rather than complement each other in the literature of infanticide. John Rogers's colleagues turned to the language of sexuality to stigmatize the youth cohort as the most vulnerable part of community, one that might "cross over" to a threatening outside community or let in contagion; in the imagery of their sermons, sexual uncleanness seems to invade the body thoroughly, corrupting every cell, as it were. Theirs is a view of a community under threat, with potentially permeable boundaries; the remedy is either to keep young people tightly controlled within family structures, or, to the extent youth bands together to become a separate social entity, to turn it into its own anti-community, with sinful sexual practices, to lop it off, casting out its representative member, the convicted infanticide.

John Rogers, in contrast, neither stigmatizes youth nor concentrates on illicit sexuality. His focus, instead, is on the capital crime of murder and therefore on the maternal bond, the breaking of which is merely an instance of the violent breach of community that is the condition of the post-lapsarian world. Moreover, maternal images themselves correlate, within this literature, with a conception of a whole community, while sexual imagery more easily suggests opposing community and anti-community (represented by Wisdom and the harlot) and lends itself to that process of group stigmatizing. As I have suggested, it is no coincidence that the former more inclusive language produced a conversion in a condemned infanticide, while the latter did not.

John Rogers was only thirty-five when Esther died. Hubbard, who preached during that month about fornication, was eighty, and Noyes and Gerrish, who commented approvingly about that sermon, were in their fifties. Perhaps John Rogers's youth goes some way toward explaining his more welcoming approach to his pastoral subject and namesake, Esther Rogers. His location at Ipswich put him at some remove from the concerns of the colonial capital, concerns that entered more directly into the thinking of his older and better-connected colleagues. As we saw earlier, the loss of the Massachusetts Charter in the 1680s issued in a wrenching reconsideration of colonial boundaries and communal definition, and perhaps pushed them toward the sexual language of anti-community, reflecting their interest in the drawing of precise and exclusionary boundaries.[43] It is not surprising that in later years, John Rogers endorsed the Great Awakening revivals: his early interest in taking lay testimony, even of sinners, seriously and in fostering an inclusive *communitas* spirit rather than an exclusionary, highly structured church conception would have predicted as much.[44] It is striking as well, in this regard, that in Esther Rogers's own account of her spiritual experience, she uses a vocabulary that we associate with the evangelical revivalism of the 1730s and 1740s, reporting in her conversion a feeling of "delight and pleasure" in "the Excellency of Gods ways" (130), or "much sweetness in [the] society" of the "Christians in the Town" (131); "I feel the greatest incomes of joy and sweetness" (132).[45] Even in 1701 Ipswich, the techniques and vocabulary of evangelical outreach were in use. In the context of the infanticide literature of the 1690s, these techniques included the vocabulary of maternity, which conveyed, in John Rogers's pulpit, both a common guilt for the sin of Cain and the interconnectedness of the human community through genealogical bonds.

The immediate result of this homiletics is that John Rogers accords Esther Rogers a spiritual dignity that is lacking in the sermons of his colleagues, as well as in the prefatory material to *Death the Certain Wages of Sin*, where Noyes and Gerrish describe her as a "leud, and rude and wretched Sinner." John Rogers's very last address to her illustrates this. His words start out harsh ("O Unclean! Unclean!"), but he quickly moves away from the dwelling on sin implicit in the leper's cry. Instead, he moves her attention for these her last moments to the subject of salvation rather than that of sin. "Is thy time of Bondage now expired?" "Admire, admire divine mercy" (*DCWS*, 125). "Once more then, Esther, look unto that Jesus" (*DCWS*, 127). The sermon, preached just a few minutes before Esther's execution, then, ends with words of encouragement, words that for the most part could be addressed to anyone approaching death.

The Passion of Esther Rogers:
"Freedom of spirit, and liberty of speech"

The youthful John Rogers is the only minister Esther Rogers mentions in her own conversion narrative; that fact, together with his tone and the testimony of the other ministers, lets us know that the relationship between the two Rogerses is central to this extended drama. The intimacy of that relationship, so well symbolized in the coincidence of surnames between John and Esther, surely would have caught the imagination of Nathaniel Hawthorne 150 years later if he came across *Death the Certain Wages of Sin* in his readings in New England history in the Salem Athenaeum; it would have piqued his interest in the erotic potential of the pastoral relationship as well as suggesting, perhaps, the name he chose for his own colonial heroine. But as in the encounter between Hester Prynne and her ministerial counselor in the opening scene of *The Scarlet Letter*, when no one dreams that they are more than a pastor and his parishioner, the full intensity of the pastoral relationship between John and Esther Rogers is muted in *Death the Certain Wages of Sin*. The complicated documents that come after the sermons—more than thirty pages—are set up to minimize John Rogers's role, and to emphasize instead the role of a multitextured community in helping Esther Rogers through her conversion experience.[46] John Rogers's homiletic practices, as reflected in the sermons here, had helped forge that community in Ipswich, a community that was willing to embrace Esther as she waited in its prison, and indeed, to look to her as an exemplar. It is ironic but in a real sense deeply appropriate that the Ipswich publication, though listed under John Rogers's name, should confirm the community's role, and not a celebrity minister's role, in pastoral conversation. But while John Rogers's teachings of a coherent community had prepared the way for Ipswich's embrace of Esther Rogers, the communal remembrances provide a complex picture of the pastoral practices of the community, practices that clash at times with what seems to have been John Rogers's agenda.

It is often unclear who has written any particular part in this section; since Samuel Belcher, minister from a neighboring town, wrote an introduction and closing notes, perhaps we can assume that he was responsible for collecting these remembrances together. Some sections represent conversations between Esther and others: John Wise and the elders of Ipswich are among the participants, as well as the woman who was, Belcher says, Esther's "peculiar visitant." Presumably, the fragmented documents that Belcher prints come from these pens. Again, significantly, he does not identify John Rogers as a contributor.

It is also in this section, of course, that Esther Rogers's words are represented. In addition to these accounts of conversation, there is a criminal narrative, several conversion narratives, an account of her walk to the site of execution, a last dying warning, and her final prayers. All of these are described as dictated, or "taken from her own mouth"; perhaps she could not write, although apparently she was able to read. We are entitled to a healthy skepticism about the authenticity of her represented testimony. However, the account as it is written stresses her ability to answer such inquiries satisfactorily in her own words, and it includes many direct quotations from her as an evidence of that ability. Indeed, the community's pastoral technique was to generate a lot of testimony from Esther Rogers, and throughout her imprisonment, as we shall see, her counselors continually asked her to give new conversion accounts and to answer new questions designed to test her fluency in the Christian idiom. Likewise, the persuasive strategy of *Death the Certain Wages of Sin* is to reproduce many of Esther Rogers's utterances. While her voice appears in multiple genres, conforming, more or less, to the formulaic demands of each, the editor of this material did not take care to weave all of his sources together into a seamless whole. The texts are repetitive and fragmentary, suggesting that he collected everything he could find from various pens and printed it. This lack of editorial control, or perhaps we could say, this principle of editorial conservation, together with the dialogue's status as evidence, means that we can have a fair amount of confidence in the relative authenticity of Esther Rogers's testimony. Because of the multivocalic nature of the printed book, we can disentangle, moreover, the threads that make up this complex fabric and expose the multitextured community that coalesces around Esther Rogers, sharing for the moment an interest in dramatizing a process of coming into communion, but betraying also other interests that are varied. This representation of pastoral dialogue allows us to see the complex workings of a community as it engages in the pastoral care of a soul, exposing the ways in which it closed about her, and the ways in which it stood apart. If we dare to hear the voice of Esther Rogers as well, we detect a similarly ambivalent or double story: a story of coming into communion and remaining apart, of fluid conversation and self-protective estrangement.[47]

The first piece in this section is a first-person criminal narrative, inflected by legal and religious forms and full of the sensational details that suggest the true crime narratives that would become more popular later in the century, eclipsing the importance of religious content of earlier execution literature. Esther Rogers was originally from outlying Kittery, Maine, and was apprenticed at the age of thirteen to the Woodbridges, a family in Newbury, down the coast. There she was given a Christian education, learning to read and being schooled in John Cotton's catechism, *Spiritual Milk for Babes*. But teenaged Esther Rogers evidently was not overly concerned with the things of religion. Like other criminals and like ministers making observations on criminal behaviors, she mentions neglecting the Sabbath and prayer as a prelude to the more serious events: "I was left to fall into that foul Sin of Uncleanness, suffering my self to be defiled by a Negro Lad living in the same House." The child of that union was born living, but Esther "stop[ped] the breath of it," in an act of murder that was premeditated and went undetected: she "kept it hid in an upper Room, till the Darkness of the Night following, gave advantage for a Private Burial in the Garden" (*DCWS*, 122), referring, presumably, to the grounds of the Woodbridge house. "[A]ll this was done in Secret," she adds, and even the father, that "Negro lad," knew nothing of it, nor even of the pregnancy itself. Esther was seventeen years old.

"Left to fall into that foul sin of uncleanness": this is highly formulaic language, and in some ways it tells a formulaic story of a fall. The confession also shows, however, an ambivalent and vacillating connection to her community. In some respects it draws on the language that was so central to the Boston infanticide sermons, for Esther Rogers depicts Woodbridge's home as a place of stability with the opportunity for godly living, from which she "fell" into "wicked company and the ways of evil." After the initial incident, she relates, she moved her residence a number of times, leaving Newbury for Piscatequa, returning to Woodbridge's house about a year later only to move again to another place in Newbury. In each instance Woodbridge's house seems to have potential spiritual value for her, as the site of her earlier Christian education, but as she tells it, she kept running away from Woodbridge precisely to avoid confronting the spiritual implications of her acts, forsaking the Christian environment for a more dangerous one, pursuing, in fact, an anti-community. Initially, she did have some stirrings of consciousness of sin, "but" left Mr. Woodbridge, she says, only to forget her first fears and fall into more dangerous habits. Later, returning to Newbury and Woodbridge from Piscatequa, "my former Sins came fresh to Remembrance, and troubled me a while; which together with other reasons, occasioned my Removal to another place in the Town." As Rogers describes it, she again rejects the Christian, godly environment and way of life, represented by Woodbridge's house, for its clear alternative, "another place," a godless, disorderly life away from Woodbridge, an anti-community recalling the descriptions of Mather and Williams, that will lead her to more sin: "my old Trade," as she calls it, a phrase that Defoe's Moll Flanders will use in a similar narrative of sin and reformation, "running out a Nights, or entertaining my sinful Companions in the back part of the House" (*DCWS*, 123–24).

But at the same time the narrative complicates this moral geography. While Esther Rogers paints herself as reacting carelessly to the first infanticide, we may speculate on those "other reasons" for her move. Woodbridge's house was, after all, a site of danger as well as of Christian training. Having had a sexual entanglement with her fellow servant, Esther Rogers knew well the dangers to which her sexuality exposed her, and her move may have been an effort to protect herself from temptation (or possibly, assault) and, incidentally, from another pregnancy. If this is so, her attempt did not succeed, for at her new residence, she says, "I fell into the like horrible Pit (as before) *viz.* of Carnal Pollution with the Negro man belonging to that House" (*DCWS*, 124). The language here is ambiguous. Did "the" Negro man belong to "that" house where she lived now? Or was this the same man, attached to Woodbridge's house, who had impregnated her before, the man whom she kept leaving Woodbridge's house to get away from? Whether we imagine a continuing sexual involvement with one man or simply the repeated pull of her own sexual impulses, Esther Rogers's account suggests her awareness of her vulnerability to sexual disaster. Her repeated movements, alternately flee-ing and approaching the sexually charged situation, reflect an ambivalence toward sexuality borne of a recognition of its peril, especially for an unmar-ried female servant. Like Pamela in Richardson's novel, although apparently not, like Pamela, sexually exploited by her master, Esther's youth, her servant status, and her sex combined to make her among the least esteemed people in her community, at once invisible to it, deprived of its protections, and bound by its most stringent expectations. The nervous agitation betrayed in the lan-guage finally finds its correlate in her description of her sexual experience: "I fell into the horrible Pit"—at once an apt Christian formulation of sin and an emblem of her social isolation. We may also read the pit as the resulting pregnancy itself, which sealed her isolation from the community, a Christian community that, ironically, would embrace her only after it labeled her a mur-derer. For expecting no help but only condemnation, Esther decided again to kill her newborn infant.

While Esther Rogers's assessment of the spiritual meaning of the first death had amounted to dismissal, her language describing the second betrays a lot more uncertainty, and perhaps unsettledness, after a traumatic event: she "did not so soon resolve the Murdering of it, but was continually hurried in my thoughts, and undetermined till the last hour." Her account of the crime echoes the breathless, feverish activity, suggested earlier by her moves: "I went forth to be delivered in the Field, and dropping my child by the side of a little Pond (whether alive, or still Born I cannot tell) I covered it over with Dirt and Snow, and speedily returned home again" (*DCWS*, 124). Her suspicious behav-ior attracted attention; moreover, the "little Pond," a contemporary source tells us, was next to the meetinghouse: the child's body was found almost immedi-ately. Rogers's indecision, her haste, and especially her carelessness—leaving the body where it certainly would be found—suggest again an ambivalence, a sense of entrapment, as well as a desire to overcome that estrangement and isolation by letting herself get caught. Her isolation is poignantly underscored by the fact that at the time she was undergoing this crisis, the residents of

Newbury were engaged in the common New England tribal ritual of assigning seats in the meetinghouse: to that end, a list of Newbury's most prominent citizens, including Joseph Woodbridge, appears in the town records. Servants like Esther Rogers of course are normally invisible in such rituals and in the records of them; perhaps she might have been considered a member of Woodbridge's household. But her own name does appear in the town clerk's records that same month, for the constable, John Pike, submitted a bill for the confinement of a Hester Rodgers for November, before she was bundled off to stand trial in Ipswich, the county seat.[48] In a sense, it was only with the discovery of her infant's body that Esther Rogers herself began to be visible to her community—visible, and capable of entering its discourse, albeit, by being labeled a criminal. And, as we've already seen, it would take John Rogers's preaching to complete the process of making her pregnancy into an occasion for reconnecting Esther Rogers to community, rather than isolating her.

It is, of course, one of the ironies of *Death the Certain Wages of Sin* that silence and isolation during her pregnancy at Newbury should be followed by such an excess of talk afterwards at Ipswich. The community's procedure in tending to their prisoner's spiritual health seems to have been to elicit endless testimony from her; likewise, the persuasive strategy of *Death the Certain Wages of Sin* is to reproduce many of her statements. That criminal confession is followed directly by her conversion narrative, taken, we are told, "from her own mouth," apparently by the Ipswich woman who was "her peculiar visitant."

Unlike the criminal narrative, the conversion narrative contains little external detail, instead relating almost solely Esther Rogers's own interior motions. Here again, however, the theme of inner agitation and bodily restlessness—"hurries," in Esther's word—continues to control her account of her experience. John Rogers's published sermons are inclusive and welcoming, even setting up Esther as an exemplary convert; but Esther Rogers's narrative reports that his pastoral visits to her in prison were harsh, counselling her on the "odiousness of sin." In any event, he does nothing beyond acting as an initial catalyst, for the conversion story she tells is one of inner spiritual struggle that took place "after he was gone." In its structure, it conforms to the traditional morphology of conversion: conviction and despair followed by detachment, denial of human agency, and the beginnings of confidence and constructive spiritual exercise.

As in the criminal narrative, Esther Rogers's language initially conveys a sense of restlessness and agitation, as well as a panicky preoccupation with those very perceptions: "I began to think that I never loathed Sin so much yet . . . I could not Rest, I was so dreadfully hurried . . . I could not Read, nor Sleep, nor have any Rest night nor day" (*DCWS*, 125–26). This description of the first step in the morphology, conviction of sin, exemplifies what John O. King has usefully called the unproductive, "alienated labor" characteristic of the preconversion stage: it is dominated by a series of first-person pronouns attached to verbs describing various activities—rest, read, sleep—none of which she can do.[49] The language describing the subsequent steps in the morphology begins to reflect her growing consciousness of the immanent presence of spiritual powers in her own psychological struggle, shaping her sentences so that the true authors of those motions are grammatical subjects: "Satan made me believe that it was impossible such a Sinner, should be Saved"; "God made me to think that it was Satan's Temptation to keep me from Repentance"; "God has made me to see that there is nothing that I can do to save me." The subject "I" is almost gone. Rather than trying frantically (and unproductively) to act herself, she is acted upon. Finally, after this struggle between supernatural beings over Esther Rogers's soul is accomplished, she falls into the balanced though dependent clauses of the convert who understands the true relationship between human endeavor and God's agency: "*If I could* Repent . . . *I might* find mercy"; "*although I am* such a vile sinner, *I hope* God has made me sensible of my sins" (emphasis added).

This very precise syntax expresses a very precise understanding of the relationship between grace, which comes from God, and repentance, which starts in the person; and a perfectly orthodox proportion in the speaker between consciousness of her sin and a pious but not presumptuous hope of salvation. The retrospective conversion narrative demonstrates, therefore, that Esther Rogers has achieved both spiritual insight *and* fluency in an important cultural idiom. The condition of salvation, repentance, is described in conditional, dependent clauses, but even then it is not guaranteed, as the tentative main verbs attest ("I might find," "I hope"). Rogers also uses the easy scriptural quotations that are notably absent from the earlier criminal narrative: toward the end of this short section, biblical passages relating to hope of pardon alternate with her sentences, one for one.

Yet another section then retraces in the third person Rogers's movement through the conversion process. Probably compiled by Esther's woman friend, her "peculiar visitant," it amplifies the conversion narrative and further establishes the conjunction between Christian experience and Christian language. The account confirms that after her initial encounter with John Rogers, Esther was both inarticulate and fearful. From the community's perspective, she was "very much reserved," giving "little Encouragement" to her visitors that she could be saved, because she would not talk to them. As the writer puts it, "she could not open her mind" (*DCWS*, 127). She further isolated herself by refusing to go to services twice weekly, as she was allowed. When she spoke at all, she spoke "of her sins with aggravation"; later, she would admit that during this period of silence she had many "distracting, and almost despairing thoughts" (*DCWS*, 128). These twin afflictions, silence and despair, are both signs of estrangement from God and from the community. Like Cotton Mather, who had depicted sin as a linguistic offense—sinners "call things by wrong names"—the community around Esther Rogers measures her spiritual progress by measuring her speech. The rest of this narrative is the detailed story of how she overcame both types of estrangement, attaining both a spiritual equilibrium, that is, a proper balance of humility and hope, and the linguistic prowess of a converted Christian, or, as the writer puts it, both "freedom of spirit, and liberty of speech" (127). As she overcame her estrangement from Ipswich, she overcame her estrangement from God.

Because of the importance of Christian speech to spiritual progress, Esther Rogers's speech is given a prominent place in this account of her conversion. As it is represented, the pastoral encounter that nurtured the conversion consisted not of lectures but of questions, not of religious exhortation but of attempts to prod her into talking. Rogers's visitors seem to have been quite disturbed by her silence at the early stages of her imprisonment. Early on, the writer notes, Rogers was unable to "make any other answer to Questions propounded, than yes or no." Her visitors preferred more expansive answers, and asked open-ended questions, like "what she thought or experienced about Conversion" (*DCWS*, 130), which she was to answer not with doctrinal responses, which would merely mimic clerical speech, but in her own laywoman's words. Not interested in catechistic answers per se, they were listening instead for an idiom, a way of constructing sentences, that would confirm her spiritual progress. Her speech in the Christian idiom would be a sign of the genuineness of her spiritual testimony; her participating in dialogue at all, breaking her isolating silence, was a sign of her integration into the Christian community. Moreover, this procedure suggests the crucial role that dialogue and lay language played in validating community identity as well as individual experience. It is precisely through the representation of many voices, including Esther Rogers's voice, that *Death the Certain Wages of Sin* testifies to the faithfulness of the community of Ipswich.

During the period of her imprisonment, Rogers achieved this fluency only gradually. The writer notes, for example, that when Rogers began to hope she was saved, she still "could not so well express the reasons and grounds of her hope, as was desired" (129). This period of partial fluency is also a period of partial spiritual calm, "tho' sometimes she felt a sinking fear come upon her [like the 'hurries' she had experienced before], yet that did not long abide" (129). By the time of her condemnation, she was entirely in control of her language, being, the account says, "much more free and enlarged in discourse than before" (*DCWS*, 132).

As Rogers got closer to her execution, the dialogues continued, and even stepped up in intensity, and the questions were much more pointed. On the night before her execution, it is reported, "One of the company asked her, what she thought of the poor murdered Infants, whom she was instrumental to bring into the world, and then perhaps of sending them to Hell. . . . *How do you think to answer the Cry of their Blood?*" (*DCWS*, 137). The next morning, that is, the day of her execution, John Wise, from neighboring Chebacco parish, visited her before she went to hear John Rogers's lecture. After he was with her for a time, the "gentlewoman" who was "her peculiar Visitant" came in and "asked her how she found her self this morning?" Wise's qustions were considerably less benign. In the transcript of the conversation printed in *Death the Certain Wages of Sin* (presumably taken down by that Gentlewoman), Wise tells her that he is reluctant to "molest your Spiritual quiet," (DCWS, 140) but in fact that is precisely his mission. He asks, "Whether, when her Coffin was brought in, it did not daunt her" (*DCWS*, 139). He gets her to tell yet another version of the conversion story, which *Death the Certain Wages of Sin* prints, and asks yet more questions, like "Whether she found it hard to believe" (*DCWS*, 143). On the walk to execution, a number of Neighboring ministers accompany her and attempt her "Terrification": "O *Esther*, How can your heart abide? Dont you here behold terrible displays of Justice; you are surrounded with Armed men, which signifies that God and man has determined to rid the World of you; and you are thus beset, that you may no ways escape." Or, they go on, "The terrible place and Engines of Destuction, are but a little before us, where you must in a few Minutes Expire; and there lyes your *Coffin* that must receive your perishing body: How can you bear the sight of all these things?" (*DCWS*, 144)

We might find these tactics macabre, and cruel: on the last day of Esther Rogers's life, while John Rogers did his best to reinforce her confidence ("look unto that Jesus"), the community of interlocutors did its best to shake it ("look unto the gallows"). But in its own way, this group, no less than the perhaps more tender-hearted John Rogers, was trying to construct a contemporary saint's life out of Esther Rogers's story. Christian hagiographies typically end with the saint dying a good death, that is, remaining confident and serene in her last moments. Esther's companions question her repeatedly because they don't want to be deceived about her salvation, and they don't want her to be deceived either. Perhaps we might say that ultimately they show more confidence in her spiritual integrity by putting her faith to a trial than does John Rogers, who spares her feelings. It is precisely by attempting to "molest her spiritual quiet" that they gather more evidence that her hopeful conversion is genuine. Esther's responses, together with the account of her faith above, indeed show that what she has achieved by execution day is an unshakeable peace of mind.

But if "liberty of speech" meant fluency in an approved Christian idiom, the capacity to partake in dialogue, Esther's accompanying "freedom of spirit," we may imagine, went beyond what the community might have anticipated. As in the criminal and conversion narratives, in this final section she continues to describe her former spiritual state in the terms of bodily confinement; her present status is preeminently one of freedom from fear, from "hurries" and agitation. In the words reported here, she elaborates that figure with the language of possession, heightening the sense of entrapment and locating the real object of terror within the body: her "hurries" come from unwanted bodily energy and her fears from unwelcome thoughts. Her account of her experience after her conversion employs a consistent imagery of possession to describe the spiritual calm, or more properly, freedom from agitation she feels—freedom even from fear of her impending execution: "neither have I been troubled," she reports, "with terrifying Dreams or Fancies, as formerly I was; nor can I possess my self with fearfulness, when I endeavour it by thinking on the most awful circumstances of my Condition and manner of Death which I am to suffer" (*DCWS*, 132). Even on the morning of her execution, she confirms her state of mind in similar terms: "When I think of my Sins they disappear, and fly from me. I many times have endeavoured to terrify my self with the thoughts of Death, and my Execution, it seems rather a matter of comfort than terror to me" (*DCWS*, 142). This is "freedom of spirit" indeed. Her language, in fact, suggests an insular self, one to which troublesome, invasive thoughts—of impending painful death, of past sin—simply won't stick. Whereas before she had been hurried, oppressed with "horrours," "Great and dire Conflicts in my Spirit" (141), she is now possessed with pleasure and delight and sweetness, and successfully insulated against all kinds of afflictions. To the question about the blood of the children, she answers, "I trust I have an Advocate." To "Whether she found it hard to believe?", "Yes, but yet she desired to roul herself upon the Mercy of God, for He has said, *Come unto me all ye that are weary and heavy laden, and I will give you Rest."* To "How can you bear the sight of all these things? She turns about, and looking him in the face with a very smiling countenance, sayes, I know I am going to the Lord Jesus Christ."

Like Sarah Smith, who had slept through her execution sermon, Esther Rogers is "unconcerned"—but while Smith's reaction was read as a sign of her estrangement, Rogers's equanimity here is a sign of hopeful conversion. The body had contained a contaminant, but it has now successfully been emptied. Whereas in the criminal narrative the verbs are active, suggesting the agency of a self that was nevertheless blocked ("I could not rest, nor sleep, nor read"), here the verbs attached to the subject "I" are verbs of perception only: "I see," "I discern," "I find." It is this paradoxical detachment from its own subjectivity that typically distinguishes the converted self. Like the cage that has expelled its bird, like the once-pregnant body that has expelled its sinful seed, the converted self Esther describes is free because it is now inert, emptied of energy, untouchable, and, it seems, impenetrable from the outside. This is a body that is no longer vulnerable to incursions, and is no longer capable of harboring dangers. It is no longer "hurried," or, we might say, although Esther does not, no longer "quickened." In Esther's spiritual idiom, bodily images reminiscent of pregnancy—containing, waiting, being emptied—describe the spiritual experience of sinfulness and redemption.

This, as we have seen, is John Rogers's particular idiom; it is language that Esther Rogers has heard in the sermons of which she was the subject; it is the language that the community of Ipswich has been taught to accept, and they believe they recognize a sinner brought to salvation when they hear her using it. In John Rogers's sermons, such language—attention to the maternal bond, images reminiscent of the processes of pregnancy—signaled both a self that is ultimately inviolable and the wholeness of a community, a community that included Esther Rogers, for her sin merely tied her to all of the created world rather than alienating her from it. And yet that idiom, when Esther Rogers uses it, is in its own way just as self-protective, just as self-isolating as Sarah Smith's sleep; she does not participate in dialogue so much as turn it back. Just as she is speaking in the community's approved language—and just as they are ready to say that she has overcome her estrangement, that she has "opened her mind" and is talking fluently to them, accepting their notions of sin and grace—just as all this is consummated, she is also saying that they can't touch her. While for them, the whole pastoral episode, and the volume itself, celebrates her integration, what we may hear in her language—this language that they repeat and approve—is not integration into the community but insulation from it—"perfect freedom," in John Rogers's phrase, from anything outside that might trouble her, including the rope that will soon be around her neck. She has learned well the discourse of sin and salvation that they have spent eight months teaching her. But as execution day approaches, she uses it, we may imagine, to her own purposes, all the while keeping them at bay while letting them believe that she dies in their embrace.

Belcher's admiring closing remark captures the paradox: "Her undaunted Courage and unshaken Confidence she modestly enough expressed, yet stedfastly held unto the end." For while the story of Esther Rogers's last hours presented here is a story of maintaining conversational fluency, it is also a story of endurance, pure and simple. Those persistent interlocutors admire her ability to speak so clearly, in that familiar Christian idiom of her salvation under the pressure of an impending death. In some ways the literary model for the narrative is the walk of Christ to Golgotha: John Rogers's references to the good thief crucified there readily suggest that context, and Belcher's very last remark confirms that Esther is being presented as a model Christian: "he must needs want Faith for himself, that wants Charity for such an one." (*DCWS*, p. 153). For Esther Rogers's part, she briefly began "to flag and faulter," but quickly regained her equanimity, and her ability to keep speaking, making replies to her companions' constant questions that were "suitable though short," recalling the three falls of Christ on his walk to execution. (*DCWS*, p. 145–46).

But Belcher suggests an alternative parallel for Esther Rogers, not the Christian martyr, but the Roman soldier, her courageousness "out doing all the old Roman Masculine Bravery and showing what grace can do, in, and for the weaker Sex" (*DCWS*, 119). Belcher's gendering of Esther's virtue is unique among all the ministers who comment. But his comment is interesting because it suggests as well an alternative exemplary behavior: not fluency but stoicism. The latter implies not, as has been the burden of *Death the Certain Wages of Sin* all along, her integration within a Christian community through dialogue, but her insularity. That she keeps her composure throughout her ordeal is very important. It was her ability to stand up under repeated harassment that finally allows both Wise in the cell before John Rogers's final sermon and the group of ministers accompanying her to the gallows to give her the stamp of approval, to concede to her that it appears that she has a good chance of being saved. Her "Radiant countenance, so unconcerned with the business of Death" at the gallows, and Belcher's words, signal this, and signal that even as she was speaking what sounded to most of those in Ipswich as the language of integration, she was, we may like to imagine, far, far away.

A Note on the Negro Lad

Though John Rogers does not stigmatize the youth cohort, as so many of his contemporaries did, he also makes no mention of the father of Esther Rogers's dead children, "the Negro Lad" that she mentions in her narrative. This father's identity, while unknown to us today, did elicit the comment of some contemporaries. Esther Rogers herself refers to his race, and in two contemporary diaries that mentioned the Rogers case, the writers make note of it parenthetically. One journal mentions that Rogers had "murdered her bastard-child (had by a Negro)" and another says that she had murdered "her child (a mulatto)" and enlarges on that theme: "It may be noted she was a poor sinful Creature as vile as ordinarily any are that live under the light of the Gospel, and one who had a child by a negro at Newbury when she was about 17."[50] These comments indicate that race was a significant marker for these writers. They tell us, first, that Esther herself was white, and second, that the race of the father was quite worthy of note, its sensational nature merely heightened, in fact, by the parentheses. The remarks suggest that the community of Ipswich that welcomes Esther Rogers, perhaps with the help of John Rogers's inclusive language, may define itself also by exclusion. The distinction between enslaved blacks and black and white servants in colonial New England is somewhat difficult to establish. William Piersen notes that black slaves, like all servants, were considered part of the household (as Esther was at Woodbridge's). Moreover, since many families "bound out" their own children to other families for a number of years, the practice among slave children was not peculiar.[51] So, what was the distinction between Esther Rogers, servant, and the "Negro lad"?

A tantalizing note in the Newbury town records the October after Esther's execution, tells us that one "Thomas Mossum, a colored man, was ordered to leave town with his family."[52] The circumstances under which the Mossums were expelled are unspecified, and it is unlikely that they had anything to do with the case of Esther Rogers (although we might imagine a son in this family, bound out as a servant, being the "lad"). But their expulsion suggests how much more marginal and ineligible for ritual coming into communion the "Negro lad" would have been than was Esther Rogers. Even John Rogers's sermons, which describe community in such inclusive language that it may include even a white servant girl who has murdered her child, gives some hint as to the limits of that community. Although I have argued that the discourse of sin in *Death the Certain Wages of Sin* preserves the integrity of the body (and therefore of the community) so that sin may be readily washed

off, those same figures of speech leave room for imagining what may be outside that cosmically ordered universe. "Can a man touch Pitch, and not be
defiled forth with?" John Rogers asks. Since the race of Esther's partner was so
much in the minds of other contemporary commentators, it is hard not to
hear such a reference to it in John Rogers's language here, suggesting that the
language of filth, however noninvasive, marks that source of sin outside the
community in the "Negro lad," the "Pitch" that Esther has "touched" (or, as
is described alternately in the same passage, "as a Sow wallowing in the mire")
and whose effects may be washed off.

"To Prevent Lives Being Lost": Community Responsibility and the Bastard Neonaticide Act

The Esther Rogers documents are anomalous among turn-of-the-century cases
in giving any hint whatever of the character of the sexual encounter that led to
the pregnancy, or indeed of the identity of the father, including his race.
Although the majority of ministers preaching in the 1690s, by emphasizing
sexuality in their sermons, did not single out the special sinfulness of women,
in fact the cluster of infanticide prosecutions in that decade does suggest that
in legal terms the sexuality of women was perceived to need a special kind of
policing. In general, patterns of law enforcement changed in the latter seventeenth century so that cases brought before the law were less likely to concern
sexual misbehavior itself and more apt to involve illegitimate births, in a
"trend," as Carol Karlsen describes it, "toward holding women responsible for
the more general failure to adhere to community sexual norms."[53] There is
indeed plenty of evidence of extramarital sexual conduct in early New England
communities: bridal pregnancies, prosecutions for fornication, and suits for
breach of promise, for example.[54] Trying to hear "a Voice of God unto the
Country," Cotton Mather went even further in his 1715 sermon for Margaret
Gallaucher when he painted a picture of towns and byways littered with un-
claimed dead babies: "Several *Bastard Children* have been *Murdered* in this
Place: But there has not unto this Day been any Detection of the *Murderers*."[55]
Mather's unspoken claim is that these undetected murderers are mothers, and
the cluster of infanticide prosecutions in the 1690s reflects the increased
enforcement of a statute known to historians as the Bastard Neonaticide Act
against them. This law, originally instituted in England in 1624 by a Puritan-
dominated Parliament, was followed in New England practice in the seventeenth century and was formally instituted in the Massachusetts Code in

1696. That the frequency of prosecutions under it coincides with the witchcraft prosecutions may reflect a general increase in anxiety about controlling women's behavior in this decade, or an over-scrupulosity in enforcing the English statute after the loss of the Charter. The act specified that for an unmarried woman, a dead infant's body was presumptive evidence, in the case of a concealed pregnancy, of murder. As a result, maternal bastard neonaticide was the only instance of capital murder that did not require two witnesses: the infant corpse alone was enough evidence for a conviction. Unless she could produce at least one witness to the birth, even a stillbirth would put her at risk for a capital charge. Concealment of birth, that is, became tantamount to murder.[56]

The Bastard Neonaticide Act is a chilling literalization of what Karlsen is talking about: a mechanism for discriminatory enforcement of community sexual norms, for of course only women could be held responsible by it for the fate of their illegitimate sexual issue. To a great extent, the published infanticide literature seems to work in tandem with this law. When Cotton Mather told Elizabeth Emerson, "You shed the Blood of your own Children to cover your Uncleanness," subordinating, as we have seen, killing to sexual sin, he embraced the theory of the Bastard Neonaticide Act, which infers murderous intent (motive) in the case of a concealed nonmarital pregnancy. According to the Act, moreover, it did not matter if Esther Rogers abandoned her infant "whether alive, or dead, I could not tell," for an unwitnessed stillbirth convicted an unmarried mother of murder just as surely as would a deliberate, witnessed act of strangulation or drowning, for example. As written, the Act transforms the infant death into a kind of perverse, unknowing speech act, both an attempt at concealment and then, when found, a public disclosure, or unwitting confession—not to violent killing, but to sex or uncleanness. So if ministers preached about sex and not murder, they were saying no more than what may have been the legal truth. The Bastard Neonaticide Act redefined evidence of sex (a birth) as evidence of murder, and in turn the execution sermons associated with it redefined conviction of murder as evidence of sex. When Samuel Willard indicts his auditor for "adding murder to whoredome," when Noyes and Gerrish warn "those who indulge themselves in the breach of the seventh commandment" that they may face the gallows for a breach of the sixth, they reproduce the action of the law, displacing murder with whoredom, conflating the killing of babies with sexual misconduct, or "uncleanness."

The rationale written into the statute puts forth a sociological analysis in miniature, one that all but admits it targets women innocent of conventional murder: "Many Lewd women, that have been Delivered of Bastard Children, to avoid their Shame, and to escape Punishment, do secretly Bury or Conceal the Death of their Children; and after, if the Child be found Dead, the said Women do allege that the said Child was born dead; whereas it falleth out sometimes (although hardly is to be proved) that the said Child or Children were Murdered by the Said Women their Lewd Mothers, or by their Assent or Procurement." The statute, that is, also directs its ire at the stubbornness of those "lewd mothers" who, like those depicted in most infanticide sermons ("as good speak to a stone"), deliberately remove themselves from the care of the community for fear of its censure, excommunicating themselves through lying. While the origins of the act surely lie in the need to deter the incidence of chargeable bastardy to English parishes, its focus on concealment has a special resonance in the latter-day New England context.[57] By making concealment, not violence, the determinative factor, the murder statute widens its scope and changes its social meaning: concealment describes not just an individual's culpable acts, but a failed relationship to a wider community. Further, it suggests not only the individual's obligation to tell but the community's obligation to hear, and to be present at a birth. The final clause of the law is an attempt to resist those tendencies antithetical to communion by providing an avenue to reattach those "lewd mothers" to community: "in every such case the mother so offending shall suffer death as in the case of murder, except such mother can make proof by one witness at the least that the child whose death was by her so intended to be concealed was born dead." This clause makes the Act an anomalous murder statute, the only murder charge that does not need two witnesses as evidence. It is the lack of witnesses that describes the crime; and witnesses are defined as exculpatory, a defense against the charge of lying. Although circumstantial evidence (usually medical testimony of a true stillbirth) could lead to acquital, as a practical matter, this "one witness at the least" means a midwife who was present at the birth.[58]

Writing in the midwife as, in effect, the court's surrogate, raises the question of community awareness, for how could any pregnancy be successfully kept secret in the first place? Who would hope to "hide her shame" by concealing the death of a bastard if she had not hoped to have concealed the entire pregnancy first? The traditions of neighborly watch in New England communities make the question all the more difficult. Although many recent studies of New England community life have focused on the famed New England litigiousness or the social functions of gossip and slander—in short, on the meddlesomeness of neighbors—the positive ideal operating in these communities was that individuals lived in community with a sense of neighborliness and mutual responsibility—mutual responsibility that included attending to each others' childbirths. Nevertheless, by 1700, the traditions of neighborly watch had begun to deteriorate, along with the communal ethos that made them possible and desirable; such changing boundaries of public and private responsibilities, which Helena Wall calls a "fundamental shift in our history," were accompanied by a certain degree of social discomfort and unease.[59] In some ways, while the infanticide case is a sign of the self-destructive sinfulness of an individual who willfully estranges herself from community, it is a sign as well of community failure to enforce its norms and make its institutions of care accessible to those in its orbit. Interestingly, by the 1730s, juries both in England and in New England tended to look beyond the presence of a witness for reasons to acquit. Evolving standards of medical evidence, a general increase in the prerogatives of defendants, and a growth in what Thomas Laqueur calls a "humanitarian" rather than punitive attitude toward unmarried pregnant women, all contributed to this trend, according to the most comprehensive study of the eighteenth-century British literature.[60] Both in England and America, some infanticide proceedings contained reports of infants found in privy vaults. In such cases, English juries, though inconsistent, would sometimes acquit the accused mother, deciding that she was not aware that she was pregnant and so could not be held to any standard of premeditation necessary for most murder convictions. Or, they would invoke the principle of "benefit of linen": if the woman could show that she had prepared clothes and other linens for the expected baby, they would interpret that as evidence that she did not intend to murder the child and acquit her, even if there was no witness, as the law stipulated, to the stillbirth or neonatal death.[61] That the Bastard Neonaticide Act seemed less credible to juries in these early decades of the eighteenth century betrays, within the New England context, the anxiety to which Wall points. As she remarks, even in more urbanized, cosmopolitan areas in colonial America, "neighbors were less intimate, and midwifery was a business—but the community still owed something to women in childbed."[62] And by 1733, when the last woman convicted in Massachusetts under the Bastard Neonaticide Act, Rebekah Chamblit, was executed, juries had become very reluctant to convict, reflecting, perhaps public ambivalence about this very question: the execution sermon for Chamblit actually prints the text of the law, "for the spreading of Knowledge of it, and to prevent lives being lost." The comment signals communal ambivalence about its own role in such infant deaths (and in exposing unmarried mothers to capital prosecution), an ambivalence that may explain the falling off in convictions.

Esther Rogers's criminal confession, published in *Death the Certain Wages of Sin*, seems tailored to the Bastard Neonaticide Act, but in that very fact exposes the complex and ambivalent role her surrounding community plays in the construction of infant murder as defined by that statute. While Esther's active voice in this section highlights her own evasions of community, the contrast between outcomes in her two pregnancies raises important questions about the roles played by those surrounding her as well. While living during her first pregnancy in what she herself had described as a paternalistically supervisory household, one that had carefully provided her with a culturally appropriate education, Rogers was able to avoid detection. But for the second pregnancy, living in a more public place, one that presumably took less notice of her, she is comparably more exposed, and is caught. It was the neighborly watch that found the second child's body and used it to accuse her, however diligently she tried to evade it. But it was the absence of witnesses to that birth, a lack of attention to a pregnancy, that exposed Esther Rogers to the consequences of the Bastard Neonaticide Act in the first place.

Rogers's confession, therefore, depicts not only her own ambivalence toward community, but its ambivalence toward her: it is eerily unconcerned and intrusively supervisory, absent and present, clamoring about her to answer its accusations and as silent as a stone. Mather's comment—"Several *Bastard Children* have been *murdered* in this Place: But there has not unto this Day been any Detection of the *Murderers*"—gets to the heart of a paradox. In this community with a long tradition of neighborly watch, what is visible to that community's detection? Esther successfully hides all the "hurries" associated with her pregnancy, including birth pains and trips out to the garden or pond, all of which proceed without interference; the infant body itself, on the other hand, issues in a rather triumphant accusation: "The Child being found by some Neighbors was brought in & laid before my Face." (*DCWS*, p. 124). If after the fact the execution sermons typically focused on sexuality, not maternity, the legal inquiries reflect communal interest in the bodies of dead infants, not of pregnant women. It is the finding of the infant body that brings a woman within the reaches of the law. But the pregnant woman's body, if it had only been noticed early enough to command the attention of those charged with overseeing childbirth, might have avoided that legal arm.

Judge Sewall's diary records a tantalizing observation about the Rogers trial. After hearing the evidence on July 15, he writes, "Jury next morn ask'd advice, then after, brought her in Guilty of murdering her Bastard daughter."[63] Court records survive in summary form only, giving no hint as to what the jury wanted to know. But it is tempting to imagine that their difficulty was with understanding the Bastard Neonaticide Act, under which Rogers was charged. Were they wondering if she could really be held responsible unto death for the demise of a child the circumstances of whose birth were unclear? Did her story suggest not just a wayward girl but also a failure of community supervision?

The conviction record itself, while written in highly formulaic language, captures some of this ambivalence. On the one hand, complying with the definitions within the Bastard Neonaticide Act, it carefully notes the absence of midwife witnesses: "Ester being great with Child, with a certain living Bastard Child the Twelfth Day of November . . . a female living Child Secretly without the Knowledge and Company of any other Woman or person whatsoever, brought forth." But, while the confession in *Death the Certain Wages of Sin* agrees that she did indeed have the baby alone and "not knowing whether it was alive or dead" hurriedly "left it by the pond," the legal record adds an element of deliberate aggression: "upon the said Living Child" it reads, "the sd Ester Rogers being led by Instigation of the Devil and not having the fear of God before her eyes, of her Malice forethought an Assault did make and the sd female Child being so borne alive and in a natural Way then and there that is to say Immediately after the birth of the sd Child feloniously did kill and murther and there, that is to say, by the Meetinghouse pond in Newbury aforesd secretly bury."[64] Technically, the Bastard Neonaticide Act required no more than concealment of the newborn to convict; constructing the "lewd mother" as violent may, however, have satisfied reluctant or doubting juries.[65]

The full court file for Esther Rogers's case is missing. But other cases for which there is a fuller record extant also tend to contain such mixed language, indicating that however vigorously the legal machinery directs guilt at the single woman in question, it often preserves traces of alternative stories, and alternative theories of responsibility. The record illustrates the processes through which alternative stories are molded in favor of the one the legal system can assimilate. As in the clerical literature, the legal literature as well reflects a tension, a competition between two theories of responsibility: either a woman who has loved and made a lie, and who now must be cut off from communion; or a difficult maternity, for which the surrounding community has failed in its responsibilities. In this tension they reveal as well a segmented community, one whose members are unsure of their primary obligations, often reluctant to participate in that legal process, reluctant to declare that evidence of lewdness is evidence of murder, reluctant, perhaps, to find the girl solely responsible. Most often, these ambivalent community members are women.[66]

Juries of Women

Margaret Gallaucher, an Irish woman, was a servant in the household of John and Mary Catta who was charged with infanticide in 1715. As in the Rogers case, the verdict against her relies on legal formulas implying violence, but it also mixes in narrative details suggesting merely a fatalistic passivity. Using the standard legal language for crimes of this type, it finds first that Gallaucher "of her own Malice forethought with force [of]? Arms an assault made up on the Body of an Infant child born alive." The more specific details that follow, on the other hand, tell a story of neglect rather than one of aggression: she "then wilfully unnaturally and feloniously deposed the said Infant new born child naked in the open air [?] Extremity of the Weather so that the sd. new born Child then and there instantly perished and Dyed."[67] It is neglect and not violence that seem to finish off the child. Cotton Mather's sermon publication about Gallaucher, *A Sorrowful Spectacle*, is similarly ambivalent in its characterization of her, ascribing to her both "Satanic Energie" and a stone-like silence: while "a very Violent Spirit," full of "Transports and Furies," she remains unmoved by his exhortations, "Obstinately all along den[ying]" the crime of which she is accused.[68] These legal and ecclesiastical accounts distilled from court testimony are hardly supported by the statements gathered in evidence, however.

The papers filed with the Suffolk Court about Gallaucher's case—indictment, conviction, death warrant—are written in the practiced legal hand, familiar to anyone who reads through these court records, of the magistrates and trained legal clerks. One evidentiary statement, though signed by the magistrate at the bottom, is written by another hand, one rounder and clumsier, with fewer flourishes—and it is signed in that same hand, "Bethiah Wharton." Bethiah was also a member of the Catta household: another servant, perhaps, or, more likely, if she did write her own statement and sign her name, a relative.

> Ruth Ripne who was then a nursing in the house to make the bed
> of Margaret Callegherne who had kept her bed the greatest part of
> the day before by reason of a pain in her leg as she said ocasioned
> by a fall in the street but when we came found her gone for which

reason with some others gave us great cause of suspicion that she
had had a child which put us upon searching narrowly for it when
we found her up the pair of stairs but found none there but afterwards being in the chamber where she lay with Mrs. Mary Catta
who examined her whether she had had a child which she utterly
deneyed but in little time after Mrs. Catta spying something under
the bed asked me what cloath that was that was there upon which I
looked under the bed and see something and pulled out the cloth
which by the bigness and weight of it I supposed to be child upon
which I told her I had found somthing and asked her whether it
was born alive she told me it was not. I then desired Mrs. Catta to
take and open the cloath which she refused saying she did not know
whether it was safe to doe it upon which Mrs. Mercy Rolstone and
Mrs. Mary Gibbs was sent for who was desired to open it to whom
I refer you for further information for I was not present when they
opened it but afterwards see a child which she owned to be hers
before the Gentlemen of the Jury.[69]

The woman's testimony makes no mention of the kind of aggressiveness or
violence remarked on in both Mather's sermon and the legal record; rather, it
paints a picture of a woman who has immobilized herself in bed, assuming
the posture of sickness but refusing the attempts of the women around her to
help. The legally significant focus of Bethiah's statement is the interest in the
infant body, which Margaret had hidden in the bedclothes. When discovered,
it is treated with totemic significance. Its "bigness and weight" suggest what it
is; the women turn it over and discuss whether they should open its coverings; and its revelation seals the evidence against Margaret Gallaucher, prompting as well her confession of maternity, which she had previously "utterly
deneyed."

Most important, Bethiah Wharton's statement in evidence indicates that
the search for the infant that they attach to this unmarried woman com-
mences only after its birth: no one, it seems, had inquired after Gallaucher's
condition when she was still pregnant. We had "a great suspicion," Bethiah
says, "that she *had had* a child." The infant body is definitive, setting in
motion an inexorable process that culminates in Gallaucher's condemnation
and death; Margaret's own body, her pregnant body, which might have set off
alarms, had no such effect.

As we have already seen, Cotton Mather, who preached for Margaret
Gallaucher after she was condemned to die, depicted her as silent, stubbornly

uncommunicative, and isolated. But Margaret's social isolation began well before her condemnation. In important respects, the experiences of Margaret Gallaucher, like those of Esther Rogers, did not conform to what we know of childbirth practices in early America. What scant evidence we have tells us that before the intrusion of the male medical specialist, childbirth was a social affair. An expectant mother would be attended for several days or weeks by a midwife and her female relatives and neighbors. During this period, known as the "lying-in," the pregnant woman might serve food, and other women would be there to help with the birth, offering technical experience and social comfort. The lying-in, then, was "the primary occasion for female solidarity," a time when knowledge about the birth process was shared among women, a realm in which women had sole authority and from which men were pointedly excluded. Although pregnancy could be life-threatening to early modern women, this elaborate female ritual helped compensate for fears and uncertainties, as well as inexpertise in the new mother.[70]

Although historians of childbirth have frequently favorably contrasted seventeenth-century "social childbirth" with later practices of isolating the mother in a male-dominated environment, Esther Rogers's and Margaret Gallaucher's experience exposes some of its limitations. For if overseeing childbirth was the responsibility of a supportive community of women, it is very clear that that community failed these women miserably. One thing we do not know about childbirth practices, as Laurel Thatcher Ulrich has pointed out, was the way in which specific tasks in the lying-in were assigned, or the way in which the event could serve as a rite of passage, a form of initiation into adult female experience, for young women.[71] We do not know, for example, whether, as a teenager, servant, and single woman, Esther Rogers would ever have been invited to be present at a lying-in in Newbury. We do not know what sort of access Margaret Gallaucher, a servant and an Irish woman, would have had to the information and comforts the ritual of the lying-in would have afforded.

The willingness of juries, as the century progressed, to acquit after concluding that the accused infanticide might not have been aware of the signs of her pregnancy suggests that young servant girls might have been excluded from these female rituals and therefore ignorant of the knowledge of the reproductive process that lyings-in served to pass on.[72] Thus, although lyings-in were for women only, they were perhaps not for all women: some, like Esther or Margaret, may have been excluded from this primary female community because of their age and class. Some of them may therefore have been ignorant of what was happening to them; ignorant or not, when they became pregnant they did not have a supportive female community to rely on for help.[73]

Indeed, for many of them, that female community was not only absent but positively hostile. According to the law, both in Massachusetts and in Old England, midwives played an important role in the legal system, being called upon to testify in court about such matters as the cause of an infant's death, the probable date of conception, and confessions in childbed, which were supposed to be particularly credible, of the identity of the father of an illegitimate child.[74] One historian has observed that for young unmarried servants, the midwife was a "quasi-judicial, inquisitorial" figure:[75] in short, not a helper but an enemy. Mary Rolstone and Mary Gibbs seem to have performed this function in Margaret Gallaucher's case; her filed conviction was witnessed by these two women, by the Cattas, and by a Mrs. Wakefield, "the midwife." When an unmarried woman was suspected of concealing a pregnancy or birth, it was often a woman, like Bethiah Wharton or Mary Catta, who became suspicious, and who first made the legal accusation.

So, while childbirth was a realm from which men were excluded, the law exploited the institution of social childbirth as a mechanism of enforcement. Bethiah notes that Margaret Gallaucher has admitted "before the Gentlemen of the Jury" that the child was hers. The Bastard Neonaticide Act, which as we have seen treated an unwitnessed stillbirth as evidence of deliberate murder, meant that an unmarried woman concealed her pregnancy from this community of midwives at her own peril. She needed the midwife and community women as witnesses in case of the death by natural causes of her infant.

In a sense, we have warring stereotypes: one in which midwives and neighbor women eagerly do the work of the law and the community by bringing to light illicit sexual behavior, thus helping to deter the births of chargeable bastards; on the other, a community of helpers who, before the invasion of the medical specialist, function to share knowledge, administer care, and preserve the life and health of women and infants. In these cases, the midwives and birth-women have a supervisory legal function after the fact, but they also have a supervisory function before it, one that they have not fulfilled. The institutions of the law and social childbirth together were inhospitable to pregnant unmarried women, who were perhaps at most risk, medically and socially, for producing a dead infant. The excommunication that Mather and others depicted in their execution sermons, the isolation of these often young, poor servant girls, extends also to their access to services, services usually provided by a female community. The focus on the discovered infant body merely points up the absence of interest in the pregnant body previously.[76]

While midwives could play an important role in convicting women of infanticide, New England court records suggest, in their fragmentary way, that the people surrounding these accused women were at times reluctant participants in the legal process, a process that could work to convert midwives' supervisory role to its own purposes. Even in Margaret Gallaucher's case, the testimony of women indicates that they were unsure at first what to do with that wrapped-up cloth, unsure of their obligations; Bethiah Wharton's testimony suggests that from the women's point of view, neglect and not aggression was the dominant feature of Margaret's experience. And in the well-documented Elizabeth Emerson case, conflicting reports of what the neighboring women found give evidence of divergent desires to affect the legal outcome.[77]

A report in the Emerson files shows that half a dozen men and women arrived at the Emerson house at once to investigate a suspicion of infanticide. The women, charged with examining Elizabeth to see if she had recently given birth, seem to allow her a chance to escape their inspection: "one of us asked her and said betty it may be you may save us a great dele of trouble and pray now tell us plainly how the case is with you whether you are now with child as is commonly reported and famd." Emerson's precipitous response shows an awareness of those "common reports," and of the legal ramifications of an unwitnessed birth: "I never murdered any child in my life. . . . I never committed murther that I know of." Her answer apparently being unsatisfactory, the women did a physical examination, and "she did seem to go willingly with them." Meanwhile, the men went outside and, finding some newly broken ground, dug and found two infants wrapped up in a cloth. At this point the focus of the women's investigation shifted from Elizabeth's body to the bodies of these infants. An inquest done by a panel that included the four women who participated in the search at the Emerson home, found "that the children was at their ful time," but that "upon our exam of their bodies could not find on them any mark of blows, or signs of their being violently put to death."[78]

These same four, however, testified somewhat differently at the trial: Hannah Browne, Hannah Swan, Judith Webster, and Mary Neff made their marks at the bottom of a statement in evidence for that proceeding, saying that they "cannot but believe them to be born Alive; for one of them had the Navell string twisted about the neck, on of its hands clapt upon the same which was apprehended and not be if the child had been born dead or still born, and the other hand the Navell string wrapt about its thigh what was the absolute means of the Death." The gruesome details seem to suggest that there were marks of violence on these bodies, and even that they may have been deliberately strangled with the cord, an implication made more dramatic by the detail of the little hand clasped on the cord at the neck.[79] The midwives' statement goes on to admit that "we cannot learn wheather it were a willful act of murder by the mother or any else but if not . . . we do certainly believe that the children perished for want of help and caer [?] att time of travell which she owned to be so." This point as we know is sufficient for Elizabeth's conviction. Why then, are the grisly details of the disposition of the bodies included, if not to drive home the point that Elizabeth should be held legally culpable? It may have been an opinion that was not shared by all, however. Below the women's marks, there is a carefully noted demurrer: "Mary Neff signs to all the above except only that she did not see the childs hands claspt upon the Navel string that was about the neck of it." Scrupulousness on Mary Neff's part may explain the presence of that notation, or perhaps, an awareness that despite the letter of the Bastard Neonaticide Act, the disposition of the cord would be used as evidence of Elizabeth's deliberate violence, making conviction easier. Neff, perhaps, participated less enthusiastically than her sisters in the whole legal machinery that would condemn Betty.[80]

One undated and fragmentary court paper in the Suffolk Court files, though it gives us only a frustratingly partial glimpse of its subject, illustrates just how ambivalent a role the community of neighboring women could play in such a case. It concerns Abiah Comfort, who having been suspected of having recently given birth, was questioned by the magistrate about her recent activities.

Quest.	Whether she had a child yea or nay
Answer.	She had something but did not know whether it was a child or not
Q.	Where she brought it fourth
A.	In passing from Zecheus house to Sarah Chillering's House. She fell very Ill by the Way and there brought forth Something and was so ill that she scarcely arrived at the sd. House there leaving what she brought forth
Ques.	Who was at the House when she came there
A.	Sary Zechaus whom she tried to wak up but could not
Q.	In the morning did you tell Sary Zacheus what befell you in the night

A.	I told her I was not well and that was all she getting up early and going away to work
Q.	Who did you see next
A.	Old Sarah Chillring, Bethya [?] and Lizzie Jakers at the next house whereunto I was sent for they being informed that I was unwell by a little girl [?] that was sent to the house of an arrant [errand] and I went
Q.	Did you tell them what had befell you
A.	Yes
Q.	And what said they
A.	They took little or not heed to it. I offered them to go and shew them but they refused alledging I should get could and so would not go with me
Q.	When and with whom you went to fetch or Bury it
A.	Last Tuesday I went with Betty Harrey and she brought it to the burying place by [Davies?] and there about noon in the company of two Squaws and two Indian men did bury it

And it being late at night the said Abiah Comfort was committed to the Constables care till tomorrow morning[81]

So far the document provides mixed evidence about the role of Abiah Comfort's community. On the one hand, the neighbors seem distant and unavailable to her, resisting at first her efforts to get the help she requests of them. However, they seem most interested in helping Abiah take care of herself. To that end, they discourage her from recovering whatever infant remains there may be— because it is most important that she rest, but also, perhaps, to keep the whole incident hidden from legal authorities. The fascinating detail about the burial—attended only by one friend and four Indians—suggests that Abiah must turn to people very peripheral in the community for help, but also perhaps, that her English neighbors didn't want to be forced, like Mary Rolstone or Bethiah Wharton, to testify against her by learning swearable details.

Obviously, someone did bring the magistrate in, leading to this document. But something changed after his first day of questioning, for the next day, an entirely different story emerged.

March the 29th the said Abia Comfort being further examined after the Jury of women had found she had a child [and did] Confess she killed the child
Q.   What did you put the string round the childs neck for
Answer   To keep it from Crying

Q.	Did it cry
A.	Yes very much
Q.	What made you kill your own child
Answer	Because I laid it to the rong man for I knew I was with child before he was concerned with me

Whether the "jury of women" who conducted a physical examination could definitively determine that this was a full-term live delivery, and not a miscarriage, premature delivery or stillbirth is perhaps questionable. In this case, though, in the absence of the infant body, the postpartum body becomes evidence before that female panel, and its exposure stimulates an entirely new confessional narrative: after the midwives' official intervention, a young man is apparently off the hook, and the delivery is a live birth, not abandoned along the way to a neighbor's house by a confused and sick girl, but deliberately and secretly strangled by its "lewd" mother.

We, however, have no reason to credit one story over the other. The women here fill that "quasi-judicial" role, and we may imagine Abiah Comfort waking up the morning after her arrest to confront a more coercive and hostile group of inquisitors than she had faced with the magistrate the previous day. Her confession illustrates the tendency of the legal documents, already remarked upon, to establish more than is required by the Bastard Neonaticide Act for conviction, namely, a claim of direct violence by the mother on the infant's body. So this jury of women, finding that Comfort's was a full-term delivery, drag out the story that she had actually put a string around the infant's neck. In addition, as a collaboration between the "jury of women" and the law, the second story, whether truthful or not, dramatizes the community's interest in establishing paternity—or more to the point, in protecting someone from that responsibility. The two-part structure to Comfort's examination and to the document functions here to expose her as a liar, and catching her in a lie about the disposition of the infant casts doubt on her identification of the father as well.

Legal historians have suggested that the shift in the attention in New England courts from punishing simple sexual transgressions to prosecuting those involving conception reflects the community's interest in protecting itself from having to support fatherless children.[82] Therefore, it would be logical that all social institutions together—church, court, and birth-women— would work together to try to identify these fathers. Most frequently, though, the references in these documents to paternity, like those in Abiah Comfort's case, involve repudiation of the mother's word. Increase Mather notes in one of his sermons for Sarah Threeneedles that she also has possibly accused the wrong man of fathering the child that she is condemned for killing. "You have accused one who not only denies what you have charged him with, but has appealed to God concerning his Innocency."[83] "Stand not in any lye," he cautions her as she nears her own death on the scaffold, hoping perhaps that she, like Abiah, will clear the young man before she dies. Cotton Mather introduces his *Pillars of Salt* with the note that most of the criminals he describes "go out of the World with *Lyes* in their *Mouths*."[84] For the infanticides in his collection, which includes Sarah Threeneedles and Sarah Smith, this surely implies in part lies about paternity. So the young woman's naming of her partner in sin becomes yet another instance of linguistic trespass, cutting her off from communion, rather than an opportunity to widen social responsibility for a pregnancy gone horribly wrong.

This snapshot of Abiah Comfort's case, with its two-part narrative, nicely illustrates, through its very clumsiness, the processes of legal narrative construction and how in its final disposition, a story of a difficult travail is replaced by the familiar narrative of a lewd woman who has loved and made a lie. Although in this case the former story finds its way into the magistrate's document, it did not easily fit into legal requirements for disposing of the case. So, when Abiah Comfort arrived at her neighbor's house, and told them that she "had something but did not know whether it was a child or not," perhaps they knew enough that the more prudent course was not to pursue the matter, not to bring forth details that could not be heard. They were willing to collaborate with Abiah, who as it turned out was too forthcoming for her own good, in a safer silence. In all, the document reflects the dispersion of motive and actions among different members of the community. As in the clerical literature, two interpretations compete, loving and making a lie, for which the "lewd woman" herself was to be held solely responsible, and difficult maternity, which would connect the woman in question to other elements of the community responsible for maternity care.

A rather full record survives for the case of Sarah Smith, the Deerfield woman for whom John Williams preached *Warnings to the Unclean* in 1698. Smith, though married, was prosecuted under the Bastard Neonaticide Act because her husband, as the court papers noted, had been "in captivity [among the Native Americans], absent then being, and had been by the space of more than two years."[85] Therefore, her child, as the law says, would have been "by law a bastard." The Smith case, though unusual because of Smith's marital status, further elucidates the ambivalent community involvement in such cases. The court records and Williams's sermon together paint an extraordinary picture of a woman living on the frontier, vulnerable to the Indian attacks that destroyed her family but also exercising the freedom that comes from that kind of communal devastation. Williams constructs a narrative of Sarah's life that both illustrates the threats facing her frontier community and asserts its enduring stability, showing that it is vulnerable to a special kind of incursion, but able to keep its boundaries, if not its borders, intact. "In the day of the Lord's anger, you have sinned more and more: when God had driven you out of one Plantation, into another, by the Enemy; when God had taken away your first Husband by Death, and suffered your second to be carried into Captivity; when he was in bondage, you were wantonly doting on your Lovers; yea though you could not look out at your door, but the Garrison and Souldiers before your eyes proclaimed it to be a day of God's anger."[86] In the terms of the jeremiad, the Indian raids are signs of disapprobation from God and of the need for a special watchfulness; the armed garrison well symbolizes the community's continuing commitment to order in the face of these forces of destruction and chaos. Smith offends her community, according to Williams, by not recognizing that continuing commitment. In not submitting to order's recognizable authorities—father, minister, husband—she violates the hierarchical binaries that are the mainstays of the social order, especially "in a day of God's anger." "You would not hearken to the voice of your eminently pious Father-in-law"; most offensive to Williams personally, "you closed your eyes, and would not see, tho' for many years you lived under an eminently Soul-searching Ministry"; and most immediately relevant, "Your sin is very great, in violating your marriage covenant," committing in her husband's absence the adultery that led to the illicit pregnancy.[87] Like other execution sermons that emphasize sex, *Warnings to the Unclean* heaps opprobrium upon one isolated sinner, casting her out so that the community itself may remain whole.

But Williams's sermon also reveals that that community is not so cohesive after all, for Sarah is not the only one who has ignored these authorities. He admonishes others, whom he does not identify: "I would fain have clarity, that there is but one in this Assembly, that hath been guilty of Murder in the highest degree of it; yet I fear there are several that have Murdered in their hearts, and some who have been guilty of interpretive Murder, for hiding and concealing the Uncleanness of which this poor Condemned One was guilty, before she became guilty of Murder, for which she is to dye."[88] Others, that is, have known about her adultery and also, perhaps, about her pregnancy, but did not come forward, thus collaborating in the lie. Williams's term, "interpretive murder," suggests, despite the standard cast-out rhetoric, some diffusion of responsibility.[89] In chastising Sarah's neighbors, he suggests that by looking the other way, they have transgressed their responsibilities not only to the community's value on truth—exposing uncleanness—but to Sarah and that "murder" victim, the newborn itself. Indeed, the legal record implies that Sarah Smith, far from being isolated, was embedded in the Springfield community in a way that potentially would make others responsible for the survival of her illegitimate child—and suggests that that part of the community to which Williams refers as being guilty of "interpretive murder," is the community of women.

For one thing, Smith had affirmed, in a recorded interrogation, that she had confided in one person, Mary Lyes[?], who had advised her "to conceale it." The midwives' testimony duly notes—as does the official conviction record—that they eventually found the infant body, "being tyed up in an apron four corners together." But here more than in other cases there is much more attention to Smith herself as a patient. Mercy Allene testified, for example, that "I heard that Sarah Smith of Deerfield was sick I went to her and found her in such a state that I thought she was in travail and the child nere birth for her water was Broken." They come to her bedside, that is, to help with the birth, not to accuse her after the fact. A joint statement by three of the attending women adds these details: "Wee told her she was in travaile she sayd she was not wee told her that we would have the truth and see her up, she sd she could & goe out of Dores and that she was only all of an ague that she was better. She began to sweat when she got up she came to the fire wee all saw by the sheete that which caused us to tell her that it could not be so unless a childe borne." While their testimony, depicting a very sick woman and stained sheets, suggests that they arrived there very soon after the birth, Sarah's own statement implies that there was a lapse of a few hours. It notes very carefully, too, that she "owned she did not Look after it, thought it was Dead," and, in what is the unfortunate determinative detail, "owned she Denyed haveing a child to the women."[90] Cotton Mather says disgustedly in *Pillars of Salt* that Smith "made the usual pretence" that the baby was born dead.[91] But there is in fact some ambiguity here. "Why," Sarah is asked during that interrogation, "did you not call help of the women," and her doleful reply is "I should have done well to have done," implying that it was perhaps all a matter of unfortunate timing that they did not arrive at the moment they were needed, and in her shaky state Smith had neglected the baby that she thought was already dead and tried to hide it.[92] The midwives' testimony about shakes, sweats, and a bloody sheet might have been taken for evidence of a difficult birth that might very well have yielded a dead infant; but in the legal form, it functioned only to prove Sarah a liar, and the legal conviction record describes that desperate act this way: "with intent to conceale her

Lewdnesse the said Childe did strangle and smother, of which strangleing and smothering the said Childe then and there dyed."[93] The record reflects, that is, both a decline in the neighborly watch in New England—and an ambivalence about that decline—and, paradoxically, some concomitant tendency within the record for a more sympathetic reading of the accused woman.[94]

The ambiguities of the communal role in Sarah Smith's sad end are captured in the official documents of her case, both legal and religious. As part of his litany of Smith's sins, John Williams declares, in a fascinating locution, "You refused to be prevented from Murder, by covering your adultery with lying."[95] Williams's familiar redefinition of infanticide as a lie about illicit sex deflects responsibility back on Smith alone, but it suggests as well the way in which the community is implicated in her story. What's wrong with lying to the birthwomen is that it prevents the community from exercising its responsibilities—responsibilities to witness births and provide care for mother and neonate. Similarly, the conviction record uses the usual formulaic language of violence to describe the so-called murder—"with force and armes upon the sd Child an assault did make," but then the court secretary adds, in between the lines of that set form in handwriting almost too small to make out, that Sarah Smith, "withholding her natural Affection, neglected and refused all necessary help to preseve the life of the Child." The onus again is on Sarah Smith, for separating herself from community, specifically the community of women, "refusing all necessary help," but the language is more than a little defensive about the community's failure to provide that help, to "prevent lives being lost."

Lessons of Caution for Young Sinners: Silencing a "Child of the Town"

Interestingly, at the moment when New England infanticide prosecutions seemed to decline, the 1730s, three publications on infanticide appeared in the New England presses after a long hiatus. Together these books provide a last window on this communal ambivalence about mutual obligations between estranged sinner and caring community. As we've seen before, in these cases a maternal (rather than sexual) narrative tends to be associated with the possibilty of communal interconnectedness, and therefore responsibility.

No execution sermons for infanticide had appeared in Boston for eighteen years when Thomas Foxcroft, co-minister of the First Church, published *Lessons of Caution to Young Sinners*, preached for the execution of Rebekah Chamblit in 1733.[96] Like *Death the Certain Wages of Sin, Lessons of Caution* is a hybrid text, containing not only Foxcroft's execution sermon, but also an introduction by his colleague William Cooper, the reconstruction by Mather Byles, another minister, of his conversation with Rebekah as he walked with her to the gallows, and Chamblit's own "last dying warning." Although like *Death the Certain Wages of Sin*, the diverse parts of *Lessons of Caution* reflect different pastoral techniques, ultimately all these parts work together to produce the same effect. *Death the Certain Wages of Sin* dramatized a woman's coming into communion, her voice achieving a fluency in a Christian idiom. *Lessons of Caution*, in contrast, dramatizes its silencing.

The "last dying warning" attributed to Rebekah Chamblit follows the demands of the form, describing in the first person her path through a life of sins—including uncleanness—that have led to the present disastrous results. It also, however, presents some interesting details about what happened with the pregnancy, details that should by now ring familiar: a young unmarried servant, a problematic delivery during which the absence of an attending nursing group not only seals her legal fate but also, perhaps, explains the unhappy outcome for the newborn.

> On Saturday the Fifth day of *May* last, being then something more than Eight Months gone with Child, as I was about my Household Business reaching some Sand from out of a large Cask, I received considerable Hurt, which put me into great Pain, and so I continued till the Tuesday following; in all which time I am not sensible I felt any Life or Motion in the Child within me; when on the Said Tuesday the Eighth of *May*, I was Deliver'd when alone of a Male infant; in whom I did not perceive Life; but still uncertain of Life in it, I threw it into the Vault about two or three Minutes after it was born; *uncertain*, I say, whether it was a living or dead child; tho' I confess it was probable there was Life in it, and some Circumstances seem to confirm it. I therefore own the Justice of GOD and Man in my Condemnation, and take Shame to my *self*, as I have none but my self to Blame; and am Sorry for any rash Expressions I have at any time uttered since my Condemnation; and I am verily perswaded there is no Place in the World, where there is a more strict regard to Justice than in this Province.[97]

The details provided here seem calculated to illustrate the strictures of the Bastard Neonaticide Act as written. Concealment, not violence, convicted Rebekah Chamblit. But apart from her confession earlier to "uncleanness," and her status as a single woman, there is no recorded intention here to conceal the birth. If the jury had been so inclined, it could have chosen to interpret the law more loosely, finding in Rebekah's report of an injury and in her ambiguous statements about the infant's being alive or not evidence for a possible stillbirth. Rebekah, instead, was convicted, and her confession underscores that the very ambiguity about the newborn's postpartum status is precisely what led to that result: "uncertain, I say, whether it was a living or dead child." The details provided in her "last dying warning," then, illustrate a very strict application of the law, one that juries were becoming less willing to accept.

The most tantalizing part of Chamblit's "last dying warning" is her apology for her "rash expressions" of protest and resentment after her condemnation. If she did not expect to be convicted under the law, that expectation, given the sharp decline in convictions, was not unreasonable. Moreover, it is possible that others shared her surprise. The record of Chamblit's conviction itself starkly describes the capital offense in language that seems to point up what had become the counterintuitive nature of the law: she "did conceal the Death of the said Bastard child and so did murder it."[98] The details of Rebekah's pregnancy may indicate an absent and in fact derelict Puritan community. But, just as Rebekah herself retracts those "rash expressions" in the last dying warning, *Lessons of Caution* disavows such responsibility, isolating Rebekah and giving responsibility to her and her alone. While her community may have been unavailable to her during her pregnancy so that she did not have access to its care, either obstetrical or spiritual, the publication through its clerical voices constructs that community as aggressively present, foregrounding the ministerial prerogative to reclaim this "child of the town," only to drown out her voice with its own. This dynamic is dramatized most effectively in the conversation on the walk to the gallows, contributed by Mather Byles. Cooper had commented in his introduction, "her Answers indeed were but short; as she never us'd to say much when we discoursed with her" (*LC*, ii); Byles's transcript reflects this assessment. As we have seen with Esther Rogers, the pastoral goal of the conversation on the way to the gallows is to test the accused woman to see whether she is remaining strong, and to remind her to focus attention on God and salvation and not on her fear. Accordingly, Byles asks Chamblit a series of questions guiding her through a theological progression from acknowledgement of sin to hope in salvation: "Do you feel yourself a slave to sin and lust"; "[Do] you see, and feel, and own it, that you have nothing in your self to recommend you to GOD?"; "Should not *you* hope in this free grace of God in Christ, as well as any sinner in the World?" He also speaks to her encouragingly: "I am glad to hear you before-hand with *me*" (*LC*, 63–4); "Thou hast well answer'd" (66). And yet as they get closer and closer to the gallows, Byles's speeches and questions get longer, and Chamblit's answers shorter. She punctuates their conversations with expressions of panic: "Oh! I'm afraid, I'm Afraid." "Alas, I've been a dreadful Sinner" (*LC*, 64). "Am I come to this? Lord, whither am I going?" (*LC*, 67). Finally, as they come in sight of the gallows, Byles reports that "the Prisoner grew disordered and faint, and not capable of attending further to continu'd discourse——Only short words of encouragement were now and then spoken to compose and animate her, till she arriv'd at the place of Execution" (*LC*, 68). Whatever resemblance this transcript bore to what really happened, the laywoman's voice depicted here, in contrast to that in *Death the Certain Wages of Sin*, is a feeble voice, dramatically overwhelmed by the language of the minister, however pastoral and sympathetic, and by the mechanisms of the law.

Foxcroft's title sermon plays, of course, an important part in that construction. Self-consciously working in the tradition of Boston infanticide literature, Foxcroft echoes Cotton Mather's sermon titles, claiming, for example, that "many have made themselves into Pillars of Salt" (*LC*, 25); moreover, the sight of Rebekah Chamblit in front of the congregation is "A sorrowful spectacle" (*LC*, 60). Following his colleagues, Foxcroft takes youth—with their propensity to sexual misbehavior—as the chief audience for his sermon, choosing as his sermon text, "They die in youth, and their life is among the unclean" (Job 36.14). Like his forebears in the Boston pulpits, and unlike John Rogers of Ipswich, Foxcroft's discussions of the sins peculiar to youth describe a distinct youth culture, of which for him a tendency toward sexual incontinence is only a part. Ticking off a list of other sins—disobedience, pride, lying, anger—he explains for each one how young people are particularly prone to them. "Intemperance . . . has bro't Multitudes even of young Persons into an untimely & miserable End" (*LC*, 44). Idleness "is a common Inlet to many other Sins," he warns. "It is very much a *City-Sin*, and a Sin of *Youth*" (*LC*, 46). Over and over again, he seems to be telling Rebekah Chamblit's contemporaries that their life in an increasingly cosmopolitan Boston, where the churches are already on the wane, is particularly dangerous. "Beware those growing Sins of the Times," he warns them, detailing all the ways in which the churches are losing influence: "profane Swearing and taking the Name of God in vain, Sabbath-breaking, despising the Gospel of Christ, neglecting the Publick Worship of God, mocking at the Messengers of the Lord, deriding serious Devotion and a tender Conscience, and turning Sacramental Mysteries into Banter" (*LC*, 32). Young people are exposed to being tempted away from religious concentration by a bustling economic life and by the newer tastes of an increasingly cosmopolitan society: "Hear this, O ye that say, When will the Sabbath be Over, that we may sell Corn, may return to Business or Diversion? that say, what a Weariness is it? that snuff at God's alter, and call his Table contemptible: *Behold, he will cut off the man that doth this*" (*LC*, 33). He warns them as well to beware of "tell[ing] Lies for *Profit*; in matters of Trade speaking falsely, to get Gain by cheating others" (*LC*, 38). Equally dangerous are the new fashions that young people are guilty of. "Some people seem to fancy it a piece of *Gentility*, the sign of a polite Education, to be always at Leasure & above Business and therefore *affect* an idle life" (*LC*, 46). Young people who aspire to "gentility" and value the new fashion of "polite education" "may be Masters," he says, "of a great deal of Knowledge (Science, falsely so called) and yet have very *wrong Notions*, in divine matters of the greatest Importance" (29).

In short, Foxcroft inveighs against all the centrifugal forces in newly cosmopolitan Boston, one in which the Harvard brotherhood has lost its determinative influence and young people are drawn away from the churches of their parents by new ideas, opportunities, and fashions. He rebukes them with the Scripture text, "*I have loved Strangers, and after them I will go.*" The gallows awaiting one of their number—this child of the town—gives him a very good rhetorical opportunity to thrust that old church structure back on them, to portray it as a present and pervasive influence, not one from which they can so easily be distracted. Severe though it is, the sermon nonetheless sounds like the last gasp of a church rapidly losing its influence, and as a fourth generation Boston minister desperately asserting his and its continuing relevance.[99] In doing so, he ascribes all the changes to the younger generation, essentially repeating the gesture of his Boston forebears, who had so thoroughly stigmatized young people. And Foxcroft identifies cosmopolitan Boston itself as an anti-community, in competition with church-centered life rather than in step with it.

While stigmatizing young people in a familiar way, Foxcroft adds the category of gender, which potentially stigmatizes women (and women's sexuality) more directly than had his forebears, who as we saw had divested "uncleanness" of any gender specificity. Though fairly evenhanded, admonishing young men and women equally, Foxcroft addresses them separately, ascribing to each different sets of sinful behavior. Lasciviousness, for example, is a gendered quality, as Foxcroft chooses separate biblical warnings about it for men and women: "Let our Sons remember & take Warning from the awful Death of abominable *Onan.* . . . And let our Daughters remember and take Warning from the tragical Story of the *Damsel of Bethlehem-Judah*, who *played the Whore*" (*LC*, 42). Infanticide, as we have seen in the past, is a form of lying; but Foxcroft ascribes that lie not to a stubborn self-excommunication, a turning away from community, but rather to pride, claiming that young women lie in a misguided attempt to maintain communal status. Aptly enough for today's occasion, pride "has tempted many a Young Woman to destroy the Fruit of her own Body, that she might avoid the Scandal of a Spurious Child" (*LC*, 35). In this context, the very presence of childbirth language in this execution sermon sets Foxcroft apart from his forebears of the 1690s. Foxcroft employs maternal language here to suggest a more thorough corruption of social roles than did either the language of sexuality (which suggested a cutting off) or John Rogers's language, where the presence of maternal imagery signaled a vision of a whole and united church. For Foxcroft, in contrast, childbirth language functions as part of his elaboration of a broken, sinful community. Seeing an entire developing culture, and not just a generation, as hostile to church authority, Foxcroft employs such imagery to suggest that all relationships are tainted. Beware, he tells youth, of the sudden destruction that a just God can visit upon you, "as travail upon a Woman with Child. Thou knowest not what a Day may bring forth" (*LC*, 13). Look to Jesus, he tells Rebekah as she contemplates the gallows, "and mourn as a woman for the loss of her first-born" (*LC*, 57). And he threatens her with a sentence from God that would reverse the thrust of the Bastard Neonaticide Act and the earlier infanticide literature, replacing the debauched pleasure of sinful sexuality with the pangs of maternity: "*I gave her a Space to repent of her Fornication, and she repented not: Behold I will cast her into a Bed* Ah! not the Bed of Lust and Pleasure, but of Travail & Pain, a bed of Fire & Torment, without Deliverance for ever" (*LC*, 56).

"A Witness against Myself": The Challenge of Reconnection through Maternity

In the same decade, two other publications about infanticide appeared in the New England presses. Neither Katherine Garret nor Patience Boston, the women whose executions they describe, were "children of the town" in the way Rebekah Chamblit was; instead, they were Native American women in outlying areas, York County and New London, Connecticut.[100] Nevertheless, both experienced the same isolation that Chamblit did in pregnancy, and the law came down on them both with the same sureness and harshness that it did on her. However, while in *Lessons of Caution* the Boston clergy had asserted, perhaps against all evidence, its control over its youth by dramatizing the silencing of Chamblit's voice, in these books the same topic—child murder—became a vehicle for the inscription of a voice in the public discourse for these Native American women in the more distant provinces. Each of these texts is remarkable for how it tips the balance of voices within it back to the individuals, for both Garret and Boston are portrayed as strong and insistent speakers. Each thus signals a different relationship between the sponsoring minister and the lay voice, and a different clerical strategy for using that lay voice for professional aggrandizement: the ministers associated with each woman, Eliphalet Adams, and Samuel and Joseph Moody respectively, were all associated with evangelical activities, and so were attuned to the importance of lay testimony, even from those most marginalized.[101] Moreover, the represented words of Katherine Garret and Patience Boston in these books implicitly challenge the processes of ritual condemnation enacted in them, for they call their respective communities to account for a lack of engagement with them, even as they are condemned for their own estrangement from community norms. While in each case the woman has a religious conversion and joins, as did Esther Rogers, in the larger religious community, overtly accepting in the process its judgment and condemnation for her actions, it may be more accurate to say that in each case the woman challenges the community to take her in.

Katherine Garret, according to the narrative attached to Eliphalet Adams's sermon, was a Pequot, "descended from one of the[ir] best Families," and lived as a servant in a minister's family. It is not clear that she was prosecuted under the Bastard Neonaticide Act (which did have force in Connecticut), for the facts of her case don't seem to fit it. The account of her troubles, though, evokes the same ambiguity as Rebekah Chamblit's on the question of how much oversight this community provided before it condemned her to death:

> Having Unhappily fallen into the Sin of Fornication & being with Child, it pass'd for a while without Suspicion by any in the family, at length being Question'd about it she deny'd it & turn'd it off, assigning *other causes* for the appearances that were observ'd, so that the suspicions about her were thereby *very much* laid asleep. When her hour was Come, she was Delivered alone by her self in the Barn; upon search the Infant was found, with marks upon it of Violence, that had been used, of which wounds it soon Dyed.[102]

Unlike in Chamblit's situation, it appears that here a live infant was found, and that there was evidence of deliberate wounding, so a stillbirth was not a possibility. Here too, there were reports of suspicion of a pregnancy before this fatal event, suspicions, though, that Garret was able apparently to turn back.

It appears, therefore, that unlike Rebekah Chamblit, Katherine Garret starts out surrounded by an involved community, albeit, for her, an adopted one. Eliphalet Adams's sermon reflects the presence of this community in a curious way, putting forth the correct parameters for communal involvement. He reminds his audience of its obligation to do justice, and chides witnesses who would lie to protect the guilty, lawyers and juries who would manipulate the truth, and communities who sometimes would rally around a criminal, even concealing her from the law. Even the criminal's family, he says, though "their hearts will ake" (*SP*, 11) should not suppress the truth. His remarks suggest that the community was sympathetic and protective, reluctant even to cooperate with the mechanisms of the law. To counter that impulse, he argues that it is appropriate for the community to take legal action against a murderer, as well as to counsel him or her. For him, the scripture text "he shall flee to the Pit" means not that a criminal or sinner will be isolated and cast out, but that she shall be embraced by a community whose task it is not to ignore her but to supervise and judge her. Paradoxically, Adams's emphasis on the communal responsibilities rather than the individual's trangressions mutes the "cast-out" theme of the sermon, distinguishing it from Foxcroft's.

The narrative appended to Adams's sermon tells us that "when the Court for her Tryal was appointed to be held at *Saybrook*" [where her master's family lived], "she seemed to Entertain a full Expectation that she should be Cleared." Perhaps Garret was counting on the English community that she had come to be a part of to acquit her. Perhaps, if the evidence had been similar to that which convicted Rebekah Chamblit, she might have been acquitted. But at the trial, "the proofs of her Guilt appeared so plain and full to the Jury and the Court," that she was indeed found guilty. From the wording here and from Adams's attention to the importance of the truth in his sermon, we may infer either that this was a reluctant jury—or that Katherine's community was not ultimately as loyal to this Pequot orphan as she had assumed they would be. Garret herself did not, intially, react well to the verdict. Like Rebekah Chamblit, who would later repudiate her "rash Expressions" after conviction, Garret "was thrown into the utmost Confusion & Distress, Her Expressions were rash and unguarded & she scarce forebore throwing blame on all sorts of persons" (*SP*, 39). Not only is her life threatened by the verdict, but her place in this community, whose support she had assumed, is called into question. She responds by sputtering out her confusion, desperately blaming others to try to plead her own innocence and to regain her old place, or, perhaps, cursing them for their betrayal.

In the logic of the account, of course, all this is prelude to the most important event, Garret's conversion; and it reports that after reading the Bible, listening to sermons, and attending religious meetings in various houses in the neighborhood, Katherine, "it is to be hoped . . . [had] quite another sight and sense of things than she had before" (*SP*, 39), leaving behind, presumably, those "rash expressions" and, like Esther Rogers, learning appropriate Christian idiom. The remarkable part of this story is that in coming around, as it were, to the community's point of view, as articulated by Adams, experiencing a spiritual regeneration and accepting its legal judgment, Garret becomes an aggressive and vocal pursuer of that community. She is able to secure a delay of execution for six months, and all but demands during that time to be given full church membership. "Having never been *Baptized,* she was Earnestly Desirous of that" (*SP*, 39) Adams writes. "She was Extreamly Desirous to partake with us at our *Lord's Table before she Suffer'd*" (*SP*, 40). She does join his congregation on two sacrament days (normally spaced monthly). "When I visited her in her prison," Adams recounts, "she seldom could part with me, without Desiring that I would Pray with her before I went, which favour she Desired of others also, who Visited her during her Confinement" (*SP*, 40). While these are on the one hand the desperate actions of a condemned prisoner, trying to get whatever attention and comfort she could, they also convey her aggressiveness. She seems to be like a gnat buzzing around Adams, tugging at his sleeve to demand his attention. This account reads less as an affirmation of communal values through the dramatizing of a sinner accepting its judgment than as an account of an isolated and marginalized woman demanding access to the institutions of care of a community that has betrayed her. Hers is a forceful and relentless argument, and while Adams's sermon admonishes her for those "rash expressions" she had made at her conviction, it also acknowledges the power of her language. Now her words, no longer "rash," threaten to take over that short account. "Many of her Expressions," he says, "were valuable and worth the Preserving," and he prints a number of statements made by her during these pastoral visits. One of the more interesting ones is her comment on the trial. "Some (she said) had reported of her things that were false; but she heartily forgave them; she Entertained no grudge or malice against any person or any account for that alone, she knew, would ruin her, if she did." Here she is not retracting her protest, but maintaining that at least some of that testimony against her was false. These and other comments quoted by Adams threaten to take over his own narrative, for he abruptly cuts them off, saying "But I forebear gathering up any more of her Expressions, That I be not too tedious" (*SP*, 40–1).

His remark of course illustrates the obvious, that it is Adams who has control over the presentation of Katherine Garret and her words. But Garret's struggle to maintain her voice and demand full access to the benefits of the community that has assumed the right to condemn her pushes into Adams's narrative, despite his efforts to retain control himself. The book dramatizes, as we have seen before, a competition between clerical and criminal voices: this is a competition, however, in which Katherine Garret does quite well for herself. While her conviction perhaps exposes her own marginality in her adopted community, the very tenuousness of her connection itself prompts her aggressive argument; hers is an energy that cannot easily be edited out.

The most extraordinary case of child murder in the 1730s is that of Patience Boston, another Native American servant woman. In the publication about her, the standard textual relationship between condemned criminal and minister is reversed. This is not a sermon published under the name of a minister with a short account of the condemned woman attached at the end. Rather, the publication is called *A Faithful Narrative of the Wicked Life and the Remarkable Conversion of Patience Boston*, and that narrative is told in the first person. There is only a short introductory note by ministers Samuel and Joseph Moody, and no sermon at all. While the ministers, of course, had ultimate control over the presentation of Boston's words, it is significant that they chose to structure the book not to illustrate a woman responding to the counselings or sermons of a minister, but to represent a woman's autonomous voice. The Moodys were linked to the evangelical movement that would culminate in the Great Awakening, and so, for them, this lay conversion narrative functions more credibly than would a clerical sermon.[103] The evangelical agenda, that is, seems best suited by a minimizing of the ministerial role and putting forward as writer the most marginalized of voices. In the context of infanticide specifically, there is a supreme irony, of course, in that it is only in these extreme circumstances of a capital sentence that this woman's voice becomes audible, that she emerges out of invisibility. However, aside from the clerical agenda governing the form of *A Faithful Narrative*, Patience Boston's own represented voice tells of her aggressive pursuit of an audience for her story. By representing her strenuous efforts to be listened to, the book indicts not only the individual's sinfulness but the community for its absence during her troubles. Hers is a voice that clamors for dialogue with a community that too often proves deaf.

The Moodys tell us in their introduction that the narrative had of necessity been rephrased, although "taken from her Mouth" and read back to her for her approval. "It could not," they say, "be exactly taken in her own way of expressing herself." One wishes, as usual, that they had not exercised such editorial control over Boston's text, or that we could know something more about the process of its editing. The most spectacular section from the Moodys' point of view, that describing the conversion, is written very much in the familiar idiom of the religious awakenings that were already sweeping through western Massachusetts and would soon spread further. Boston reports a sense of terror that alternates with a sense of "light and joy, so sweet and good."[104] The conventional language, similar to that used by Esther Rogers thirty-five years previously, points us to Boston's own success in schooling herself in the religious idiom recognizable to her church audience; or, it perhaps represents the efforts of the Moodys, fluent in that idiom, to recast her story. But the narrative contains such a plenitude of detail, so many alternations between light and darkness, that in spite of the Moodys' editorial pen, it must retain much of Patience in it.[105]

Patience Boston was not convicted of killing a newborn. Rather, the title page announces that she was "executed July 24, 1735 for the Murder of BENJAMIN TROT of Falmouth in *Casco Bay*, a Child of about Eight Years of Age, whom she Drowned in a Well." This was the grandson of her master, and she confesses in her narrative to the deliberate murder of this child. Her conversion takes place while she is awaiting the trial, but it is the extraordinary narrative of the life leading up to that crime that first demands our attention. For the story that she tells of her long spiritual struggle is intertwined with the story of her struggle with her own maternity. It is the story of a woman who today we would judge troubled, one who has repeatedly had, as she puts it, "Murder in my heart" toward children; until now these thoughts were directed not at the children of her various masters, but at her own. While not prosecuted under the Bastard Neonaticide Act, Boston makes numerous attempts in her narrative to portray herself as the "lewd mother" described in that law, and to accuse herself of neonaticide. The difference is that while the Bastard Neonaticide Act reaches into the anonymous lives of isolated women, constructing criminality out of neglect, ignorance, fear, and even lack of evidence, Patience Boston's narrative is the story of a troubled and outcast woman making repeated attempts to bring those arms of the law around her, and to force acknowledgment from it. Significantly, troubled maternity plays an important role in this plea for reconnection with a community that had been long absent.

She was born Patience Samson, she writes, and her mother, who had been connected with one of the Indian churches, died when she was three. She was placed in a minister's home, and had a close relationship with the woman in that household, who "was a Mother to me" (*FN*, 2). But she was in her words "a wicked, mischievous and rebellious servant" (*FN*, 2) who broke the Sabbath, lied, and set fires. After her mistress's death, her story is one of alternating license and stability: like Esther Rogers, she moves around a great deal, passing from one master to another, falling into "strong and violent corruptions," yet also seeking out family structures. Though free of a master for a while, with "no Body to command me," she marries a Negro servant and binds herself voluntarily to his master. During her first pregnancy, however, she reports breaking out of the stable structures that have been built around her:

> I had tho'ts of murdering it, and whilst I was big I ran away from my Master, my Husband being Absent on a Whaling Voyage; and I drank hard, and broke the Marriage Covenant, being wicked above Measure. After I got Home, I was delivered of a Child, which I had hurt in my Rambling, so that both its Arms were broken, as was found in Dressing the Child; and it died in a few Weeks, so that I now think I am Guilty of its Death. (*FN*, 3)

Boston's "rambling"—straying from her marriage, from her home, from her maternal responsibilities—has in her interpretation disastrous consequences for her child, and from this point on, the narrative is conditioned by this maternal ambivalence. She repeatedly has thoughts of killing her infant children and actually claims, at various points during the narrative, to have done so.

During a second pregnancy, she begins to reform her behavior and turn her attention to religion; but she says she "soon returned to wicked Courses, drowning all good tho'ts, desires, Purposes, and beginnings of Reformation"— and again, she has thoughts of killing her child. This child dies suddenly, though not through her fault; but, in a drunken quarrel with her husband, in order "to vex him," she says, she "told him that I had Murdered our last Child" (*FN*, 5). Thus begins Patience Boston's long engagement with public authorities. The husband at first disregarded her claim, but then called in a magistrate, who examined her numerous times. For all her claims that she has committed murder, the magistrates seem reluctant to believe her (partly because they "perceived that she was in Drink" [*FN*, 5]), but eventually her repeated insistences on her guilt land her in prison on the charge. However, at the trial itself she resolves not to lie, and so pleads not guilty, and is acquitted. Patience perceives the whole episode as her attempt to commit suicide. Still expecting to be executed, she says, she prays "for the Pardon of all my sins, especially that of lying so often against my Conscience, and thereby destroying my own Life. This I thought was a greater Sin, than if I had indeed murdered my child" (*FN*, 5-6). (Perhaps she found some consolation in the fact that, though acquitted, she was ordered to pay court costs.[106]) Despite her resolve, when she moves to a new place she raises the issue again by telling people there that she has killed her baby. Again, the authorities look into the matter but are skeptical. A search for the body yields nothing, and she is examined by a panel of women who say they find no signs of a recent delivery.

While Boston's self-accusations are the strategies of a desperate and troubled woman, possibly wracked with guilt over that early "rambling," they are also repeated attempts to engage the community around her, and perhaps around her dead infant. Those binary structures that in theory should have lent stability to her life—marriage and servitude—did no such thing once she became pregnant. Further, no minister assisted her in turning her experience to her spiritual benefit; no midwife or other community of women supported her to allay her fears about bearing and losing children. While unexplained infant deaths had propelled other women, like Rebekah Chamblit, into public scrutiny in the past, it had not done so for Patience Boston. In her case, the community responds to her self-accusations inadequately. It makes a legal inquiry but still does not respond in any way to the distress of someone who has lost several children while already in the throes of a spiritual crisis. Therefore, Patience follows the only means of engagement that she knows, self-criminalization. An infanticide accusation has not been an avenue to bring her to communion: something more drastic is required. She resolves, therefore, to kill a child—not her own this time, but the grandson of her master.

The details of this story are chilling. She lured the boy to the well and drowned him, keeping him under water with a pole. She relates, "When I saw he was dead, I lifted my Hands with my Eyes towards Heaven, speaking after this Manner, Now am I guilty of Murder indeed; though formerly I accused my self falsely, yet now has God left me" (*FN*, 8). In this dramatic and eerie scene, which sounds like something out of Charles Brockden Brown's gothic novel *Wieland,* the relation between this deliberate murder and Boston's previous self-accusations becomes clear. Accusing herself of responsibility for the deaths of her own children has not worked, but this crime, an interracial, interclass killing, is sufficiently sensational finally to inscribe her firmly in the public consciousness. "I went forthwith," she says, "and informed the Authority." Just as she had believed that her own child's broken limbs testified to her guilt, now she fears that this child's body will bleed, accusing her, if she touches it during the inquiry. To avoid this gruesome scene, she says, "I resolved to be a witness against myself" and confesses directly to the crime. She has always been such a witness, but has not been heard until now.

Patience Boston's book signals both the growing demand in publications about crime for these sensational details, and the ascription of such sensationalism to more marginalized individuals. The Bastard Neonaticide Act did not demand an act of violence, and indeed in Rebekah Chamblit's account, for example, it is very clear that she did not commit one. But Patience Boston's conviction and her narrative recast the definition of female infanticidal criminality so that it does include such sensational violence—"murder indeed." The tragic part of this story is that Boston has overcome her social isolation by criminalizing herself: ironically, her construction of an even more sensationalist crime for herself has the double effect of giving her voice more prominence in her book than either Katherine Garret or Rebekah Chamblit can achieve in theirs while at the same time reinforcing her own marginality.

Whatever fascination with the gothic-style details of the murder may have drawn the reader to this *Faithful Narrative*, it is Patience Boston's conversion experience, the most prominent part of the book, that finally links her back to that audience. Significantly, however, that conversion story is also the story of a reconstituted maternity. For as she cares for her one remaining child in prison, Boston begins to confront in a new way the meaning of her connection to her offspring. When the child becomes ill, she says, "I examined my self, whether I was willing to part with it; and hoping God would take it to himself, I think I was willing" (*FN*, 25). Her willingness to lose the child, an important step in her own religious experience, also evinces a maternal care of a kind she has rebuked herself for lacking in the past. She is particularly concerned about what may happen to the child after she dies; perhaps, she thinks, if it did die of this illness, "my own Death would be easier" (*FN*, 26). After the child's recovery, Boston takes yet another step in her conversion: "one Night, as I was sitting with my Child in my Lap, and looking on it, I think it was made plain to me that my Child had the same sinful Nature that I had, and stood in as much need of a Saviour; and that it would be just with God to damn it" (*FN*, 28–29). By now she is looking at the child not just as an object in her own life toward which for her own spiritual health she must adopt the right attitude, but rather as someone with whom, in the terms of the Christian idiom she has adopted, she shares a common humanity. She has, that is, overcome the estrangement from communion that had tortured her throughout the rest of her sad narrative. "And I hope," she adds, "I have been enabled to believe for my Child, as well as for myself" (*FN*, 29). For the rest of her stay in prison, she responds to this child in a maternal, care-giving way. After a lifelong struggle, it seems, Patience Boston has finally resolved her maternal ambivalence and can now articulate her profound implication in, rather than her estrangement from, the human community. Thus the *Faithful Narrative* does conclude, like other examples of execution literature, by reconstructing communal identity, not through casting out the sinner, but by emphasizing her reconciliation. Once again, it underscores that communal reconciliation through an affirmation of the maternal relation.

Even so, that reconciliation itself contains a subtle indictment of the community it is set up to affirm. On execution day itself, Boston continues to struggle to accept the loss of her child, and it is reported that "Mr Moody read to her the Passage of *Abraham*'s offering up his Son" (*FN*, 33). And her final prayer is for that child, "that it might be brought up in the Fear of an infinite God, and gave it up to Him. Lord, said she; It is not my Child, but thine. The Lord hath given, and the Lord hath taken away, blessed be the Name of the Lord" (*FN*, 34). Sadly, her prayer, and the invocation of the story of Abraham and Isaac, seem more appropriate to mourn a separation by the death of the child than by the death of its mother. If Patience Boston had earlier been given the pastoral help she is given here to mourn appropriately the deaths of her other two children, she might not have wound up facing death while holding another infant in her arms.

Chapter 2

On Wedlock and the Birth of Children

The "Pious and Ingenious" Jane Colman Turell

In the same year that Patience Boston died on the gallows, another young New England woman of a very different social class, Jane Colman Turell, met her death in a more private, and perhaps, commonplace way. She had had four pregnancies by the time of her death at age twenty-seven; although she did not die in childbed, all her pregnancies had been problematic, and only one child had survived infancy, though he would die at age six, soon after his mother. In what was perhaps a related circumstance, her family reported that she had been afflicted for years with a "hysteric distemper," by which they meant a condition of gynecological origin that resulted in both physical and psychological weakness. In her last days, her husband wrote, "as is Common in Hysterick Cases," Jane Colman Turell had not only had "Oppressions at the Breast & the Bowels," but "Faintness," "Paroxysms," pains in the back and shoulder, and intermittent stupor.[1]

Maternity, then, could be problematic not only for the marginalized women we looked at in the previous chapter, but for the most privileged women in early New England society as well. Jane Colman Turell was educated and well-read, the daughter of the most prominent minister of his generation; she was accustomed to meeting prominent Bostonians, including the governor, in her childhood home; she had made a socially advantageous marriage; and she is known to us today as a poet, considered second among colonial women poets only to Anne Bradstreet.[2] But as different as Patience Boston and Jane Turell were, the coincidence of their deaths in 1735 invites us to consider this commonality between them: that for both, problematic maternity played a significant role in their spiritual lives and writings.

89

Jane Turell's most frequently anthologized poem is "Lines on Child-birth," and it tells the sad story of her reproductive life. That story, if characterized less by "rambling" and melodrama than Patience's, has its own kind of pathos, for each of the first three stanzas tells of a successive problematic pregnancy ending in stillbirth or neonatal death. Patience Boston's pregnancies play important roles as spiritual markers in her narrative; ultimately, as we saw, her possibilities for redemption are measured by her relationship to her remaining living child. Likewise, Jane Turell's poem seems to unite her hopes for a living child—a live delivery—with language of spiritual deliverance. In the final stanza, the speaker, pregnant now again, prays for a different result this time:

> That I may deliverance have, and joy to see
> A living child, to dedicate to thee.

I will argue below that the topos of deliverance, with its double meanings, was central not only to the well-known poem, but to Turell's life-long struggle with her spiritual identity. Like Patience Boston, and, in a different way, like Esther Rogers and John Rogers, for Jane Turell maternal language played an important role in her attempts not only to articulate her own spiritual identity but also to articulate her ideal of the religious community.

Another characteristic Turell shares with Patience Boston, Esther Rogers, and the other infanticides is that her literary "remains" seem no less compromised than her biological offspring: we know as much as we do about Turell only because after her death, some sympathetic ministers, in her case her own father and husband, were moved to make her story public in a memorial volume. In the book, called *Reliquiae Turellae et Lachrymae Paternae. The Father's Tears over his Daughter's Remains . . . to which are added, Some large Memoirs of her Life and Death*, her husband, Ebenezer Turell, excerpted her diary, letters, and poems, and added his own running commentary; her famous father, Benjamin Colman, provided a preface, two funeral sermons, and a postscript consisting of his letters to her; and a fellow poet, John Adams, contributed a consolatory poem.

Reliquiae Turellae thus belongs to a genre of publications that became increasingly common in the first decades of the eighteenth century: the portrait of the virtuous woman. These were, typically, funeral sermons for prominent women—or the wives or mothers of prominent men—sometimes bound, as they are in *Reliquiae Turellae*, with their own writings or a short biographical precis. As Laurel Ulrich and others have written, these books put forth a generalized portrait of a female saint, referring, often, to the passage in

Ecclesiastes, taken to be a portrait of Solomon's mother, Bathsheba, that begins "How shall I find a vertuous woman"; typically, they display the features enumerated in that passage, such as devotion to family, humility, good household management, and exemplary piety. As with all classic hagiographical literature, there is a sameness to these portraits, one that amplifies their teaching and memorial functions: like gravestone inscriptions, their purpose, in Ulrich's words, was "not to commemorate, but to transcend personality. A good wife earned the dignity of anonymity."[3] In his preface to *Reliquiae Turellae*, Benjamin Colman remarks on the paradox of making the portrait public. During Jane Turell's lifetime these traits were kept, in Colman's words, "always under the Veil of great Modesty and Reserve" (*RT*, 48). But now, he says, "She *being dead* speaks *to You in what is here publish'd, after a short and* silent *Life among you*" (*RT*, iv).

And yet we know that Jane Turell did not exactly live a "short and silent Life." Rather, she was one of a circle of poets who regularly exchanged their work. Her work was produced, in fact, not for her own closeted edification nor for publication in the press but for a middle ground, publicity in this circle. Elaine Hobby and Margaret Ezell have shown that early modern women writers often produced in this way, so that a strict division between public and private writing did not obtain for them. David Shields's recent study, *Civil Tongues and Polite Letters*, establishes the importance to eighteenth-century American culture of widespread literary activities that did not necessarily issue in publication in the press; poets like Jane Turell could have an audience among an active and well-connected society of interested people, in her case, "Boston and Harvard literati."[4]

Of course, this understanding of the production of women's literature does not do away with the editorial dynamic at play as Jane Turell's works found their way, posthumously, into the public press. But to the extent that Benjamin Colman's introductory material directs us to that reading, it exposes a tension within the publication, as Benjamin Colman and Ebenezer Turell try to fit her quasi-public voice into a very different format, the portrait of the female exemplar. As described by Ulrich, the exemplar is a frozen, static figure, one that the reader is invited to look at and admire. However, Ebenezer Turell, like other early American editors (including those who edited the infanticide literature), evidently felt little need to integrate his diverse, heterogeneous material into a coherent, univocal text. Therefore, we can recognize the ways in which Jane Turell, even as she is being used posthumously in the volume, does not conform entirely to the programmatic portait being drawn of her there. As I will show, the voice that comes through is not merely one interested in cultivating private virtues fitted to the passive female exemplar, but rather one that assumes a more aggressive public role and a public audience. The religious poems in the volume, even the most seemingly conventional and imitative of them, position Jane Turell's voice as an interactive, semi-public one, rather than that of a remote exemplar. They make significant and unconflicted claims to a public voice, despite Benjamin Colman's remark about her "short and silent life."

But the most important drama that can be reconstructed from *Reliquiae Turellae* is the story of the central crisis of Jane Turell's spiritual life, her decision to become a full member of her husband's Medford church by taking the Lord's Supper there. The three-way dialogue on that subject revealed in the book is a more traditional pastoral encounter, like the ones narrated in *Death the Certain Wages of Sin* (though with different effect). Again, the book's preservation of multiple voices gives us a rare opportunity to witness a pastoral conversation. Here again, as with the poetry, we witness a complex interaction of shared ideas and divergent emphases. It has been the argument of this book that pastoral conversation reveals the multivalent exercises of power, rather than the brute suppression of one voice by another. This is the dynamic that we find in *Reliquiae Turellae et Lachrymae Paternae*, one that is best recovered by examining the interacting parts of this volume.

Significantly, in both the "ingenious" poems and the "pious" biography, the language of pregnancy and childbirth figures prominently, paralleling the appearance of such language in the infanticide literature, for it signals not just a private spiritual struggle but an awareness of corporate church identity. For both areas, Turell's thematizing of community through childbirth metaphors is not an original contribution to discourse. It is my contention, though, that in examining the interaction of voices in books such as these, we should look not for original discursive contributions in what is after all a Bible-based culture, but rather for ways in which different groups or individuals inflected that received discourse, and the ramifications of those inflections.

Piety or Ingenuity?

As I have remarked, Ebenezer Turell's incomplete editing makes *Reliquiae Turellae* not a seamless piece of propaganda but a complex work of interactive and sometimes dissonant voices. Most obviously, there is a clear disparity in aim between Benjamin Colman and Ebenezer Turell, much like the disparity between John Rogers and his elder colleagues in the pages of *Death the Certain*

Wages of Sin. Their respective sections in the volume reveal a posthumous struggle of sorts taking place in its pages, in which husband and father each advances his own version of Jane Turell's life. Ebenezer Turell divides his portion of the book, the *Memoirs*, into discrete sections. First he describes Jane's very early education and prints some of her early writings, and then moves on to her "Composures," as he calls them, "between these and her *Eighteenth year*" (*RT*, 66), sorted into poetry and prose. Next he recounts the story of their courtship and marriage in 1726; and then again excerpts more letters, diaries, and poems written after that time. He has sorted her literary remains and divided her biography into premarriage and marriage periods. In other words, for Ebenezer, the climactic event in Jane's life is her marriage to him. Predictably enough, he has less respect for her achievements in the former than the latter period. He apologizes for the "early *Essays* of her Youth," which contain, according to him, "a great deal low and juvenile" (*RT*, 75), useful, perhaps, as models for children, but not as expressions of adult, even female adult, piety. And although we, doubtless like Turell himself, are very aware of the "turning point" as a result of his comments, we have less of a sense, from his account, of the chronology of events within each individual period itself.

Benjamin Colman's contribution, on the other hand, gives a much clearer idea of that chronology. His eight letters included in the postscript are meant to be examples of successful parental and pastoral counseling. Six were written after Jane's marriage, and most of these concern her spiritual life, especially her scruples about taking communion, which she finally did about a year after her marriage. During this crisis, Colman commended her to Turell's care and, as the day approached (it coincided exactly with the 1727 earthquake), sent her a cluster of encouraging letters. Colman's material reads like a corrective to Ebenezer Turell's interpretation, for it suggests a different shape to Jane Turell's life, one that chooses to emphasize not her marriage but her spiritual struggle instead.

Internal evidence shows us, then, that the two men had different agendas for publication, and different understandings of the life of Jane Colman Turell. Even what the two have in common betrays an ambiguity on the crucial question of what it means to present a female exemplar to the public. For the epithet that the title page applies to Jane Turell, "pious and ingenious," implies that she will be praised here for both her religious devotion and her poetic talent. However, in the book's actual pages, it is her ingenuity rather than her piety that is praised unstintingly.

In fact, for both father and husband, Jane Turell's spiritual excesses seriously compromised her authority as a religious exemplar. Both agreed that she was physically weak; they imply that she was also emotionally fragile, exceedingly dependent on them, subject to physically debilitating reactions to loss, and, most tragically to them, characterized by a serious imbalance in her spiritual life. They were particularly disapproving of the role the Lord's Supper played in her religious life. Neither could understand, first of all, why after marrying Ebenezer she was initially so reluctant to become a communicant in the Medford church—why "her *timorous* Disposition," as Colman wrote, "restrain'd her" (*RT*, 52). And both clearly disapproved of her devotions to the Supper afterward. She evidently offended her father's sense of decorum with her zeal; as Colman wrote, "She afterward *exceeded*, to her *own* and her *Consort's* great Discomfort in her Preparations for Communion Days; which was her *Infirmity*, and I do not praise her for it" (*RT*, 52). Turell notes also, "considering her tender Make and often Infirmities she *exceeded* in Devotion. And I have tho't my self oblig'd sometimes (in Compassion to her) to call her off, and put her in mind of God's *delighting in Mercy more than in Sacrifice*" (*RT*, 116). Turell even recalls ruefully some of the more distressing moments of his marriage, when his wife's scrupulosity—also excessive, in his view—disturbed the domestic peace, keeping him up all night: "How often has she lain whole *Nights* by me mourning for Sin, calling upon God, and praising him, or discoursing of Christ and Heaven?" (*RT*, 116). Bewildered until the end by her spiritual troubles, both ministers finally responded by choosing not to take them all that seriously; Colman attributed them to a womanly, "hysteric" disease rather than to religious conscientiousness: "her Temper was exceeding *timorous*, and her Distemper *Hysteric*, the Accidents of which all know to be a *Swimming* of the Head and *Inquietude* of Mind. This naturally both *clouded & frighten'd* her in her Sickness" (*RT*, 53).

How could such spiritual flaws find their way into a book that was supposed to be an exemplary portrait? The two ministers' extensive disclaimers may signal their own professional self-aggrandizement, for they suggest that dependence on clerical guidance rather than spiritual autonomy is the mark of a virtuous woman. Could Colman and Turell be more interested in presenting the "ingenious" Jane Turell, memorializing her for her poetic achievements, than in presenting her as a pious exemplar? For all the condescension and indeed misogynist overtones of such remarks, however, the demurrers on Jane Turell's spiritual practices, especially those from Benjamin Colman, are remarkable in that they do *not* adversely affect his assessment of her intellectual activities. Neither Ebenezer Turell nor Benjamin Colman makes the link between her literary productivity and her health, so tempting to commentators on women's letters from John Winthrop (who maintained that Mistress

Hopkins had "fallen into a sad infirmity, the loss of her understanding and reason . . . by reason for her giving herself wholly to reading and writing, and had written many books")[5] to S. Weir Mitchell (responsible for the "rest cure" famously described by Charlotte Perkins Gilman in "The Yellow Wallpaper"). Although Jane Turell "spent whole Nights in reading" (*RT*, 78), neither Colman nor Turell suggests that this was the cause of her physical and emotional distress. Ebenezer Turell, in fact, explicitly denies that her physical infirmities were linked to intellectual achievement, either positively or negatively: "her Constitution from her early Infancy was wonderful weak and tender, yet the Organs of her Body so form'd as not to obstruct the free Operations of the active and capacious Spirit within" (*RT*, 61). Rather than censure her intellectual activity, both ministers endorse it.

To be sure, some of Ebenezer's comments on the poetry are only grudgingly complimentary. But the book as a whole, and certainly Benjamin Colman's contributions, show that Jane Turell's literary skills received a great deal of encouragement. Colman gave his daughter the best education a girl could get—she couldn't go to Harvard College, but she did have access to his library, and he encouraged her in her efforts to educate herself, exchanging letters and poems with her when she was a child. He assured her that if she had had a university education, she might have surpassed his own achievements. Here again we see some difference between husband and father, for Turell is careful to assure us that his wife's intellectual pursuit, including poetry, was a "*Recreation* and not a *Business*" (*RT*, 79) and took second place to housekeeping. But even Turell routinely read to her after their marriage, and comes close to admitting that he was intimidated by her ability at paraphrasing psalms during their courtship. Colman is more unstinting in his praise of her literary abilities, adopting in his compliment the language of the Song of Songs: "her *Pen* as well as her *Lips*, both . . . drop'd as the *Honey-comb*" (*RT*, 51).

Even the biographical sections of the *Memoirs*, written by Ebenezer Turell, thematize speech, and indeed, public speech, making it an integral part of Jane Turell's portrait. One incident in Jane's infancy, for instance, is presented as foretelling both her lifelong invalidism and her talent for language. Gravely ill, given up by the family for dead, the baby signalled her recovery when "she half opened one of her sunk Eyes, and answered unto the *Barrow* in the Street, repeating what was cry'd there to be Sold." Colman says he knew from that moment that the child would be "a Blessing and remarkable in her Life" (*RT*, 50). According to another favorite family story, recounted by both Colman and Ebenezer Turell, Jane as a child didn't need to use a prayerbook for children, but told her father that "God gave her Words to speak when she began to pray" (*RT,* 51). And such hints of verbal precocity only are corroborated further by the achievements of later years: at two she could speak, recite the letters, and tell scripture stories; at four she could read and recite psalms and poetry, and "make pertinent Remarks on many things she read" (*RT,* 61); at that same age she was speaking publically, diverting her father's houseguests, including the governor, with her performances. Clearly, Benjamin Colman valued his daughter's verbal mastery, and encouraged it. When, after a few years she had gotten a little shy, Colman admonished her in a letter, "When I last saw you you were too shame-fac'd; Look People in the Face, speak freely and behave decently" (*RT,* 63).

The biographical account, therefore, belies Colman's claim that his daughter's was a "short and silent life among you." On the contrary, it seems he encouraged her in modes of self-representation that were self-assured and public, and prepared her for those literary circles of which she would be a part. Moreover, notwithstanding Ebenezer Turell's editorial decisions, it is clear that both he and his father-in-law thoroughly approved and delighted in Jane Turell's intellectual achievements, and in her capacity to present herself in at least a semi-public way.

It was her spiritual life, instead—the piety, not the ingenuity—that needed, according to the *Memoirs,* constant supervision and correction by her pastors. Despite the epithet "pious and ingenious" that appears on the title page of *Reliquiae Turellae,* Jane Turell is actually presented to readers as an exemplar with only fragmented authority: she is a good poet, but a less than adequate religious figure. This is undoubtedly a strange result, whatever Ebenezer's and Benjamin's loyalties to their mourning literary friends. But the notion that a woman's exemplariness is only partial is a familiar idea. Anne Bradstreet's publishing career is instructive in this regard. As Ivy Schweitzer has shown, the admiring male relatives who controlled Bradstreet's public presentation through the press, driven by their own political agendas, were unwilling to allow Bradstreet both biological womanhood and literary pro-ductivity, or as Schweitzer says provocatively, "patriarchal culture severs . . . woman's body and her brain."[6]

Clearly, a similar dynamic—though on somewhat different terms—obtains in *Reliquiae Turellae et Lachrymae Paternae.* But, I will argue here, it is the religious poetry included in the book that reunites the two strands kept separate by Colman and Turell; in spite of her editors' efforts, Jane Turell asserts, through these poems, not merely a partial authority but rather a full power to use both piety and ingenuity in her poetic enterprise.

Piety and Ingenuity: Jane Colman Turell and
the Tradition of Women's Religious Poetry

To some degree, Turell's own letters, as well as her husband's comments, depict her as adopting a subordinate, student-like posture with respect to her intellectual life. Both before and after her marriage, she sent poems to her father "for correction," and she chose subjects (according to Ebenezer Turell) with her father in mind. Yet such evidence of intellectual dependency is belied by the complete absence of statements of uncertainty in the poems themselves. There is no counterpart among the surviving poems to Anne Bradstreet's references to "my mean pen," no laments, ironic or not, over the probable reception of woman's writing by "carping tongues," no expressions of dissatisfaction with an "ill-formed offspring" of a "feeble brain." Bradstreet's language suggests that the speaking or writing woman is a paradox—an invocation of the Renaissance modesty topos, and more specifically, a way to appease the prejudices of male readers. In contrast, in the two poems in which Jane Turell addresses with most self-consciousness the subject of her poetic role, she unapologetically claims an exalted position of authority for herself and other women writers. Moreover, these two poems, "To My Muse," and "On Reading the Warning by Mrs. Singer," conclude that piety and ingenuity are closely linked indeed. In their claims of both poetic mastery and spiritual authority, in the self-assurance of the speaking personae, in the vigorous tone they both exhibit, they contrast with the fragmented authority Colman and Turell are willing to give her.

Schweitzer comments that Bradstreet's editors, in calling her the "Tenth Muse," put her in the standard position of inspirational woman to a poet that remains defined as male.[7] Jane Turell preempts such a move by addressing one of her poems "To My Muse." In that poem, the speaker, not doubting her own ability and worthiness to write important poetry, petitions—indeed, orders—her muse to "Instruct me in those Secret arts that lie/Unseen to all but to a Poet's Eye." Although she invokes a distinct tradition of women poets—Sappho, Orinda (Katherine Philips), and Philomela (Elizabeth Singer Rowe), she makes no apology for this tradition, nor does she imply in this poem that women poets are restricted in subject matter or limited by a lack of education or skill. She promises to "devote thee to a fair *Virtues* Fame," but only after the Muse has taken her to "*Parnassus* shady Top" (*RT*, 74–75): in other words, to be favored with poetic insight, even by a woman's muse, is not automatically to write of pious subjects and with sentiments appropriate to the stereotype of the godly woman; rather, that emphasis is a deliberate choice on the part of the already-inspired poet. Both piety and ingenuity are equally important sources of power and autonomy. Ingenuity does not depend on piety, but the two certainly coexist in Turell's ambitions for herself.

A second poem, "On Reading the Warning by Mrs. Singer," makes an even stronger argument that an inspired woman poet may utilize her gifts for moral purposes not only to enhance "fair Virtue's fame," as in "To My Muse," but also to teach and admonish in a very public way. The poem claims that Rowe, in criticizing the corruptions of her society, "vie[s] with the fam'd prophetess of old," identified by Ebenezer Turell's note as Huldah, who admonished the people of Judah for forsaking the law (2 Kings 22). Colman Turell describes Rowe's poetic skill as an aggressive force:

> Each noble Line a pleasing Terror gives
> A secret Force in every Sentence lives.

While her speaker begins "Surpriz'd" that a woman should be such an outspoken social critic, by the end of the poem the speaker has demonstrated that that role is not surprising at all: the role, deliberately chosen by the woman poet, is also biblically sanctioned. Thus the role that Turell envisions for an "ingenious" woman poet is a pious, certainly, but even more, a prophetic one. In fact, she participates here, as does Rowe in the poem she cites, in the tradition of the prophecy, a literary form used most frequently by early modern British women writers to comment on important public matters, such as revolutionary politics.[8] Indeed, the most striking lines in Turell's poem, the closing couplet, make an aggressive claim for the public moral function of the woman poet, in language that is particularly powerful:

> A *Woman's* Pen strikes the curs'd *Serpents* Head
> And lays the Monster gaping, if not dead.

Here Colman Turell intricately reworks one of the most magisterial images of woman in the Bible, adumbrating its complex exegetical history. After the sin in the garden, God tells the serpent, "I will put enmity between thee and the woman, and between thy seed and her seed; it shall bruise thy head, and thou shalt bruise his heel" (Gen. 3.15). This passage became important to Christian exegetes, who saw in it a prophecy of the Incarnation and an allegory of the struggle between Satan and Christ. It was linked typologically to Revelation 12, a vision in which a woman appears in the sky, gives birth, and is pursued by a dragon. In both biblical texts, the enmity between serpent and woman is finally enacted by the seed or male offspring, Jesus in the Christian interpretation. The woman escapes, and the dragon, enraged, goes "to make war with the remnant of her seed" (v. 17).[9] Turell's poem captures all the violence and cosmic sweep of these collated texts. The difference is that by converting the reproductive language of the Bible to a metaphor for literary production—a "woman's pen"—she makes the woman the direct antagonist of sin, attributing to her all the aggression, violence, and public action that that entails. Unlike the speaking yet silent Jane Turell depicted in the *Memoirs*, the speaker in "On Reading the Warning" exercises both poetic skill and moral authority to public effect without ambivalence.

Her praise of Singer Rowe, and for the string of women poets she wishes to invoke, makes clear the ambitions that Jane Turell had for her own poetry: to utilize her undoubted technical skill to "vie with the famed prophetess of old," Huldah. This model of female behavior is of a very different order from the "virtuous woman" Bathsheba, for it assumes an active teaching function, rather than a purely domestic heroine who appears as a passive exemplar to be admired and imitated. In aligning herself both with a tradition of aggressive women poets and with the Old Testament prophets, Turell seems to desire not only to delight in exercising her ingenuity to write admirable poems but also to use them as vehicles for participating in a public discourse—this despite what Colman called her "veil of modesty and reserve."

"The Voice Leisurely Ascends": Jane Colman Turell and Psalm Paraphrasing

As spectacular as "On Reading the Warning" is in this regard, Turell's ambition for her poetry to take on a public meaning is also evident in another group of poems, the psalm paraphrases. Poems in this highly conventional genre are often thought of as mere exercises for fledgling poets, and Jane Turell's choice to write such poems—or Ebenezer's choice to print them— seems like more evidence of her submission to clerically imposed guidance. Or, as Madeline Marshall and Elaine Hobby have noted of such genres, they may have been of particular use to women writing religious poetry, since they allowed them to mask their creativity in seemingly innocent form, simple translation of a sacred text.[10]

However, in the context of latter-day Puritan New England, the gesture of paraphrasing the psalms was by no means a simple one. In fact, I would argue, instead, that they function for Jane Turell in much the same way that the prophecies functioned for the women of the Civil War sects, as vehicles through which to comment on important matters of public and political concern. The psalms Turell chooses to paraphrase are very self-reflexive, for they both meditate on the subject of the psalms themselves and connect the activity of translating the written psalms into poetry to the activity of singing them in communal worship. They take on even more significance because during the decade in which they were written, the 1720s, the place of the psalms in worship services became a locus of dispute in the Boston-area churches. Long before the rumblings in Northampton, the psalm-singing controversy, as it was called, predicted the conflicts that would come dramatically to the fore in the Great Awakening, most particularly the renegotiation of power between the clergy and the laity. All the crucial issues that would become dramatically visible during the Great Awakening, five years after Jane Turell's death—the propriety of the use of emotions in spiritual experience, lay initiative colliding with clerical direction, and the very nature of the corporate whole—are expressed in the psalm-singing controversy, and they are also part of the dynamic of *Reliquiae Turellae et Lachrymae Paternae.*

The psalms were always an important part of Reformed Protestant worship, and they were especially associated with its anti-sacerdotal character. Singing psalms in worship was a way to introduce an aesthetic element into a service that avoided ritual. It was also a way to pay homage to the Protestant vernacular Bible, and to allow the laity to participate actively in the sermon-laden service. According to Natalie Davis, the party badge, as it were, of the French Protestants was their psalm-singing, considered especially noxious by the Catholic majority.[11] The first book published in New England was, of course, the Bay Psalm Book. Using a plain-style vernacular Bible; translating closely from the Hebrew; incorporating biblical songs rather than original hymns into worship: all were ways to enact the pious idea that, in the words of the psalter's preface, "God's altar needs not our polishing."[12] Singing psalms in the congregation mediated, as Protestant worship had to do, between communal and individualistic expressions of spirituality. Within the context of a worship service, then, it fulfilled the same function as did paraphrasing scripture for a religous poet: believers recreated canonical sacred texts.

That mediation proved no longer adequate by the early eighteenth century, however, and the psalm-singing controversy of the 1720s arose from an attempt to tip the balance away from individualized engagement with the Bible in favor of a more orchestrated communalism. By that time, singing in the Boston-area churches had evolved in this way. Typically, a layman, acting as precentor, would "line out" the psalm line, and the congregation would repeat it, but with ornaments to the tune such as grace notes and intervals added, not by prearranged plan, but haphazardly by individuals at will.

In the early decades of the eighteenth century, this had begun to sound too disorderly to some. In 1721,[13] John Tufts of Medford, where thirteen-year-old Jane Colman was one day to be minister's wife, published a psalm-singing manual that suggested that a little polishing needn't be such a dangerous thing. If people would only set about learning some tunes in an organized way, congregations would actually start singing together and would finish together; the whole congregation would sing the same tune; and psalm tunes would be recognizable from one congregation to another: none of these conditions obtained in the New England churches. It made perfect sense to the Boston elite, including much of the clergy. Cotton Mather wrote, "We ought certainly to serve our God with our *Best,* and *Regular Singing* must needs be *Better* than the confused Noise of a Wilderness."[14]

But not everyone saw it that way. To judge from the number of polemics published by advocates of so-called "regular singing" in the 1720s, the innovation met with stiff resistance from many congregations. First, the aesthetic judgment implied in Mather's remark was by no means universally shared. In particular, rural congregations balked at this newfangled way touted by those with polite educations from urban areas.[15] In the language of theological controversy, the conservative resistance saw the Regular Singing movement as an attempt by the clergy to introduce an idolatrous set form, and thereby seize more control over worship services by regulating a part of the worship that properly arose spontaneously from a lay congregation.

Since young people were especially enamored of the New, Regular Way, the controversy was also expressive of generational tensions.[16] It may have enacted the growing alliance between women and ministers, since the New Way advocates made it a point to assert that women, who were otherwise biblically enjoined not to speak in church, could certainly sing psalms; moreover, the New Way singing techniques tended to allow softer women's voices to be heard more readily than did Old Way techniques.[17] The Singing Quarrel became yet another occasion for the kind of contention within the churches that was so common in this period; like arguments over assigning seats in meetinghouses, it had the potential for splitting congregations.[18] The controversy, then, encapsulates many tensions important in the years before the Great Awakening.[19]

The controversy is especially suggestive because it underscores the connection the psalms had to lay spirituality. In the years before the Great Awakening, there were various moves on the part of the clergy to replace the congregational with a presbyterian model. In an attempt to maintain power and personal prestige in an increasingly diverse society, clergymen formed professional associations, held conventions, and evolved elaborate ordination ceremonies.[20] That is, they attempted to establish a new power relation with the laity: to centralize power in the ministry, to make it more sacerdotal in character, and to hold themselves accountable to each other, through synods and professional organizations, rather than to the local laypeople. Part of the impetus behind the Great Awakening, which would occur in the 1740s, was an anticlerical backlash, a restoration to the churches of the lay basis of religious authority, which was the genius of congregationalism. Likewise, pro-Awakening New Light ministers (Benjamin Colman among them) tended to have been open to innovative pastoral activity, to new ways of involving the laity and encouraging and affirming their spiritual experiences, in contrast to their more conservative (anti-Awakening) Old Light counterparts, who maintained a more distant and authoritarian posture. In fact, this difference in pastoral style may have been more important than doctrinal differences in precipitating the controversies surrounding the Great Awakening.[21]

Jane Turell's immediate clerical influence, Benjamin Colman, would become a tentative supporter of the awakenings. It was to Colman that Jonathan Edwards would write one of the earliest accounts of the frontier conversions, those precursors to the Great Awakening, that occurred in the year of Jane's death, and when the movement started affecting Boston, Colman endorsed it, sending Edwards's accounts to Isaac Watts and others for publication in England. He did eventually withdraw his support somewhat, joining other Boston clergy in denouncing James Davenport, an enthusiast who had led a New London crowd in a feverish burning of books and luxury items.[22] Colman's cautious support of the revivals is predicted in an early work, composed before his daughter was born, *The Government and Improvement of Mirth*. This work, which takes as its scripture text James 5.13: "Is any among you afflicted? let him pray. Is any merry? let him sing psalms," endorses the importance of emotion in cultivating spirituality, but argues as well that such emotion needs careful regulation.

What Perry Miller found most interesting in *The Government and Improvement of Mirth* was the mark of secularization in its pages. Colman's special legacy, Miller believed, was the stylistic consequence of his liberalized theology: "By a studied avoidance of overemphasis, Colman softened the colors of both rhetoric and religious emotion, yet he liberated colonial prose for the expression of other emotions."[23] Colman's intention, however, was precisely the opposite: to tap emergent aesthetic sensibilities, to "liberate" them, one might say, for the enrichment of religious feeling. He acknowleges, therefore, the role that emotion does play in spirituality. However, that text from

James provides him with a vehicle with which to advise his flock on the instability of religious emotion, which he believed to be one of the most perplex-
ing aspects of the Christian life. Aimed primarily at young people who have
cultivated the polite social skills of singing and reading poetry, and penning
verses—a group that would include his own daughter—*The Government and
Improvement of Mirth* endorses the psalms, both as sung and as paraphrased,
as an important vehicle for regulating religious emotion. As Teresa Toulouse
has shown, Colman shared this interest in exploiting the aesthetic pleasures of
poetry and song with his English friends and correspondents Isaac Watts and
Elizabeth Singer Rowe, Jane Turell's model in "On Reading the Warning." As
Toulouse notes, all these three were interested in using set forms, like the
psalms, to evoke but also to control such emotions, confining them to a safely
narrow compass, far removed from the dangers of religious enthusiasm.[24] It is
that emphasis on control that characterizes *The Government and Improvement
of Mirth*, striking that cautionary note that would continue through Colman's
career.

The scripture text, he writes, gives us "a Law how to behave our selves"
to counteract "our Danger in Either Extream, of Sorrow or Joy."[25] Because
one engages in it with "*Deliberateness* & Leisure," Colman saw singing in particular as having great spiritual value in combatting religious instability: "The
Mind has time allow'd it to Pause on the Sacred Passages: Every *Sillable* is distinctly utter'd, and *drawn out* in its proper *Note*, that the Mind may fix and
fasten and dwell on the holy Tho't. And as the Voice leisurely Ascends, so
may the Soul with it towards Heaven" (*M*, 148–49). Such ascension was
especially crucial for those whose souls were of Jane's spiritual temperament,
as Colman would understand it. Some Christians, he had written, are "Dull
and heavy, sad and disconsolate, sour and morose" (*M*, preface). Admonishing the "*Sad Spirited Saint*" (*M*, 158) of the "Duty, *to Exhibit . . . the Joyes
of Religion*" (*M*, 155), he urged them to follow the example of the psalms and
praise God openly, for to do otherwise would show ingratitude for God's mer-
cies. And urging the benefits of a mirthful approach to religion, he even came
close to saying that singing was a converting ordinance: it "sweetly dilates the
Soul, and God often comes into the op'ned heart" (*M*, 145). It is useful, then,
not only to channel naturally occuring emotions in proper ways ("is any
merry? let him sing psalms"), but also to create proper frames of mind.

Colman's intention, then, is to use the psalms in particular to harness
lay energies and emotions, in very controlled ways, to encourage a spirituality
that bears the peculiar Colman stamp. The goal of the spiritual exercise
Colman and his text recommend is the deliberate manipulation of naturally

occuring spiritual moods, minimizing emotional flux, so as to maintain an uninterrupted walk with God (*M*, 7). He forecasts, even at this early stage of his career, exactly the misgivings that moderate clergy like himself would have about Awakening spirituality: appreciation for the role of emotion but concern about restricting its anarchic possibilities. And it was precisely such emotional instability that Benjamin Colman would anxiously observe in his daughter, in the decades leading up to the awakenings, and that he would admonish her about in *Reliquiae Turellae*.

To a great degree, Jane Colman tried to adopt her father's vision of the Christian life, writing to him in a letter that she yearned for that stability and wished to "be instructed how to behave my Self in all the Changes and conditions of Life, as becomes a *Christian*, not to be too elated in *Prosperity*, nor sunk under *Adversity*, but ever resigned to the Will of God in all things" (*RT*, 78). But if the psalms were for Benjamin Colman convenient vehicles for regulating religious emotion, Jane Colman's paraphrases, written during the 1720s, suggest that for her, the psalms held the potential for articulating a lay-centered vision of church polity, one that mirrored the program of "Old Way" congregational singing and anticipated the thrust of Great Awakening lay aspirations.

In two paraphrases written in the 1720s, Jane Colman Turell adopts a stance similar to the one she adopts in "On Reading the Warning." The speaker is not simply an observer or exemplar, looking at her community or being looked at by it; that is, she steps out of the role assigned to her in *Reliquiae Turellae*. In each of these psalm paraphrases, she adopts a persona that interacts with community and is embedded in it, one that, moreover, is interested in articulating not an individual, but a corporate relation to God.

For example, Colman Turell begins her paraphrase of Psalm 8, a hymn to creation, with a version of verse 1 that emphasizes the cosmic scope of the poem; all creation, heaven and earth, is both a sign of and a vehicle for praise of the creator. The next verse is by far the most elaborate, with poetic additions that go well beyond the ornamental adjectives that characterize the rest of her lines. Where the King James Version says, "Out of the mouths of babes and sucklings hast thou ordained strength because of thine enemies, that thou mightest still the enemy and the avenger," Colman Turell interpolates:

> From thence thou scatterest all thy Blessing round,
> And in an *Infants Lips* thy Praises sound.
> Thy gracious Care to *Sucking Babes* extends,
> And feeble ones thy Providence defends.

O from a *Suckling's* Mouth now strength ordain,
Nor Praises from a lisping Muse disdain!
Assist me Saviour, thou the *Babe* whose Breath
Struck the *Avenger* to Eternal Death!
Inspire thy Babe in this my sacred Theme,
And *still* the Foe, whose Curse is to blaspheme.
(*RT*, 73–74)

The force of the biblical text is that even infants, part of the order of creation, join in a cosmic hymn of praise for God; here, Colman Turell identifies the poetic speaker as one of these "feeble ones," relying on "a lisping Muse."[26]

Although the poetic posture here is not the same self-assertive one Colman Turell adopts in the feminist poems—the "Suckling Mouth" might be that of a young apprentice poet—neither is it particularly an expression of weakness. In this poem, the "lisping Muse," denigrated by Benjamin Colman and Ebenezer Turell, is not another woman but another infant, the Saviour, "the Babe whose Breath/Struck the Avenger to Eternal Death." Though the speaker hardly aspires to "strike the avenger," her song will have some effect in "still[ing] the Foe, whose Curse is to blaspheme." The paradoxical identification of a childlike speaker with the object of praise, Jesus, anticipates Blake's "Song of Innocence" ("I a child & thou a lamb,/We are called by his name"), but with an important difference. The insertion of the incarnate Jesus into this Old Testament text underscores not the weakness of the speaker but the cosmic dimension of the poem. His appearance as an infant suggests that the speaker is describing not only herself but all humanity as infants, participating in the cosmic hymn to creation as a chorus of feeble, lisping voices, of which she is one.

Most important, her paraphrase of Psalm 8 underscores the gesture of congregational singing of psalms, which was, as the psalm-singing controversy demonstrates, no vacuous cliché but a culturally important image, whatever its precise form, of the essence of the Christian communal ideal. It is unclear whether the infants in her poem are New Way or Old Way singers. Given her urban roots, her polite education, and her clerical family connections, it seems likely that Jane Colman Turell would have been in favor of Regular Singing; the approval given by the New Way controversialists to women's psalmody may have also attracted her. Whatever her aesthetic preferences, however, her paraphrase demonstrates some sympathy, at least, with the impulses of the Old Way, or "Anti–Regular Singing" party, as it was called, to protect the prerogatives of the laity. The poem's infant chorus, including the poet, figures not subordination or apprenticeship to an earthly master, but a direct likeness to Jesus. In this congregation, New Singers or no, there is no clerical mediator directing the lay voices, no "adult," as it were, in a superior or teaching position. In this vision, lay spiritual expression is autonomous, needing no clerical supervision. A chorus of lisping, weak, and untrained voices that yet somehow resonates with the harmony of the spheres also suggests the Old Way. Despite the potentially disordered "scattering" of blessings among individual voices, the poem expresses the confidence that the elect community—or actually, since the poem's cosmic vision is less exclusive than that, the created world—*will* make harmonious beautiful music, not a "confused noise of a Wilderness," even without central direction.

It is highly significant that the poem affirms, in the midst of the psalm-singing controversy, the lay voice in chorus. The speaking infant is not a leader, but one of a group of lisping voices, all of whom have been "scattered round" with blessings. I don't mean to ascribe any anticlericalism to this dutiful daughter of a ministerial family; but the vision of the church that is described in this poem is, at the very least, devoid of the emphasis on strong clerical leadership that we might expect from the daughter of a pastor. Rather, it is an imaginative meditation, using the psalm as a text, of a vision of congregationalism with a clear emphasis on the unmediated "democracy in Christ" which that form of polity implies.[27] The speaker confidently asserts her own spiritual authority—and that of her lay community—not to dominate, but to participate in the cosmic hymn on equal terms with the rest of creation. She shares her father's commitment to recognizing and encouraging lay devotionalism, and his association between it and the psalms, but she uses this psalm not to limit lay emotionalism, as he had in *The Government and Improvement of Mirth*, but to declare that the laity is the church. She uses Psalm 8, that is, to put forth a vision of *communitas*.

Colman Turell's paraphrase of Psalm 137 ("By the rivers of Babylon"), written when she was seventeen years old, pushes her identification of the relation of the poet's voice with the lay community further. Here again, we see her locating the poet/singer squarely in the community. The argument of the poem is that in some situations, the individual poetic voice must be silent, must decline to speak:

> If I forget *Judea's* mournful Land,
> May nothing prosper that I take in Hand!
> Or if I string the Lyre, or tune my Voice,
> Till thy Deliverance cause me to rejoyce;

> O may my *Tongue* forget her art to move,
> And may I never more my Speech improve! (*RT*, 68)

Colman Turell's speaker, expressing the patriotism of the community in exile, asserts that the individual's gift must be subordinated to communal aims. Singing is not an isolated act of artistry, for it can never be divorced from context, that is, its audience, occasion, and purpose. The oppressors demand a song for their amusement:

> Come, now, they Cry, regale us with a Song
> Musick and Myrth the fleeting Hours prolong.

But the captives know that singing is a holy activity, not possible in a hostile place: "whilst Slaves we can't rejoyce." The only appropriate response is a call for more hostility, the curse on Babylon that closes the psalm.

In this psalm the movement between first-person singular and plural pronouns, preserved in Turell's paraphrase, further delineates the relationship between poet-speaker and singing community. The speaker does not really admit the possibility of the community being unfaithful to this remote God, only that she might be unfaithful. The standards of joyous singing and silence in exile, that is, are thus set not by God, or the psalmist, but by the community. The poet's task is to support those political—and therefore the poetic—imperatives, and for most of the poem, she speaks in the communal voice, "we." The elect community is united even before the psalmist goes to work; she affirms, rather than provokes, unity. Again, the persona here is one who is embedded in an interactive community, neither a passive follower nor a specially anointed leader. The most perfect singing is communal.

But it is also exclusive. Rejecting the most public, indiscriminate audience, the poet-speaker's community will "tune our voice" and "touch our lyre" only on "our" terms. "Our" silence in this captivity underscores the more communal nature of holy singing, for which the appropriate audience is ourselves: "we" turn to the captor, and to the pronoun "you," only with the curse at the end, as the speaker redirects the anger of an absent God with Israel onto the captor community:

> Thou *Babel's* daughter! Author of our Woe,
> Shalt feel the stroke of some revenging Blow;
> Thy Walls and Towers be level'd with the Ground,
> Sorrow and Grief shall in each Soul be found:
> Thrice blest the *Man*, who that auspicious Night
> Shall seize thy trembling Infants in thy sight;

> Regardless of thy flowing Tears and Moans,
> And dash the tender *Babes* against the Stones. (*RT,* 68–69)

These last two verses are always rather shocking; they are the more so here if we anticipate—as perhaps a young Jane Colman, or any woman in the early eighteenth century, could—that their author would lose three children in infancy. Despite the aggression inherent in the line, those added descriptive adjectives suggest the more mournful language of elegy, a language like that she herself would use a decade later in her elegy for her own dead child: "trembling infant," "tender babes," "flowing tears and moans." While they suggest the pathos of the loss of children, the violence of the image resonates with that which the speaker has promised in the loss of her own tongue. As in "On Reading the Warning," which associates creativity and power with a female speaker, Colman Turell's paraphrase of Psalm 137 depicts a parallel between literary and biological offspring. Neither are mere private creations, and both have public import. Here, both are grimly sacrificed, with violence, for the good of the speaker's community.

The most startling innovation in the poem, an extensive interpolation of the psalm's first line, enlarges that thematic interplay between fruitfulness and destruction. In the King James Version, the psalm begins, "By the rivers of Babylon, there we sat down, yea, we wept, when we remembered Zion. We hanged our harps upon the willows in the midst thereof." Colman Turell's greatly expanded version reads, in part:

> Born down with Woes No Friend at hand was found,
> No Helper in the waste and barren Ground;
> Only a mournful *Willow* wither'd there,
> Its aged Arms by Winter Storms made bare,
> On this our *Lyres,* now useless-grown we hung,
> Our *Lyres* by us forsaken and unstrung!

The plural "willows" of the original becomes the single "mournful" and "wither'd" tree, blasted by cold and shorn of its leaves. The tree becomes an emblem of the culture's—and of the individual speaker's—own refusal to "bear fruit" through creating music.[28] They hang up their lyres, silent, barren and unproductive, on its bare branches. Later in the paraphrase the speaker imagines the homeland being just as desolate, now that the people are in exile:

> O *Palestina*! our once dear Abode,
> Thou once wert blest with Peace, and lov'd by God

But now art desolate, a barren waste,
Thy fruitful fields by Thorns and Weeds defac'd.

This figurative language is what we would call an example of the pathetic fallacy. In each case, the landscape reflects the psychology of the exiled community. Palestine is abandoned; Babylon, the new land, is cold and equally inhospitable. Both are "barren" or unproductive of vegetation or of poetry, for no one sings in either place. For now, only the conquering Babylonian nation has any capacity for bearing fruit, the "tender babes" who, the poem threatens, will also be destroyed, making Babylonian civilization just as barren as its captive nation.

In Colman Turell's version of Psalm 137, then, an intricate imagery of fruitfulness and barrenness overlays the themes of homeland and homelessness. In any event, biological, poetic, and political fruitfulness are all intertwined; in fact, biological production is much associated with the public future of the nation, either Israel or Babylon. Turell's extrapolation of the psalm's imagery, then, issues in an intense identification between poetic speech and biological productivity, between an individual's control over language and her implication in her communal or public identity. Even as it foregrounds the maternal (or, as Benjamin Colman might have called it, the "hysterick"), the poem does not consign it to the private sphere. On the contrary, biological reproduction becomes a vehicle to foreground the union, both genetic and spiritual, of the community (much as the choral singing of infant voices does in Psalm 8), and the communal embeddedness of the individual. The poem pushes out, therefore, from the boundaries of the passive exemplar. The speaker is neither gazing out nor meant to be gazed at, but is actually united in a communal exercise.

When teenaged Jane Colman sent this poem to her father, he seemed taken aback by the extremity of its language, notwithstanding its biblical roots, and he cautioned her, in spite of his endorsement of psalm paraphrasing in *The Government and Improvement of Mirth*, not to allow even such a pious exercise to take time away from other religious devotions, like reading and prayer: in a letter printed in *Reliquiae Turellae*, he wrote to her, "as to a Poetical Flight now and then, let it be with you only a thing by the by" (*RT*, 70). Most significantly, he also corrected her most imaginative revision: "You speak of a single *wither'd Willow* which they hung their Harps on; but *Euphrates* was cover'd with Willows along the Banks of it, so that it has been called *the River of Willows*" (*RT*, 71).

Perhaps, in suggesting that her exploration of the theme of barrenness would be properly replaced by an image of fecundity, Benjamin Colman merely wanted to share his biblical erudition with her, as he would with a son or candidate for the ministry. Or, perhaps, anticipating the reservations he would express about his daughter's spiritual practices, he feared her imagination was getting too extravagant, especially since it led her to exaggerate the sorrows of exile and to overdramatize, in his view, the embattled heroism of the religious community and the speaker's own participation in its poetic and political enterprise. His response endorses his preferred form of spirituality outlined in *The Government and Improvement of Mirth*, and echoes the reservations he would express about his daughter's spiritual practices in his introduction to *Reliquiae Turellae*: that she was too inclined to a melancholy spirituality. "I hope, my Dear," he continues, "Your Lyre will not be hung on such a sorrowful *shrub*. Go on in Sacred Songs, and we'll hang it on the stately *Cedars of Lebanon*" (*RT*, 71).

This is an odd comment. Even though he had just cautioned her to limit the time she spends writing poetry, this remark clearly encourages her to write poetry or paraphrase psalms—"go on in sacred songs." Indeed, it belittles the impulse depicted in the poem to forgo poetic speech in favor of a principled silence. Instead, he tempts her with public recognition for her more cheerful poetic efforts: "we will hang it on the Cedars of Lebanon." In his rewriting of this image, the hanging lyre is a symbol not of communal barrenness and desolation but of public applause and admiration. Rather than to share a community's destiny, he urges his daughter to feel a comfortable self-satisfaction in her poetic achievement.

Colman urges her, that is, to disentangle the very threads that are so profoundly interwined in the poem. He retains in his comment the emphasis on fruitfulness that she explored in the poem, but divests it of the political character she had given it there. Approving her poetic self-consciousness, he steers her away from somber topics that implicate the poet/speaker in the communal destiny, inviting her, perhaps, to dilute that sense of communal oneness in favor of her own poetic self-aggrandizement. He promises her, that is, an audience but not a community, and the kind of publicity he envisions for her is exemplary rather than interactive.

Is it too much to hear in Colman's rebuke, despite his evident tenderness, the voice of the Babylonian captors? "Regale us with a song,/Musick and Myrth the fleeting hours prolong." At the very least, his influence is double-edged. On the one hand, his response shows just how well he read his daughter. In commenting on the willow, he notices the most significant literary innovation and the peculiar spiritual turn she gives the psalm, heightening its spiritual desolation. In paraphrasing that willow imagery with a difference, he opts for a pastorally appropriate technique, since it gently revises her argument while allowing her to set the terms of discussion. But in telling her that her imagination has led her into a dangerous theology, Colman also provides his daughter with what amounts to a serious rebuke, one that reveals that his own ambitions for her poetry—and his view of how she fits into community—are very different from her own. He discourages her vision of *communitas*.

But the pushing and pulling evident here—the responsiveness and the rebuke—underscore the delicate issues that characterize the pastoral relationship. The portrait of Jane Turell in the exchange, and perhaps in *Reliquiae Turellae* as a whole, is one of a subordinate woman who dutifully and seriously accepts the guidance of her father. The pastoral conversation seems to be a mechanism of careful minute regulation, in line with Benjamin Colman's notions of the necessity of regulating emotion, and with his reservations, which would remain throughout her life, about his daughter's emotionality. But within that conversation, two things happen: one, Jane Colman Turell's own distinctive voice and concerns do emerge even in as conventional a form as the psalm paraphrase, especially if we look at these poems against the backdrop of evolving religious and pastoral controversies. That voice, in fact, begins to adumbrate the lay backlash against clerical professional aggrandizement and the aspirations to *communitas* associated with Great Awakening spirituality and ecclesiastical ideals. And two, it is Jane Turell's voice, as I have said, that sets the terms of that conversation. In using the most conventional of literary forms and biblical language, she is able to draw Benjamin Colman into a dialogue with her: he must respond to her initiative, specifically, to her interest in using the theme of fertility to explore spiritual concerns relevant both to an individual speaker and to corporate identity.

Come to the Marriage

That subtle pastoral dynamic, in which the subordinate lay speaker exerts a considerable and discernible influence, is evident in *Reliquiae Turellae* not only with respect to Jane Turell's poetry, but with respect to her piety as well. After her marriage to Ebenezer Turell, Jane would face the central crisis of her spiritual life, her decision to become a full member of his church at Medford by taking the Lord's Supper there. Ebenezer Turell's editing does not give prominence to her sacramental dilemma, but there is enough material in the

Memoirs—some of her own letters and diary entries, Ebenezer's memories of her spiritual doubts, and, in the postscript, letters from Benjamin Colman— to suggest the outlines of the story, as well as the character of this triangle of pastoral and familial relationships. It is around the issue of the Supper that a pastoral dialogue is most clearly preserved. In that conversation—mostly between Benjamin Colman and Jane Turell, with some participation from Ebenezer—the outlines of what we see in the exchange on Psalm 137 are reproduced: directive advice from Colman steers Jane Turell in the direction of less intensity, encouraging a more relaxed persona. Turell responds grate- fully and seriously, but also with a gentle resistance, introducing other ideas that, although they hardly constitute an original theology, remind Colman of emphases that had been important in his pastoral practice but that he had omitted in his pastoral advice to her. Thus even in the printed book, intended simply to present a female exemplar of piety, the dynamism of the pastoral relationship is evident. The dialogue that I will reconstruct below is one in which lay and clerical voices interweave with and answer each other, alter- nately bringing up diverse strands drawn from the tradition from which they both come. Ultimately, in this instance, those different stances resolve into a gentle conflict, one that has theological roots and is reflected in different pref- erences for biblical imagery. Once again, Jane Colman Turell is a gentle advo- cate of *communitas*.

Jane Turell moved to Medford soon after her marriage in August 1726, but she did not immediately become a full communicating member of the Medford church. In her role as minister's wife, she had an extra social obliga- tion to take the Supper, both to ratify her new membership in the town and to support her husband's ministry. "Delay not this Duty," Colman wrote to her in December 1726 (*RT*, 123). But delay she did, for over a year, and although Ebenezer Turell doesn't print any letters or diary entries from this period, Colman's postscript includes several letters of counsel written to his daughter in September and October of 1727, letters that show that Jane Turell had expressed many doubts about her fitness to take the Supper.

Colman's letters suggest that his daughter's reluctance stemmed from her ambivalence about leaving her father's guidance, household, and church for those of her husband. She had not become a communicant at Colman's Brattle Street Church, and her doing so at Medford would signal a transfer of allegiance from father to husband. Or at least, in persuading her to take the Supper, Colman turns to an argument—and a literary figure—that promotes that psychosexual interpretation: Jane's new wifely obligations to Ebenezer parallel her spiritual obligations to Christ the bridegroom. For in these letters,

Colman introduces the image of Christ the bridegroom, suggesting that the "outstretched arms" of both Ebenezer and Christ beckon to Jane Turell to take the Supper, and subtly ascribing to his daughter a reluctance to enter that bridal embrace and a preference to remain loyal to her father. In the process of pushing her away from his own pastoral guidance, he uses gendered language, arguing that it applies both to social and spiritual relationships.

In his letter of December 1726, he commended her to Turell's guidance, implying that there was something unseemly about Jane's continuing to consult him rather than Turell, and used, for the Supper, the marital imagery that suggests the propriety of letting her earthly husband lead her to the heavenly bridegroom: "Mr. *Turell* will direct you in renewing your Espousals to *Christ* at his *Table*" (*RT*, 123).

In October 1727, two days before she was to take the Supper for the first time, he wrote to her that he would not be able to travel to Medford and preach the sermon, as he had planned. Pleading the foreboding weather, he also hinted that Turell would in any case be a more appropriate speaker, implying that Jane must fully accept her new relationship. Colman's slippery pronouns further confound the distinction between earthly and heavenly bridegroom: "I would not have you expect me, nor that Mr. *Turell* should have the least Dependence on me. I hope God will be with you in your *open Giving your self* to Him" (*RT*, 126). As written, "Him" is God, of course, but there may be more than one antecedent. Jane's obligation to covenant with the Lord in the Supper is very closely related indeed, he suggests, to her obligations to Ebenezer Turell, both as his wife and his congregant. Her taking the Supper will benefit not only herself, but the Medford congregation and its pastor: "be a Blessing in your Place, both to Mr. *Turell* and to the People among whom your Lot is cast" (*RT*, 126). Her "place," clearly, is in Medford with Ebenezer, not in Brattle Street with her father.

The marital language Colman uses emphasizes the rightness of such an arrangement, employing a string of binary relationships as analogies for the spiritual relationship Jane Turell was about to enter: "For in Covenanting with God we *joyn our selves* to Him, as *Servants to their Master* by an Indenture; as *Subjects to their King* by an Oath of Allegiance; as *Soldiers to their General* in a War against Sin and Satan; and as a *Wife to her Husband* in a Marriage Covenant; a *Covenant* of mutual, endearing, constant, and perpetual *Love*" (*RT*, 127). The order of the list of analogies suggests that the most precise metaphor for the communion covenant is the marriage relation, and, in the context of this letter, that it is all for the best that Jane Turell "renew her Espousals" in the presence of her husband rather than her father.

When he wrote that letter, Colman was facing a familiar pastoral problem, for Jane Colman Turell was not alone in her anxiety over taking the Lord's Supper. The Supper had always been a matter of controversy in New England—and in Reformed Christianity, for that matter; scruples on the part of laypeople about whether they were eligible to partake of it had been a persistent theme in New England history, and, despite minute but important differences among them about what exactly qualified someone to take the Supper, generally speaking, New England's ministers, rather than warning laypeople away, spent their time encouraging their congregations to overcome their scruples and commune.[29] What is important about Colman's letters, though, is that his comparison of the Lord's Supper to marriage raises the vexed question of how we are to interpret gendered religious symbolism.

The presence of this highly conventional language in New England homiletic literature has been important to its literary historians because it seems to promise a way to use clerical sources to uncover some sense of lay response or lay spirituality; it could potentially help us use an overwhelmingly clerical archive to serve the interests of the study of popular culture. Some studies of those lay conversion narratives that are available do find that they can be differentiated by gender.[30] Such differences suggest, in turn, that gendered language in sermons may appeal to different constituencies by preachers or suggest possibilities for varying responses by lay listeners. The figure of the bride is a primary example of female imagery that appears quite frequently in the homiletic literature, as it does in Colman's letter. Commentators, however, have interpreted the presence of such language variously, ranging from the argument that female imagery like the Holy Spouse may be used to intimidate and control women to the view that such imagery enables women's religious experience more than men's.[31] To further complicate things, the early decades of the eighteenth century saw the "feminization" of the churches—that is, more women than men became church members.[32] But the connection between that "feminization" and the language that emanated from the pulpit during those years is difficult to make. Numerous scholars point to the appearance in the New England presses in those years of more books like *Reliquiae Turellae*, describing the female saint, and thus suggesting that demographic feminization.[33] On the other hand, Amanda Porterfield has argued the opposite, that images of women prominent in seventeenth-century Puritan discourse are abandoned after the Salem witchcraft trials (1692), when they became too explosive.[34] Whatever the historical trajectory, most readers, however carefully they avoid overly simplistic generalizations, share some commonsense idea that such "female" imagery within religious discourse may have been aimed at women and had special effects on women congregants. For example, while Margaret Masson's important, often-quoted study, "The Typology of the Female as a Model for the Regenerate," carefully avoids arguing that the increasing frequency of portraits of the female saint like that in *Reliquiae Turellae* meant that sainthood itself was necessarily being typed "female," she nevertheless remarks that "the consistency between the prescribed secular and religious role for women may account for their generally high level of church membership."[35]

But, as historian of religion Caroline Walker Bynum writes, "however religious symbols 'mean,' they never simply prescribe or transcribe social status."[36] Men and women may differ in their understandings of gendered religious symbols (symbols are polysemic); and neither understanding need reflect social experience in a simple way (religious symbols point by analogy beyond social experience).[37] Bynum's own studies of medieval religious language, for example, find the presence of gendered symbolism there but conclude that to the extent that medieval women expressed their spirituality in ways distinct from men, the best way to characterize their rhetoric is as a rejection of binarism, showing *less* interest in language employing the genders. Her analysis suggests that, for New England religious culture, although there may be very interesting differences between the genders, and although these differences may be related to the ways men and women use gendered language, it need not be true that the mystical marriage metaphor or other gendered symbols are particularly "female" or particularly congenial to women. In fact, Bynum's work suggests that the opposite may be true. Gendered symbols can "mean" in any number of ways: in Bynum's words again, they "may refer to gender in ways that affirm or reverse it, support or question it; or they may, in their basic meaning have little at all to do with male and female roles."[38]

Linda Mercadente's study of gendered language in nineteenth-century Shaker discourse is similarly cautionary in this regard. Mercadente finds that despite the well-known presence within Shaker discourse of the dual-gendered God, there is little evidence that within the Shaker community that language provided special resources or meanings to women. Rather, she argues, "Shaker experience suggests that female imagery for God is not necessarily more attractive to or empowering for women than for men." She finds that men and women use such imagery in roughly equal proportions, but that for both the use is at best "uneven and sporadic."[39] Mercadente's study, like Bynum's, investigates the use of a female imagery for God, while seventeenth- and eighteenth-century Puritan discourse requires the believer to adopt the female persona. But both theorists of gendered religious language issue important cautions to students of that gendered language within New England Puritanism, because they show that the commonsense presumption, that "female" imagery speaks in a particularly salient way to women, does not always stand up to scrutiny in other historical contexts.

The Colman-Turell letters engage these issues in a particularly useful way. They constitute a very specific and traceable pastoral conversation, one that uses gendered biblical language in both conventional and surprising ways. In the interchange of images between layperson and clerical counselor, we can see not only that gendered symbols can "mean" in different ways, but that their presence in pastoral conversation may provide a helpful key to the subtle power dynamics of that relationship.

But given the range of meanings for conventional biblical language available to members of these early New England communities, the precise pastoral context in which they appear is crucial. It is necessary, therefore, to step aside from the exchange itself and examine Benjamin Colman's other pastoral practice, since it is within the context of his entire career that he turns to the marriage metaphor here, and it is in the context of that career that Jane Turell would hear his words.

Benjamin Colman and Marriage: "Union by Vision"

First, it is important to clarify the biblical sources of marriage within the Puritan discursive tradition generally. That imagery has two distinct biblical sources, and, I would argue, at least two very different potential meanings. On the one hand, nuptial eroticism, whose sourcebook is the Song of Songs, provided a language expressive of an overwhelming and mutual desire between Christ and the believer. Such intimacy, though certainly part of the Christian tradition before the Protestant Reformation, carries with it the most radical and anti-authoritarian implications of the Puritan movement: an ideal of a direct relationship with God that need not be mediated or regulated by intervening earthly authority, an ideal that led nonconforming Puritan ministers to risk their careers and their lives to defy Archbishop Laud. In a tradition just as old and just as biblically sanctioned, however, the figure of marriage may stand for the opposite: not an ideal of a union with God, a union that supersedes and indeed obviates earthly relationships, but instead a vision of social order. The fifth commandment, "Honor thy Mother and Father," implied for Puritan theorists a whole set of dichotomous and hierarchical human relationships—child to parent, servant to master, subject to prince, wife to husband—in which the posture of subservience it prescribed for the lesser partner was justified by a final analogous relationship, believer to God.[40]

Colman's use of marital language to persuade his daughter to take the Supper should not, therefore, be taken at face value, without considering its pastoral context. On the face of it, the metaphor seems to function to encourage Jane Turell to acknowledge the power of stable binary human relations. While such an appeal is consistent with the dedication to decorum Colman exhibited throughout his life, it diverges significantly from his application of marital language throughout his pastoral career. This is because most frequently, when he uses the marriage metaphor to talk about the relationship of the believer to God, and even, as in the letter to Jane Turell, the Lord's Supper, he invokes a different context for it: the sacrament as a marriage feast. This image has more in common with orderly hierarchy than with disruptive desire, but with an important difference. It lends itself to one of Colman's deepest concerns: the corporate, rather than binary, nature of the God-human relationship.

Colman's most ambitious sermon series, *The Parable of the Ten Virgins*, written before Jane Turell was born, contains his most extended use of the marriage metaphor. This work discusses the parable of the wise and foolish virgins, who await the bridegroom as attendants, not as brides. We might expect to see here Colman's most systematic exploitation of the homiletic possibilities of gendered language.[41] Into this parable, however, Colman introduces texts from the Song of Songs, and his discussion moves back and forth between the perspective of attendant guests and that of the bride, between marriage as convivial feast and marriage as union.[42] The first sermon of the series in particular draws on the language of the Song of Songs, suggesting the erotic potential of the marriage figure. However, Colman mutes the erotic potential as well as the gendered identity of the bridal figure by presenting it primarily in corporate terms. Most often, the bride of Christ is the church, not the individual believer.[43] Even the consummation of that relationship is described in a curiously abstract way, simultaneously invoking the notion of physical erotic union and weakening it by transforming the marriage into a group affair: at the final hour, "he will give his Church a *personal and bodily Meeting*."[44] Elsewhere, Colman transforms the image of Christ as lover by explicitly fusing it with the metaphor of the church as corporate body, united with Christ as head: "We are Members of his Body, of his Flesh, and of his Bones. The Reference is to those Words of *Transport* wherewith *Adam* receiv'd and welcomed *Eve*; charm'd at her sight he said, *This is now Bone of my Bone*,

&c" (*PV*, 8). While the first human marriage provides a figure for intimate bodily union ("bone of my bone"), Colman gives even that language a Pauline rather than an erotic context ("we are members of his Body"). In this first sermon, then, Colman carefully controls the tenor of the metaphor. His bride represents the corporate church, not the individual believer, with the twin results that the eroticism of the figure is diffused, and the female gender of that figurative bride is all but neutralized. In two senses of the word, then, Colman desexes marriage.

Throughout *The Parable of the Ten Virgins*, it is the wedding feast, with the corporate celebration implied there, that is Colman's concern. In sermon nine, which deals with the moment of union ("And they that were ready went in with him to the Marriage") he explicitly rejects the erotic potential that he had treated only gingerly in sermon one, cautioning his audience "that we do not so much as in Thought defile the Allusion which the Holy Ghost has sanctified. . . . Let us therefore throw out of our Souls every loose and fleshly *Idea*" (*PV*, 281). An erotic interpretation of this parable would be impure, and the resulting theology inaccurate. For the union with Christ promised in the parable ("They went in with him") is not an individualized erotic union—and is not even figured as such—but instead simply a "being with." The marriage the virgins attend is "a Time of Festival," a sumptuous meal and group celebration; they are received not individually into the arms, or bed, of the bridegroom, but as a group into his dining hall. Even then, Colman is cautious about the sensual quality of the language: "the carnality of the *Allegory* must be wholly removed out of our Thoughts. The Feast is intellec-tual" (*PV*, 282).

That Colman is most interested in using marital imagery to present a vision of corporate church, rather than an individualized relationship with God, is further evidenced by his tendency, even here, to turn away from the sensuous language of his chosen parable—whether sumptuous feast or implied eroticism—and toward a language that relies no less on sensual experience, but which does allow him to control the posture of the virgin saint: the language of sight. His collation of biblical images of sight all but overwhelms the origi-nal context of marriage. Just as "*Solomon's* Wisdom was more than all his Royalties, in the Eyes of the discerning Queen of Sheba"; just as "*Ahasuerus* [gave a] *feast* unto all his *Princes* and *Nobles*, to show the *Riches of his Glorious Kingdom*"; so this "intellectual feast" prepared by God at the last judgment will give the saint even "greater Things to look for, sure as *Eye* has not seen" (*PV*, 274, 275). Heaven is a "place of vision," salvation, finally seeing "*Face to Face*" (*PV*, 285, 273). Sight is the sensory experience most apt to serve as metaphor for spiritual experience. Final union with God consists not in sexual-like consummation, but in "having his immediate visible bodily presence"—it is a "Union by Vision" (*PV*, 283, 284). This strategy allows Colman to control the posture of his saint, presenting the saint as a calm, detached observer rather than unleashing more disruptive behavior or emotions—and resonating, therefore, with the homiletic poetics he shared with Isaac Watts and Elizabeth Singer Rowe. It suggests also, theologically speaking, that Colman's interest in the church, or corporate relation to God, overrides his interest in the individual's relationship. If heaven means union by sight, then part of the joy of heaven may come from the sight of other Christians—of a community—in heaven as well as from the sight of Christ himself.[45]

This same emphasis on control of the saint through the cultivation of sight imagery appears in *Some of the Glories of Our Lord and Saviour Jesus Christ*,[46] the later sermon series in which Colman most systematically addresses the question of the sacrament, and which he was preparing for publication when he wrote to Jane Turell at Medford. In this work, visibility once again remains at the heart of his sacramental teaching. It is primarily through visual experience, albeit imagined visual experience, that the devotional life can assimilate the meaning of the Incarnation. "To awaken us by the remembrance of his death to repent, and convert, and be saved," Colman says, "Jesus Christ is *set forth* crucified among us" on sacrament-days (*SG*, 241, emphasis added). In spite of the distancing formula (the sacrament is only a remembrance), the language he uses to point the attention to the physical body of Jesus "set forth," is extraordinarily vivid: "God sets him forth before our eye, in his death and wounds, and blood, that we should look to him" (*SG*, 241).

In saying that Jesus is "exhibited to us" (rather than "distributed to us") in the sacrament, Colman is adhering to a Reformed vocabulary, which in general deemphasizes the corporeal aspect of the sacrament and therefore, it would seem, the role that sensual experience and language would play in sacramental piety.[47] In fact, however, in doing this Colman sets up a sacramental piety that is extraordinarily pictorial. In place of a discussion of access, which would have divided the various sects within the Reformed tradition, or its concomitant, the proper response the communicants should have to the sacrament, he focuses not on the sacrament but on the thing symbolized, the physical and human body of Christ. Colman's most imaginative, sensual language is concentrated instead in those passages that call upon the congregation to "see," or imagine this beautiful physical body of Christ. Yet, even as they evoke figurative visual experience, these passages simultaneously control and limit the sensuous imagining that that appeal necessarily entails.

Two allusions to the Transfiguration illustrate this development. Teresa Toulouse has suggested that Colman's tendency in his sermons to paint "dramatic pictures" has the effect of distancing the audience from the picture, allowing it to look without being involved. Illustrating with a passage from *The Parable of the Ten Virgins* that also describes the Transfiguration, she comments, "The images do not seem intended to encourage an interpretive response—they simply describe the 'show.' Thus, while the language is sensuous, it is also static."[48] The two passages in *Some of the Glories* evoke rather than describe the Transfiguration in the context of a broader discussion so that, as Toulouse has found, Colman's theological meaning is clear and he does not invite further inquiry from his listeners. However, even his brief evocations do not diminish the scene's visual impact. In fact, the theological meaning that he so firmly enshrines is precisely the spectacular nature of the scene. And it is through this invocation of sensuous sight that Colman simultaneous draws in and immobilizes the listener.

In sermon 15, the Transfiguration illustrates the transformative power of revelation, which is particularly desirable in preparation for death; and that revelation is centered in the experience of actively seeing, either literally or imaginatively, the person of Jesus. Except for the pre–New Testament character Moses, all the believers in this passage, including the disciples on the Mount of the Transfiguration, derive faith from a spectacular view of Christ's body.

> Let us get our souls *changed, irradiated, and transfigured*; some light of the glory of God upon them, and some happy sense of the love of God to us and of communion with him, before we die. Our Lord going to his cross, took the *mount of transfiguration* in his way: the *light* whereof helped him (or rather the three favoured disciples) against the *hour of darkness* coming on. So *Moses* got a sight of *Canaan* before his easy death; and *Simeon* got a sight of *Christ* and the salvation of God, and wish'd to go in peace: and *Stephen* saw the glory of God, and *Jesus* standing on his right hand, and *kneeled* down to die. Like these happy *Saints* let us get our souls changed into the *image of Christ, from glory to glory*. Be ye *transformed* by the renewing of your mind, and so be ready, then be willing to die. (*SG*, 217)

In this passage, the faith experience is a passive yet profoundly transformative one; through the act of seeing, the "happy *Saints*" themselves are transfigured, "changed into the *image of Christ*." Moreover, while the individual scenes of spectacular revelation of the body of Jesus, including the Transfiguration, are *not* dramatized here—instead they are each listed briefly—that act of seeing a revelation scene *is* dramatized and valorized. Although in some respects the passivity the passage enforces through its emphasis on seeing rather than doing ("let us get our souls change*d,* irradiate*d,* transfigure*d*") reflects an orthodox, anti-Arminian theology, it also paradoxically deflects attention away from that transfigured Christ and onto the seeing Saint. Colman is not so dazzled by the sight of Jesus that he loses awareness of the perceiving body. Even in a passage like this one, which would seem to have the most potential for overwhelming sensuous description of the body of Christ, attention is carefully refocused back on the perceiver, but in a way that makes self-conscious aesthetic appreciation, not theological insight or devotional engagement, the most notable result.

Colman refers to the Transfiguration in an earlier sermon in the series to construct the believer as a self-conscious but passive seer rather than an actively involved devotee. His large point is that the Incarnation is revelatory. The life of Jesus illustrates a number of virtues, including "*hope, truth, dependence, reliance, confidence,* a perfect *humility, submission, and resignation.*" "These things," he says, "were display'd in all he said or did, and are conspicuous in the gracious words of my *text*": the verb applies to the human life of Jesus but echoes the language preferred by Reformed theologians for the sacrament of the Supper (*SG,* 60). The proper response of the believer, or communicant, Colman says, is therefore to look at what is displayed:

> We must set them in true light, and see them blazon'd with a *radiance* even to be drawn about the temples of the *son of man.* Draw then as well as you can the *blaze* of perfect faith, love, gratitude, hope, confidence, joy in God and devotedness to him, about the words of my text, and how gloriously must they sound in our ears, and shine in our eyes! How dazling and yet ravishing must they be to a devout soul! As the face of *Jesus* in the holy mount was to the three favour'd disciples. The adorations of men, and the *anthems* of angels are nothing to them! *Psalm* xlv.2. *Thou art fairer than the children of men; grace is poured into thy lips; God has blessed thee for ever.* (*SG,* 60–61)

The words of the biblical text, "them" in the first line of the passage, become visible in the life of Jesus—metaphorically visible, of course—but also, it seems almost literally a part of a visual scene of Jesus's body, "blazoned about his temples." The onlooker/soul allows this sight of Jesus's words, virtues, and body, to "blaze forward," to "shine in our eyes." No extra effort to incorporate or respond to what is "shown forth" is required: "seeing" is enough. Therefore, the devout soul is not so awestruck as to be, as perhaps Jonathan Edwards's saint would be, annihilated by the sight of God, but self-consciously assumes a pious posture of adoration instead. This was the sort of piety and Christian practice for which Colman was criticized by Boston's "old guard," Cotton and Increase Mather, when he first took his position at Brattle Street; it suggests the practice of "dumb readings," reading scripture passages without sermonic comment.[49] The Mathers might have found Colman's emphasis on looking within sacramental piety reminiscent of the popish practice of adoration of the sacrament bread in the ceremony of benediction. Again, paradoxically, Colman's passage enforces passivity but also acute self-consciousness. This "dazling *and yet* ravishing" experience denies the release of true dazzlement, but it also suppresses any contrary impulse to act on the desires inspired by the beautiful sight. Here, Colman's devout listeners might find themselves in the awkward position of the three favoured disciples, who wanted to do something appropriate ("Master, it is good for us to be here; and let us make three tabernacles; one for thee, and one for Moses, and one for Elijah," Luke 9.33) but were ignored, left standing impotently, and told to keep quiet. Denied both annihilation of self (figured, perhaps, as blinding light) and the active devotional response, figured elsewhere as the erotic desire of the bride, the only tenable posture left to the soul is a self-satisfied aesthetic appreciation of the sensory experience.

Despite Colman's consistent immobilization of the sensate saint, desire does remain an important ingredient in this theology of the Incarnation, and of the Supper. But in talking about desire, Colman always mutes the erotic potential of his metaphor. The language of erotic desire is potentially disruptive because it injects a motivation that is supranatural, being inspired from above by the beloved object, God, in a way that may obviate or make irrelevant other earthly relationships because of its all-consuming nature. Colman, however, describes desire itself as an orderly affair, and the analogy to earthly relationships is invoked not to surpass them, but to confirm them: our desires for Christ should be like "the desire of a child to his father, of a servant to his master, of a subject to his prince, of a wife to her husband, of a perishing sinner to a merciful and willing Saviour" (*SG*, 204). In what sense does a servant desire his master? Not with a bodily desire inspired by beauty, either literal or metaphorical, but with a sense of duty and of the value of an orderly society. Colman repeats here the standard list of binary earthly relations that, as Edmund Morgan long ago showed, dominated Puritan theories of social

organization and commonly served as analogs for the God-humanity relationship as well.[50] The marriage bond traditionally occupies, as it does here,
the culminating position in the list of these ordered pairs presented as analogies, because it is voluntary, and comes closest to uniting duty with feeling.

For Colman, then, the Supper is an important ritual enactment of corporate unity, stabilizing all the ordered relationships that constitute it while
immobilizing the communicant in a posture of pious devotion. That ideal is
dramatized in the most poignant of passages in *Parable of the Ten Virgins*, in
the closing sermon. Here Colman imagines what it would be like to be shut
out of the marriage celebration, out of heaven, to be, as it were, one of the
five foolish virgins. One of the torments would be to be able to look in at
family members and others who are at the marriage—people to whom you
were formerly linked by social and ritual bonds—and to see that that closely
knit community, that perfectly balanced, unified body, still exists but does
not include you. "To see your children there"; "to see your parents": to be
outside that complex web of relationships is the punishment. The worst, "the
last occasion of Anguish that can be," he says, would be "to see your *Pastors* in
Glory . . . and you not with them, for whom they *travailed in Soul*, and
besought with Tears to bear them Company!" (*PV*, 317).

By portraying the pastor-congregant relationship as the most critical,
and the most distressing to see broken, Colman is threatening his congregation here, demanding that they take their relationship with him seriously, and
consider solemnly the possibility of separation from him. But then he reverses
his pronouns, turning his most anguished language not on them but on himself: "And yet worse to behold many of my charge and *Flock* in Heaven, O
my Soul! as I trust I shall, and (O God forbid it!) *My self a Castaway*! . . . O
Cruel Thought and horrible as a Million Snakes folding about the *Neck*, hiss-
ing in the Ear, and striking their forked tongues into the breast!" (*PV*, 317).
In a climactic gesture of humility, Colman places himself at most risk of
being shut out of the marriage, imagining his own suffering and declaring,
too, to his congregation his dependence on them, and the overwhelming feeling of abandonment that would result from their separation. This is a picture
of heaven that is heavily dependent on the presence of a community of saints.
"My self a Castaway!" he laments, conjuring up in our minds, perhaps, the
picture of Melville's Pip who floats utterly alone on the wide sea, isolated
from the community, such as it is, of the Pequod, or Edwards's loathsome
insect, suspended, small and helpless, in a vast and threatening cosmos. But
for Colman's castaway, worse than the divine fires that torment Edwards's
insect is the loneliness, heightened by the knowledge that there *is* a full elect

community elsewhere. While Edwards's insect is abandoned—and indeed persecuted—by God, Colman's castaway is the more miserable because he has been abandoned by his community. Damnation means excommunication: not the loss of the lover, the husband, or even the face of Christ; not the loss, that is, of an individuated, binary relationship, but the loss of the group. To be damned is to be the outsider.

By favoring a communal idea of heaven rather than an individual one, Colman is of course also advancing his view of the importance of the church, of participation in its rituals, including the sacraments, and in a society that, like heaven, is orderly. Colman's avoidance of erotic language is tied to this theological goal, for such language would be more suited to a notion of a privatized, unmediated salvation, one in which the saint achieves a personal intimacy with God. Throughout his description of marriage, he insists on the context of the wedding feast rather than the Song of Songs; he adds the language of sight to further dilute the sensuousness even of that image; and he describes desire itself as a kind of corporate interlocking, rather than as an individual longing. Oddly, then, this sermon series on the metaphor of the marriage feast suggests that the marriage figure itself is inadequate to some of Colman's dearest concerns.[51] For it to work for him, he must control and qualify it; and he always subordinates it to the interest of the corporate ideal.

Even more peculiar, *Some of the Glories*, that later sermon series that most explicitly addresses sacramental theology, pays what may seem like an inordinate amount of attention, interestingly enough, to congregational psalm singing. Two entire sermons in the series are devoted to singing (taking as their text, in fact, the first verse of Psalm 8, which Jane Colman had paraphrased). And the final sermon in the series, which according to Colman's organizational logic should conclude with commentary on the Supper, instead returns to the subject of singing, taking as its text Rev. 5.9, "And they sang a new song." Even in *Some of the Glories*, it is singing, not the communion meal, that best expresses Colman's vision of congregational unity in Christ. It is as if Colman, recognizing the difficulties his scrupulous congregation has had with the Supper, was trying to shift their attention to other communal ordinances, just as expressive of the corporate vision but less fraught with theological difficulties derived from tortuous New England sacramental history. The corporate ideal itself, therefore, seems more important than even the sacrament that would enact it.

Significantly, though, at strategic moments in these two major sermon series, Colman introduces a different image whose functioning more easily accords with this theological program: an image of maternity. Gender-specific references need not represent special addresses to women, but they do show awareness of women as part of the spiritual community. For example, Colman's endorsement of singing in *Some of the Glories* cites biblical singers, pointedly including women—the songs of Miriam and Deborah, the Magnificat of Mary. Numerous references to the female figure who appears in Jane Colman's "On Reading the Warning," the woman clothed with the sun whose seed crushes the serpent, appear throughout his work.[52] Select passages use childbirth imagery to describe both the ministry ("they have *travailed in Soul*," in the castaway sermon from *Parable of the Ten Virgins*; and in *Reliquiae Turellae* itself, Colman himself has "with some Pains and throws been travailing in Birth till Christ was formed" in his daughter, ii) and even Christ's suffering on the cross. In the following striking passage from *Some of the Glories*, that comparison nicely exploits in the figure of childbirth the paradoxical union of suffering and danger of death with joy and renewed life: "*how am I straitned* (or *pained*, as a woman expecting the hour of her deliverance, and making all proper and needful preparations for it:) how do I long for the time and welcome the hour of pains and sharp *travail*, necessary to the redemption of men, that I may have the after-joy of seeing my seed, many sons born to God and brought to glory" (*SG*, 213). Christ speaks here as an expectant mother.

Even sermon 9 of *Parable of the Ten Virgins*, although it explores the imagery of marriage at greatest length, advances an image of maternity; most significantly, it does so at the *expense* of marital imagery. In two separate passages, the image of binary marriage is conspicuously absent where we would normally expect it to occur—and it is replaced by maternal imagery. In one section, Colman lists earthly analogies to that "infinite love" between God and the saint. We would expect such a list to include, and indeed culminate in, a mention of the marriage relation, but Colman does something different. "'Tis a peculiar Love: of a Friend, *I have called you Friends*: of a Brother, *Go tell my Brethren, I ascend to my Father and your Father*. It is the Love of a Father to his Family, of a Shepherd to his Flock, of an Owner to his Propriety; and the dear Gift of his Father, as well as the Price of his own Blood that has purchased us, endears us to him; as the *Travail* and *torn Bowels* of a Mother does the *Babe* to her. Finally, 'Tis the Love of the Head unto the Members, every one of which are dear to it: But, to say infinitely more than all this, it is the Love of God to his Elect. It is Heaven and Blessedness to partake in this *Love*; and Life from the Dead to read it in our Judge's Face" (*PV*, 275).

Rather than ending with marriage, he ends with the Pauline head and body image, which preserves the idea of hierarchical orderliness in a corporate, rather than individual sense. The rest of the list is rather unusual, offering a variety of patterns for the covenant relationship, suggesting both traditionally hierarchical binaries—father, shepherd, owner—and more egalitarian ones— friend, brother. The least conventional item is, of course, the mother. This analogue is particularly interesting in its theological implications, because rather than merely delineating a link between two unequal partners it adds the notion that that intimate relationship is partly dependent on the mother's experience of her own body. As he would in *Some of the Glories*, Colman compares God to the travailing woman.

Similarly, at the very end of the sermon, where one might reasonably expect Colman to refer to marriage imagery in a summary way, he again substitutes childbirth imagery. "Is Heaven Our Marriage to Christ? . . . Be not disheartened, Time flies apace . . . your Desire is at hand. . . . And *as a woman forgets* her Sorrows and Pains *for the Joy* of a living Child, so will the Believer his present Sorrows and Travel at the first Glimpse of the Face of Christ, unto whose everlasting Arms he is going" (*PV*, 287). Here the roles of metaphorical mother and child are reversed, for the believer is cast as the travailing mother, who forgets all in the "afterjoy" of the birth, as he will put it in *Some of the Glories*.

The appearance of maternal imagery in select places in these two sermon series, its substitution, in fact, for marital language, together with the varying strategies Colman uses to control marriage imagery, suggest that the presence of "female" imagery has significance beyond its possible appeal to a female constituency. The pattern in which female imagery appears confirms a pattern that Caroline Bynum has found in medieval texts: "the presence of some kinds of feminine imagery seems to have inhibited the presence of other kinds"—in this case, marital and maternal language do not appear in the same environment.[53] Instead, not only gender, but the theological quality of the image itself is important. The maternal image seems to function to give Colman more flexibility. Mother can figure either God or the saint; it suggests both joy and suffering, both consummation and waiting, and a relationship that has an evolving history: it also blurs hierarchical, binary distinctions. The list of not-so-binary binary relations in which it appears suggests a variety of patterns for the covenant relationship, including some less stratified (brothers), less dependent on exclusive, privatized matched pairs (head/body parts), and even—in the figure of the mother and child—less dualistic. Like his development of the image of corporate marriage feast and his emphasis on the controlling power of sight, it provides a useful alternative to the privatized binarism that he finds unavoidable when he uses marital imagery. Some of these results are consonant with the predictions of feminist theologians, that female images of God can subvert patriarchal theology by making possible nurturance rather than judgment, intimacy rather than distance (both of which depend on a rejection of dualism).[54] Without claiming that Colman's language appealed to women in particular or that it had the theologically subversive implications that feminist theology advocates, we can see that Colman's use of maternal imagery does seem to be appropriate to his concern with his corporate theology, precisely because it revises the dualism that so easily accompanies marital language.

What is also so interesting about the appearance of the language here, and the whole theology it supports, is that it is different from that described in his letter to Jane Turell about the Supper, and from the whole tenor of that letter. When counseling his daughter to take the Supper, Colman turned to the very language that he had so carefully controlled or avoided in his public sermon series: an image of binary marriage. Why should he change his pastoral strategy in this situation? Perhaps he believed that the more flexible figures he had used in *Some of the Glories* and *The Parable of the Ten Virgins* were more appropriate to a professional audience than a pastoral encounter. And he had, of course, used this binary language before in counselling Jane on other matters. Documents throughout *Reliquiae Turellae* show that Colman had prepared his daughter for the kind of social role this language describes. A poem he had sent her when she was seventeen praises her poetry but cautions her against too enthusiastic feelings of filial affection:

> Your Heavenly *Father* made your Tongue,
> And first his Glorious should be sung.
> Your Earthly *Parent* next may claim
> Your *Filial Praise*; a dearer Name
> You know not yet on Earth . . . (*RT*, 67)

And in a letter shortly afterward, he reminds her again that some day he may be properly displaced in her affections by a husband: "I would have you therefore careful against this Error, even when you say your Tho'ts of Reverence and Esteem to your *Father*, or to a *Spouse* if ever you should live to have one" (*RT*, 70). Whichever earthly relationship turns out to be the primary one, the model for each requires her to fit into a pattern that always describes the human condition in an orderly society. Reverence for God should surpass all human attachments, but follows the same binary pattern. The task of the spiritual life is to adapt this earthly model to one's relationship with God. To fulfill one, in fact, is to fulfill the other.

But, this language did not prove effective in settling his daughter's spiritual questions. Although she accepted such language to describe her social role, she would turn to a different resource to describe her spiritual experience— one that, in fact, she might have picked up from reading her father's published sermons.

"Tho'ts on Matrimony": Jane Turell at Medford

It is borne out by Jane Turell's own writings that at the time of the communion crisis and afterwards, even though she was nominally under the care of her husband, the Medford pastor, she more frequently turned to Benjamin Colman for spiritual advice: "I know of none in this World," she wrote to Colman on December 6, 1727, "I can so well apply to for comfort as your Self" (*RT*, 86). His arguments of two months previous, including the marital analogy, then, had failed. Nevertheless, it seems clear that at this early stage in her marriage Jane Turell continued to believe that Benjamin Colman would do better as her spiritual counselor than Ebenezer. Psychosexual explanations aside, there is evidence that hers was a wise assessment.

Besides Ebenezer's condescension, already noted, to Jane's intellectual life, there are a number of indirect evidences, both within *Reliquiae Turellae* and outside, that he was less than responsive to her spiritual needs. In the early 1740s, after initially welcoming the religious revivals that became known as the Great Awakening, Turell quickly became disenchanted with Whitefield and other itinerant preachers, and scornful of the more extreme expressions of religious ecstasy their preaching prompted. He even published a handful of anti-Awakening tracts at that time, and became associated with the Old Light party, acting as clerk to the Old Light–dominated convention in 1745.[55] If George Harper is correct in his assessment that Old Light ministers were less receptive than New Lights to different forms of lay experience, then we would expect that Ebenezer, who would become an Old Light, would have been less sympathetic than Benjamin Colman, who aligned himself (with some reservations) with the New Lights during the Awakening, to the particular forms that Jane Turell's spiritual doubts and devotions took.

An incident that took place much earlier confirms this suggestion. In September 1728, not quite a year after Jane Turell became a communicant, Ebenezer was approached by another young woman, perhaps a year younger than Jane, asking to be admitted to the Supper.[56] Although initially the woman, Elizabeth Blanchard, gave "a very good account of herself,"[57] she came back a few weeks later, the day before she was to receive the sacrament, with a startling confession. Some years earlier, as a child in another town, she had, she told Turell, shammed witchcraft possession and even accused a neighborhood woman of afflicting her. She and her sister had suffered, in Turell's wry phrase, "the usual marks of such things"—bodily wounds, faints, appearances on the roof of the house and claims to have flown there. All of these, he details, were false claims, based on elaborate deceptions by the confederate sisters, as Elizabeth now freely confessed.

The lesson Turell draws from this incident is that such stories deserve "no more faith than . . . the tales of fairies, and other idle romances." Indeed, such "foolish books, . . . trifling ballads, and . . . romantick accounts of dreams and trances, senseless palmistry and groundless astrology" might be themselves the source of the "experience" of possession, for Elizabeth Blanchard (like Jane Colman, growing up in another town at the same time), "was more than ordinarily delighted with reading." Although he condemns the girls for lying, Turell is most scornful of the credulous and indulgent adults who encouraged them. The adults bear responsibility for the deception: "had not almost any excuse or reason [for inconsistent or suspicious behavior] been swallowed, all their schemes would have been dashed to pieces." Although he insists that he believes in the invisible world, he recommends skepticism toward all such accounts.[58]

This incident must have confirmed Turell in his belief that it was unwise for people in authority to lend too much credence to claims, particularly, perhaps, by young women, of extravagant experiences of a spiritual nature. Although Ebenezer certainly did not suspect his wife of lying, he was not impressed with her complaints of spiritual distress. Later, in the *Memoirs*, he wrote wearily, "How often has she lain whole *Nights* by me mourning for Sin, calling upon God, and praising him, or discoursing of Christ and Heaven? And when under Doubts intreating me to help her (as far as I could) to full Assurance of God's love" (*RT*, 116). These doubts, he reports, were easily disposed of by his counseling, by telling her, for example, that she was simply misreading scripture. "Her Fears about her Prayers being an *Abomination* were ill-grounded; for more was intended by *Wicked* in that Scripture then she imagin'd; and I hardly thought she would own her Self the *resolved Sinner*, delighting in Sin and committing it with Greediness" (*RT*, 99–100). Like Elizabeth Blanchard, though without the same motive, Jane Turell is, according to him, overreacting, seeing personal significances in scripture where there are none, exaggerating the spiritual meaning of her petty, everyday experience, calling, perhaps, like the Blanchard children, for attention. Although by

Ebenezer Turell's own self-congratulatory account, his counselling helped her ("Upon the whole, I led her to *Christ* the true Light," *RT,* 100), Jane Turell's own writings suggest that his advice was less than adequate. For example, one excerpt from her diary reads, "In the House of God greatly distress'd on account of *Deadness* and *Dulness* under the Word preach'd. I did all I could to raise and fix my Tho'ts, but all in vain" (*RT,* 109). Although she blames herself for her "deadness" here, we should remember that the word was being preached, presumably, by Ebenezer. And Jane Turell continued to write to Benjamin Colman, hoping that she would not remain dull under counseling from Brattle Street.

On the evidence of *Reliquiae Turellae,* Colman's pastoral technique was more responsive. At his best, Colman responded minutely to Jane's requests, answering her own questions and observations point by point, engaging in active dialogue with her rather than letting his own agenda and reasoning structure his response. He even put aside, in one letter, his characteristic marital imagery and responded directly to her query. Although we don't have her letter, his response is so lengthy and minute that we can fairly reconstruct it. The letter tells us indirectly that her main worry about taking the Supper was a theological one, derived from her reading of scripture: "he that eateth and drinketh unworthily, eateth and drinketh Damnation to himself" (2 Cor. 11.27). In his response, Colman puts aside the marital imagery that had dominated his previous letters and turns his attention to her worries about this text, analyzing scripture and quoting theologians in a manner worthy of an exchange between teacher and divinity student. Generally, his argument echoes Ebenezer Turell's that the abuses to which the text refers were much more serious than anything she might worry about. And, much as we saw him do in *Some of the Glories* (substituting psalm-singing for the sacrament), he tries to move her attention away from the Supper, suggesting that it should have no special status among other parts of the spiritual life: "And think my *Dear,* Is it only by *Eating* and *Drinking unworthily,* that the Judgment of God is incurred? Is is not also by *unworthily Praying?* For it is said, That the Prayer of the wicked is an *Abomination* to the Lord" (*RT,* 125).

Ebenezer Turell might not have thanked him for this remark, for he reports, as we saw, that his wife kept him up all night worrying if indeed her prayers *were* abominations. Colman's intention, though, is to suggest that the Supper is no different from any other devotional act, and that therefore she should not demand of herself any higher standard for it. What is most interesting about it, though, is its utter difference from his previous letters to Jane Turell, which invoke marital imagery, and argue, by analogy, that her new role of communicant should fit easily on her because it is so similar to her role as wife. It was only when Jane Turell challenged him directly that he put aside that language, language he perhaps hoped would have a special social resonance for her, to address her theological concerns, showing that he could bring the same rigor and care to his pastoral conversation as he did to his more public treatises.

As it happened, Jane Turell did take the Supper on the appointed day. But this decision did not end the spiritual uncertainties it caused her. While she may have accepted Colman's intellectual reasonings, his analogical argument using marital imagery had not made her more comfortable coming to the Lord's Table. At the time she was preparing to take the Supper, it did not adequately embody her spiritual experience or constructively express her spiritual dilemma in such a way as to bring her comfort. When her father urged the metaphor on her for that purpose, she resisted it.

Not that she avoided the subject of marriage—quite the contrary. Her writings on marriage show, in fact, that she clearly accepted the authority of the image and its implications for the social order and her role within that order. The subject surfaces most directly in Ebenezer's paraphrase of her "tho'ts on Matrimony," a prose reflection, written perhaps a year before she married. Ebenezer Turell's account shows that Jane Colman wrote a deliberately reasoned description of the institution of marriage, its roots in God's plan for creation ("Man [is] a *Sociable* Creature"), its institution in Eden and development since, its benefits and requirements. She ends with a list of rules she intended to follow in making her own marriage, including requirements of a potential spouse that, presumably, Ebenezer met: the husband should be "descended of pious and credible Parents," be of sober character, a church goer, and "of a sweet and agreeable *Temper*; for if he be the Owner of all the former good Qualifications, and fails here, my Life will be still uncomfortable" (*RT*, 77).

For a girl of seventeen, this is a sober meditation indeed. It describes marriage exclusively as a social arrangement, a "momentous Affair," to be sure, "on which so much of the Comfort and Pleasure of Life depends," but one which should prompt prayer and reflection on the suitability, primarily in a social sense, of the potential spouse, and on the duties incumbent upon married people. In this it is consistent with the traditional Reformed view of marriage as a civil bond and not a sacrament. It is noticeably lacking, however, in any features that might easily feed into the marriage metaphor for religious experience: there is no marriage as union, no marriage as covenant between two parties, and certainly (perhaps because of her editor's fastidiousness) no marriage as erotic encounter.

Even Jane Colman's biblical paraphrases show that the topic of marriage had social interest but little usefulness for the spiritual introspection that her other paraphrases expressed. Her paraphrases always include the technique of interpolation, of expanding a single verse well beyond its original length with elaborations. As we saw, her interpolations in the psalms dealing with the topic of singing—Psalm 8 and Psalm 137—do so in ways that expand the possible meanings of the poem. In contrast, her psalm paraphrases that deal specifically with gender roles make interpolations that simplify the psalms' imagery, making it less rich and multidimensional, and less available, therefore, for spiritual use. For example, in her paraphrase of Psalm 128, which describes the earthly blessings of prosperity and progeny promised to the God-fearing man, her elaboration delineates the role of the virtuous helpmeet, the role that she expected to fill. In this case, the King James Version's "Thy wife shall be as a fruitful vine by the sides of thine house; thy children like olive plants about thy table," is rendered:

> The beauteous Consort of your Bed,
> Like a fair Crown shall grace your Head.
> Her softer Hours she'll improve
> With the fair Pledges of your Love;
> Round thy full Table they shall stand
> Fed by her careful tender Hand. (*RT*, 72–73)

The King James text suggests through metaphor the ideas of fruitfulness and abundance, a theme and image that Colman Turell had embellished in her paraphrase of Psalm 137. This paraphrase, in contrast, eliminates that figure, detailing instead a full picture of family life, a picture in which the wife takes charge of domestic cares, serving food and perhaps educating young children; much like Bathsheba, the "vertuous woman" of exemplar literature, she converts the abundance that is God's blessing on her husband into nourishment. Her practical administration of God's bounty enhances the family's prosperity and adds an ornament ("a fair crown") to the husband's brow. As a result of these efforts, marriage is advanced as the foundation of an orderly society.

What Colman Turell subtracts from the psalm is equally important: figurative language that suggests but does not spell out the ways in which marriage may be "fruitful" ("as a fruitful vine"). The children are arranged around the table to be fed, but are not described as productive in themselves or as products of that fruitful marital interaction. In her paraphrase of Psalm 137, a highly complex imagery of fruitfulness and barrenness had played a crucial part in her exploring the poetic and prophetic roles that linked her to the elect community. But in this psalm, she eliminates this most expansive language, with the consequence that the figure of marriage is not available to her here to explore other kinds of marital productiveness—spiritual, or literary, for example. Therefore, this psalm shows that the social arrangements of marriage may be harmonious with God's will, but it does *not* suggest that they may provide a parallel with the spiritual life.

Colman Turell's paraphrase of a passage from the Song of Songs similarly flattens rather than expands its poetic language. The biblical passage (Ct. 5.8), in which the bride describes the bridegroom, uses sensuous metaphors and similes of physical satiety to convey the sense of longing. Theological readings of the language of desire in the Song of Songs turn on an ambiguity, by which mutual erotic desire between a human bridegroom and bride can suggest the intimate relationship between the believer and Christ. Jane Colman's version, however, mutes the physical aspects of the description of the bridegroom, lessening the possibility of religio-erotic ambiguity and, paradoxically, making the bridegroom more firmly human and less potentially divine. In some verses, she drops the physical description altogether, substituting instead generalized adjectives of approbation and, especially, moral attributes. For example, the King James Version's "His head is as the most fine gold, and his locks are bushy, and black as a raven," becomes, for Jane Colman, "His Head is Wisdoms spacious Theatre,/Riches of Grace and Beauty there appear./A down his Shoulders with becoming Pride/Falls his fine hair in beauteous Ringlets ty'd." All the colors mentioned in the King James Version are gone, and the attributes "Wisdom," "Grace," "Pride" take their place (*RT*, 72).

In the King James Version, the next verse, which describes the eyes of the bridegroom, unites a variety of types of imagery to produce an effect of an overflowing of sensations from a number of realms of creation—the animal kingdom, precious jewels, fragrant and life-giving liquids: "His eyes are as the eyes of doves by the rivers of waters, washed with milk and fitly set." Jane Colman's simile is more consistent but also more pedestrian: "His sparkling Eyes in splendent lustre vie,/With the Twin Stars that grace the azure Sky." This is a bridegroom of much diminished stature, and a report of a less overwhelming experience. The moralizing of qualities in the bridegroom suggests, like the paraphrase of Psalm 128, social attributes that can be admired rather than a bodily presence that excites an overwhelming affective response and either erotic or religious ecstasy; the description is more appropriate for a respected earthly husband than for an overpowering heavenly spouse. This is a poem about Ebenezer. It is not a poem about Christ.

Interestingly, Elizabeth Singer Rowe, in so many ways Jane Colman Turell's model, has two paraphrased versions of this same Canticles passage that also lessen the ambiguity traditionally ascribed to the book by Christian exegetes, *but* in favor of the divine spouse rather than the human. Singer Rowe's versions sometimes modify the biblical images of satiety, but generally compensate in some way to convey the same sense of a breathless, overwhelming desire. For example, in her first paraphrase, which Jane Colman surely knew, Rowe adds a series of incomplete exclamations that substitute effectively for the lack of extravagance she accords the eyes of the bridegroom: "His *Eyes*, the endless *Magazines* of *Love,*/How *soft*! how *sweet*! how powerfully they move!"[59] Colman Turell's paraphrases on the marital theme, in contrast, avoid such ecstatic features. We can conclude that although she wrote frequently and with apparently little ambivalence about the religiously prescribed social role of wife, she did not adapt that language to more private spiritual subjects. In the context of these writings, then, it is not surprising at all that the conventional marital language that Benjamin Colman recommended to her does not have the resonance needed to satisfy that spiritual discomfort. Her acceptance of the covenant of marriage as an earthly bride did not make it easier for her to covenant with the heavenly bridegroom in the Lord's Supper. In short, the analogy for spiritual experience that Benjamin Colman continued to invoke—the covenant—did not express to her satisfaction this new relation she feared to enter.

Coming into Communion: Jane Colman Turell
and the Travailing Woman

On the day that Jane Colman Turell took the Lord's Supper for the first time, there was an earthquake in New England—the famous earthquake of 1727, which prompted a number of Boston ministers, including Benjamin Colman, to preach traditional jeremiads interpreting this natural cataclysm as a warning from God. Unlike Hawthorne's minister, who reads in the meteoric "A" in the sky a private message indicting him for hypocrisy and secret adultery, Jane Turell does not seem to have taken the earthquake personally. The day, in fact, was not a turning point one way or the other. Not two months after taking the Supper, a series of letters that she exchanged with Benjamin Colman—still turning to him, despite having another counselor closer to home—shows that she had not achieved the serenity that might be expected in a communicating church member.

The exchange of letters in December 1727 exhibits some features of a productive pastoral dialogue: the exchange is initiated by the layperson seeking guidance, the minister's response is attentive, sympathetic and productive, the layperson's subsequent response seems to represent an advance. This pastoral relationship, however, is one that is negotiated, not authoritarian. In fact, her December letter, which Ebenezer Turell does print, marks a significant change in that pastoral relationship itself. For even as she continues to turn toward a trusted pastoral authority, her father, Jane Turell also puts forth her own spiritual insights, ignoring, again, the language of binary marriage and focusing instead on a vision of church that she had developed in the singing paraphrases. She does this by focusing attention on her own body as a locus for spiritual perception, and by choosing biblical images, not of marriage, but of maternity.

Ebenezer Turell's introductory remarks on the letter again give an idea of why his wife thought she could turn to "none in this World" better than her father. He calls it a "long and *broken Letter*" (*RT*, 86); Jane Turell's own nicely symmetrical comment is, "This is a short and broken Account of my Soul" (*RT*, 87). As we have been led to expect, Ebenezer thinks this anguished outpouring is an excessive reaction; Jane, on the other hand, knows she can't commit the whole story to paper. The subject of the Supper is conspicuous for its absence from this letter, but the crisis of two months ago is clearly not over. Studiously avoiding any explicit mention of the sacrament, Jane nonetheless articulates some of the problems it poses: she writes of a feeling of distance from Christ, using language of union, though not erotically figured or otherwise particularly dualistic, associated with the Supper: she wants to "lay hold on him," to "join my Soul to him," and laments, "I could not go to Christ." Moreover, she remarks, in what must be a deliberate evasion, that she is trying to be hopeful about the spiritual significance of that momentous day, October 29: "I am more mortify'd to the World since the *Earthquake*, and love is less" (*RT*, 88). To comment on a regionally shared experience and draw the public lesson that had been urged from pulpits across the colony over the past few weeks is curiously to suppress the more important event, for her, of that day, her covenanting with God and with the Medford church at the Lord's Table.

These are not, whatever Ebenezer Turell might have thought, the evasive strategies of an overwrought and timorous woman. The letter resists Benjamin Colman's own formulation of her spiritual situation (the marital analogy), even as it reaches toward him for some sort of legitimation. It represents instead Jane Turell's own strenuous effort to reconceive the nature of her spiritual problem. Having reached a stumbling block in the Supper, and in marital language, she labors to shift the terms of the discussion—and of her spiritual life—to other, more productive ones. Her gesture is reminiscent of her attempt to follow Benjamin Colman's advice, using psalm paraphrasing to correct a despairing frame of mind; it is similar also to Benjamin Colman's own strategy in *The Parable of the Ten Virgins* and *Some of the Glories*, substituting a discussion of psalm-singing for one of the Supper. Rejecting both marital imagery and the centrality of the Supper, she introduces other images, drawn from her scripture reading.

In some respects anticipating the theme Jonathan Edwards would elaborate to great effect in *Sinners in the Hands of an Angry God* (1741), she writes of a dizzy sense of precariousness and impending death:

> Sometimes my Sins come pressing on my Mind, and appear so black and numerous that I am quite amazed. I look all around, and see a World of Vanities, which can yield me no Comfort, much less any Help. . . . I seem in a maze, that such a Sinner as I, am spar'd from day to day; and admire at the Patience of God in giving me a space for Repentance. O that he would give me Grace to repent!
> ——— Often in a Day I think what would become of me if I should die? I think, if it were possible, I could open my very Breast, and tear the accursed thing *Sin* out of it. But since I can't wholly take it out, or drive it out, I look to God for his Grace that I might mortify it and subdue it, and prevent it's reigning in me. (*RT*, 87)

Edwards's sinners suffer from agoraphobia. As small as "some loathsome insect" confronted by a vast and brutal cosmos, they hang in bewildered, dizzily unanchored suspension over an abyss ("a great furnace of wrath," "a wide and bottomless pit").[60] Even Edwards's happier passages, like the "little white flower" passage in the "Personal Narrative," describe the same posture: the tiniest of mites surveys an overwhelmingly large and God-filled cosmos. The figure, which as his two passages show can express either a fearsome or an ecstatic apprehension of God's sovereignty, dramatizes the great gulf separating the Calvinist God from his creatures, a gulf expressed in the orthodox Calvinist theology that Edwards reintroduced with new vigor into the New England imagination.

While Edwards's soul turns outward for that perception, the posture Jane Turell describes turns inward; whereas Edwards's terror, as well as his most ecstatic delight, is in his apprehension of vast space, Turell's is a claustrophobic, constrictive panic ("my sins come pressing on my Mind," "I seem in a Maze"). And reflecting as they do a sense that the body contains something fearsome and uncontrollable, that might burst its boundaries or explode it, Turell's inwardness and claustrophobia converge in a sense of bodily posses- sion. Her insides are inhabited by an incubus ("I could open my very Breast and tear the accursed thing *Sin* out of it"). Her greatest temptations are "wicked, revengeful, quarrelsome Tho'ts rising up in me," and "rash passion- ate Expressions ready to break thro' the doors of my Lips" (*RT*, 87). Whereas for Edwards the human subject becomes so small as almost to disappear before God (a loathsome insect, a little white flower), the center of the spiri- tual experience Jane Turell describes *is* her body.

I use Edwards's well-known language here, to which I will return in the following chapter, because in this image it is so relentlessly dualistic. In emphasizing distance from God and the smallness of the creature compared to the vastness of God, it exemplifies, of course, an orthodox Calvinist theol- ogy. Benjamin Colman, although he hardly shares Edwards's extreme Cal- vinism, shares his terror of empty space outside the body, as shown in the castaway passage in *The Parable of the Ten Virgins*. He, as we saw, draws most extensively, though, on the imagery of sight, directing the body's senses out- ward from its surface. In contrast to both Colman and Edwards, Jane Turell's language uses the body itself as a locus of spiritual meaning, showing no awareness of anything outside. Like Esther Rogers, in fact, she describes a fear of inner pollution rather than of outward filth; and like Esther Rogers, she will find spiritual comfort metaphorically in the inner spaces of the body. The relentless interiority of her language has the effect of establishing a nondualis- tic spirituality, one for which meaning is located inside and not in relation to a remote other, whether fearsomely judgmental or gazed at adoringly. And, since Mary Douglas has written, "the human body is always treated as an image of society," this language, as isolating to the body as it may seem, points back as well to the vision of a unified, undifferentiated church polity, whole in itself and not dependent on dualistic relationships for its definition.[61] It is, like her father's in *Some of the Glories* and *Parable of the Ten Virgins*, a corporate vision; and it may echo, as well, the emphasis on a unified undifferentiated *communitas* that she had developed in her psalm paraphrases on singing.

Turell also chooses biblical language that metaphorically directs atten- tion to the internal spaces of the body, the conditions within that are con- ducive (or not) to spiritual calm. She complains that her own studies have not helped her accept her new status as communicant: "I have been much at a loss about laying hold on and applying the Promises, and when I have been searching my *Bible* to find out a Promise, that Scripture has come full in my Mind, *What hast thou to do to take my Covenant into thy Mouth?*" (*RT*, 88). This is a quotation from Ps. 50.16, in which God addresses the wicked; it echoes Turell's earlier concern with the text from 2 Corinthians, "he that eateth and drinketh unworthily eateth and drinketh Damnation," and may refer, somewhat elliptically, to the physical act of taking the Supper ("in thy mouth"). Other scrupulous New Englanders were often troubled by this passage, but in Jane Turell's case it has extra resonance with her other complaints: she fears bodily pollution, a dangerous entity inside her body that can destroy her. Similarly, she notes that attending services doesn't seem to help, for things don't seem to be going at all well at the Medford church: "I dare not stay away from the *House of God*, but when I am there, my Heart is as the *Way Side*, and *Stony Ground* to the Seed sown" (*RT*, 87). (The sower, of course, was Ebenezer, and although Jane blames herself for being unreceptive, she turns to her father in her letter in the hope that another voice might more efficaciously soften her stony heart.) Her choice of biblical language here echoes the lament for barrenness in Psalm 137, implying as well that her own body is the locus of change and growth. Her emphasis, then, is on the conditions within and whether or not they are conducive to a productive spiritual life. She consistently uses an idiom that locates meaning inside, not outside, and to which dualistic language, whether Edwardsean Calvinism or Colmanesque marital order, is irrelevant.

In the climax of her letter, she turns to a different kind of image, one also drawn from the Bible, that makes explicit what is implicit in her remarks about fearing possession by a foreign, destructive agent: an image of pregnancy. "But Amidst all my Spiritual Troubles that Text has afforded me some Comfort ————— *Shall he bring to the Birth, and not cause to bring forth?*" This line is from a passage in Isaiah (66.9) in which God promises to restore Jerusalem, figuring the city as a travailing and nursing mother who will deliver and nourish the nation of Israel. This was a figure resonant, perhaps, with Colman Turell's social experience, for at this time, sixteen months into her marriage, she had already had one stillbirth, and was just pregnant a second time.[62] It was resonant also, and more importantly, with her religious experience, for it is expressive of a protracted period of waiting, irresolution, and distress, the very pain of which, however, is a sign of God's presence and of his promise that the term of suffering will end "in due time," yielding issue.

In contrast to the Pauline figure of new birth, so important to reformed Christianity, this Old Testament text suggests a gradual process of spiritual growth rather than an instantaneous and complete coming to (new) life. Although in common usage either mother or infant may be "delivered," the biblical passage as a whole figures Jerusalem (and therefore, at another level, the soul) as a travailing mother rather than a newly born infant. Turell confirms this emphasis, even assigning a gender to the Soul in her gloss: "I can't but *hope* after all that God has begun a good Work in me; and will he not carry it on and finish it? I would hope that in his own Time he will deliver my Soul from all her Sins and Fears" (*RT*, 88). Her explication suggests the fluidity of the metaphor in another sense as well, for the gestating soul, like a pregnant woman in early New England who looks forward to the birth of her child and knows also that she risks death in childbirth, is profoundly ambivalent toward her burden: it is full of danger ("he will deliver my soul from all her Sins and Fears") and promise ("God has begun a good Work in me"). Finally, and most important, as we saw in Benjamin Colman's own writings, this image resonated as well with an emphasis on a notion of corporate church identity rather than a binary individualized relationship with God. It seems particularly appropriate, then, that Jane Turell, for whom the exercise of psalm paraphrase had also been an important vehicle to explore the congregational ideal, should turn to such language here too: the theological significance of the Supper was not, as she knew if she had studied her father's own public sermons, to turn toward a superior in a binary relationship, but to assume membership in a whole community. To adjust to being a communicant, she had to direct her attention not to understanding her relationship with God and Ebenezer, but to accepting her new relationship with the Medford church. Therefore, the maternal imagery, in its association with nonbinary mutual relationships, as well as its ability to express Jane Turell's own experience of waiting and patience, served her better than conventional marital imagery.

What is important about the contrast I am developing here is that it shows, as I have already said, that marital and maternal language, though both gendered, and though both may apply to women's biographical experience, compete in this discourse, and that they have very different theological qualities. Jane Turell's biological experience of sexuality and pregnancy are not as significant to her choice of imagery, therefore, as the theological meanings that attach to these images. The most subversive potential of maternal imagery within this homiletic literature, that is, lies not in its incorporation of a feminine perspective but in the alternate theology (concept of God and concept of church community) it can imply.

This letter from Jane Turell is dated December 6, 1727. Benjamin Colman answered immediately, with a short note—all, he said, he had time to write—

to give his daughter some comfort while she awaited his more deliberate reply. With tender words he acknowledged her pain and assured her that all would be well. "My Soul grieves for you, and rejoyces in you, and I long to be with you. You are a thousand times dearer to me than ever" (*RT*, 89).

The next day, December 9, he wrote quite a long reply—it runs to almost five printed pages in the *Memoirs*, or about twice the length of Jane's own letter. Colman's letter exemplfies the best of his pastoral practice. Clearly he has read his daughter's letter with meticulous care and sympathy, and he answers each of her remarks in turn, praising her for her introspection, supplying extra scripture texts, suggesting new contexts that might be helpful. As we saw him do in his note of thanks to Jane for the Psalm 137 paraphrase, he lets himself be guided by her own choice of imagery; but here he largely confirms rather than contradicts her spiritual insights. Echoing her vocabulary, he writes, for example, "You are amaz'd that one so *Young* as you should have *heap'd* up such a Load of Guilt, you say: O stand *amaz'd* at what God has wro't in Christ Jesus for the Salvation of the greatest Sinners: having laid on Him the Iniquity of us all, and calling every *weary and heavy laden Soul* to him for rest" (*RT*, 91). Essentially, he is correcting and amplifying her reading of scripture, as did Ebenezer Turell. But unlike Turell, who had dismissed her interpretations ("I hardly thought she would own her Self the *resolved Sinner*"), Colman encourages her in her searching of scripture, underscoring the solace it can provide. Echoing his advice in *The Government and Improvement of Mirth*, and affirming Jane's own sense of the experiential ambiguity of the spiritual life, he writes, "Blessed be God for the *Comforts you taste* at times: O be very thankful for them, prize them, and live on them, when Darkness returns. And still follow God in the Dark" (*RT*, 92).

Most significantly, Colman affirms the usefulness of her own chosen figure to express this insight, the image of the travailing woman. Picking up her citation from Isaiah, he writes, "Think it not strange (my Dearest) that you are under such Pressure of Spirit, and are bow'd down heavily, for it is no more than what many of the dear Children of *God* have experienc'd, and they have been to them as the *Pangs of the New Birth*: These will be remembered with *Joy* if you are indeed *born to God*; as the sorrows of Childbed are forgotten for Joy that there is a Child born" (*RT*, 89). His gloss, like her own, construes the experience of birth loosely, recognizing its uncertain outcome and drawing simultaneously on the perspectives of infant and mother, to describe Christian conversion. The "children of God" experience a "new Birth" and are "born to God"; but the maternal "pangs of birth," and "Sorrows of Childbed," anticipate the promised deliverance. Later on he repeats the text

from Isaiah and adds other scripture texts that express the same idea of waiting with both pain and confidence: "*Shall he bring to the Birth and not cause
to bring forth? Will he quench the smoking Flax, or break the bruised Reed?* No,
no: *Be confident of this very thing, that he who hath begun a good Work in you
will perform it to the Day of Christ*" (Isa. 66.9, Isa. 42.3, Phil. 1.6; 92). The
two figures here express the two sides of the ambivalent birth figure: the soul
as bruised reed suffers but will survive; as burning flax, it begins to perceive
dimly ("a good work is begun") and will not lose its inner conviction.
Paralleling his inclusion of the mother and child in the list of analogies in *The
Parable of the Ten Virgins*, here Colman explicitly links Jesus with the image of
childbirth, since the amplification from Isaiah is from one of the "Servant
Songs," passages commonly interpreted in the Christian tradition as adumbrating the Incarnation.

Pastorally, then, Colman attempts to comfort Turell by confirming her
insights and recognizing and amplifying the richness of the images (and
therefore of the spiritual perceptions to which they point) that she has picked
out from her reading of the Bible, including those that suggest a maternal
image of God. Expressing his pastoral and fatherly concern for her, he reminds
her that God is an even more tender parent than himself: "The bowels of
Christ are mov'd infinitely more to you, if he sees you in the Mournings of a
True Repentance" (*RT*, 91–92). Although he closes with a patriarchal idea of
judgment and distance, the parental God here is a mother, whose own body
knows and responds to the pain and needs of the offspring. In place, therefore, of the language of marital binarism that Colman had originally used
during the year, Jane Turell's letter of December 6 brings him back, reminds
him, as it were, of his own preferred figure of childbirth, preferred because it
allows more flexibility, because it is less dualistic, and because it acknowledges
incompleteness and uncertainty. His response of December 9 acknowledges
the fitness of this image.

Even in this letter, though, Colman returns to the language of the
covenant, figuring the spiritual life in the terms of binary family relationships
and earthly prosperity. The image of God as mother parallels his own filial
care for Jane, and suggests to him also the social role of parenting that it
would bless her to fill: "*God Almighty bless thee*; and increase his Grace in
thee; make thee fruitful and multiply thee; . . . give the Blessing of *Abraham*
to thee and to thy Seed, and say of thee that thou *shalt be a Blessing*. Make
thee a happy Mother, and a *better Parent* to thine than *I* have been to thee"
(*RT*, 93). He cannot resist invoking once more the marital analogy, intimat-
ing that part of his daughter's spiritual calling is to preserve the domestic

tranquillity, as described in Psalm 128: "Live *cheerfully* with Him whom thou lovest, and to whom thou art espoused; with *Him in Heaven* which is Christ; and with *him on Earth* who will love thee *as Christ loved his Church*, and help thee on in thy way to Heaven. Make Mr. *Turell's* Life easy and pleasant by seeing you so" (*RT*, 93). All of these covenants have their origin, as he reminds Jane Turell, in the covenant of Abraham, the Old Testament source, in Puritan theory, for the image of binary relationships that formed the basis for covenant theology as well as for orderly human society. The figure of the covenant, Colman implies, is finally the figure she must understand to resolve her spiritual problems. Not incidently, that resolution will also bring her social prosperity and allow her to fulfill successfully the role of the virtuous woman ordained by a theory of society and spirituality that organizes spiritual and social callings in twos: "O I hope God means of his free Grace to make you a holy and happy Woman, a gracious Wife, Mother, and Mistress in your House, a Blessing in your Place, and blessed for ever" (*RT*, 90).

We have seen that this conception of spiritual and social organization, and the conception of religious experience it supported, was at odds with the most profound insights into her spiritual condition that Jane Turell came upon as a result of her introspection during troublesome times. The covenant image, common though it was in early New England culture, implied a conception of a self that turned toward a partner—either an earthly partner or a divine partner figured as earthly—to understand its spiritual identity. Jane Turell's early writings suggest that it had become her habit to describe her spiritual identity in terms of membership in a corporate whole rather than as individual partnered with God. In her only preserved letter to her father, her semantic problem was to find a language, not for the right relationship with God, but for her own experience of anxiety. In that letter, she solved that problem, adopting instead a different idiom for both sin and salvation, an idiom of pregnancy that allowed her to give voice to the experience of ambiguity, vacillation, and waiting—and the resolve to "follow God in the dark."

Aftermath

A few weeks after this exchange, Jane Turell sent a letter to her younger sister, Abigail, who was living in Boston with her parents. In contrast to Jane, Abigail, or "Nabby," as she was called, was the rebellious sister, who would briefly take her inheritance from her grandfather out of her father's control, and, later, would elope with a man unacceptable to Benjamin Colman, scandalizing both him and the town.[63] Jane Turell was doubtless aware of her adolescent sister's refractory tendencies, and wrote to "Nabby" with declarations of sisterly affection and some advice. The letter consists mainly of the standard admonitions commonly found in contemporary advice to young people: "Remember your Creator now, even *now* in the Days of your Youth"; "Fly Youthful Lusts"; emulate "the Incomparable Pattern and Example which our Lord Jesus Christ has left unto Young People to Copy after." Hinting how much she herself appreciates their father, and how much she misses his daily company, she reminds Nabby, "You have a precious Opportunity for Instruction and Improvement under the best of earthly Fathers." Filial obligations—to God and to Colman—are especially important: "Be dutiful and shew all Reverence to your Parents. O remember the *Fifth* Commandment; study the Promises and Threatenings of it." Mostly, Nabby should behave in a seemly, decorous way, as becomes a Christian. "Behave your self Womanly. . . . Indulge not a passionate or fretful Temper. . . . Be obliging, and modest, and humble, so shall you deserve and have the Esteem of every Body. Hearken to Instruction, and let your Ears be open to *Reproof*" (*RT,* 94, 95). In short, Jane lectures Nabby on the behavior that becomes a "vertuous woman." Emulating the pastoral role Benjamin Colman had taken with her, Jane Turell adopts the posture of adult counselor to her sister, and casts the reader of the letter into the complementary pose of the partner in a pair that receives spiritual advice: child, student, wife, or, more precisely, woman. That is, she adopts the same kind of rhetorical strategy she had rejected in resisting the marital analogy for her own spiritual experiences. Indeed, the letter's concern is not with spiritual introspection at all, but with outward behavior.

The letter, which conspicuously adopts the language of binary—and gendered—social relations, is a curious coda to her own struggle over the Supper. What it shows is that in the communion exchange, Jane Turell had not so much rejected the marriage language once and for all as she had made another more appropriate choice for her own situation. It was a moment of polarization, perhaps, in a long and ongoing pastoral conversation, a moment at which she reminded Benjamin Colman of an alternative language that he had used in his career but had temporarily put aside; after thus reminding him, she herself spent the rest of her life moving back and forth between both types of language. In fact, in this next exchange with Abigail, father and daughter seem to have changed places. She uses the language of binary relationships, but he, in praising her for her gesture toward Nabby, turns to maternal language. He comments in his biographical section in his sermon that she had "*travail'd in Birth*" for Nabby (52), using the same language for

Jane that he uses elsewhere to describe his own ministry. In a letter to Jane herself, praising her effusively for her efforts, he uses an interesting variation on that language: "You have done a *Sister's* part, and acted like the converted to God, desiring to carry your only & younger Sister with you" (*RT*, 96).

Jane Turell was only nineteen when she wrote this letter to her sister. For the rest of her life—only eight more years—she turned more regularly to Ebenezer for spiritual guidance, honoring her earthly spousal covenant. In one note, for example, she even apologizes to him for shutting herself up in her room and not confiding in him. To make amends, she adopts a posture of unquestioning dependence on his instruction: "What shall I do? tell me freely, and resolve me quickly" (*RT*, 98). Her diary conscientiously records her desire to keep the covenant faithfully, "for *her Self* and her *Children*" (*RT*, 103): "Make me stedfast in thy Covenant" (*RT*, 111). She continued to have problems with the Supper, undergoing lengthy preparations and sometimes enduring grave doubts about it, even the temptation, as she put it, to refrain from taking it. But in later years she was able, Ebenezer Turell tells us, to overcome these "dark & distressing" times by meditation. Her diary even records a few meditations on the sacrament using the binary Canticles imagery she had before eschewed.

Interestingly, however, her Canticles meditations are expansive and flexible, drawing more freely than did Benjamin Colman on the erotic component of that book, fluently using the image of the Holy Spouse in combination with other figures. Five years earlier, she had not been able to associate the Supper closely with marital language; but in 1732, she writes, "I bless God that I have experienc'd more outgoings of Soul towards my Saviour (in his House and at his Table) to Day, and more of the divine Afflations comforting & refreshing me than ever in my Life before. *I return'd home fill'd with Joy and Praise.* I think I could see my Interest in Christ, and the Father's reconciled Face shining on me. *My Beloved is mine and I am his! All things are mine!*" (*RT*, 113–14). Clearly, her use here draws not on the language of marital orderliness, the idiom Colman had used, but on the imagery of marital ecstasy. It draws on the language of sight ("the Father's reconciled face shining on me") used so prominently by Colman to express sensually the experience of God and at the same time to control it, but it incorporates the erotic aspect of the marital language that Colman had always avoided, allowing for a binary conception ("outgoings of Soul towards my Saviour"), but also locating spiritual experience inside the body. She is "filled with Joy and Praise," and experiences divine "afflations," an overwhelming sense of possession, of inspiriting.

Similarly, in her private meditations from the later years of her marriage, she wrote of her religious experience using both languages, the covenant language of her father, which prescribed a rigidly defined posture and set of behaviors, and the more fluid language of delivery that she had learned to use during the fall of 1727. Another of her communion meditations illustrates this, uniting the scripture texts and the imagery of the two types of religious experience: the covenant language of Canticles, which turns outward toward a remote God, and the intimate language of Isaiah, expressing an inward consciousness of God's presence: "This Day I was much affected with God's Goodness to me thro' my whole Life. I hope I can truly say I love my *Redeemer*, that he is *altogether lovely*, and I prize him above ten thousand Worlds. I trust in none but Him. I have had a *most ravishing Sight of Him!* How wonderful is his Love! He has begun a good Work in me, and will carry it on to the End" (*RT*, 114). This meditation, again, draws upon Colman's language of visual experience for desire ("the most ravishing sight of him") rather than explicit eroticism. It unites, however, a desire of the bridegroom in which spiritual sight is consummation with an account of an inward experience that is gradual, attendant, yet confident ("he has begun a good work").

The last poem included in the *Memoirs* embodies another development in Jane Turell's use of familiar biblical imagery, one that was perhaps less salutary. The poem, a paraphrase of Psalm 133, revisits the issue of the corporate church, with a quite different result than those of Psalms 8 and 137—either because her experience as the pastor's wife had induced her to change, or because in her poetry, as in her meditations, she had adopted more fluid use of biblico-political figures. This poem, Ebenezer tells us, was written at a time of "some unhappy Affairs of Medford in the years 1729 & 30" (*RT*, 115). Readers have assumed that Medford was embroiled in a seating controversy, but it could just as well have been a local singing quarrel. In any event, the conflict, according to Ebenezer, "produc'd many Prayers and Tears from her": these factional disputes among congregations, so common in this period, would of course generally involve the minister on one side or the other, and could certainly be very upsetting to the minister's wife. If Turell's comment suggests again what he thought was her tendency to become unhinged, he was grateful that his wife was also able to write this poem, which, he wrote, "I publish as a *Monument* for and *Motive* to my own *People*, to continue in *Love* and *Peace*" (*RT*, 115).

The psalm she chooses is indeed not a rebuke to a backsliding, contentious community, though there are plenty of those in the Psalms, but a paean to a perfectly harmonious society.

> Behold how *good,* how *sweet,* their Joy does prove
> Where Brethren dwell in *unity* and Love! (*RT,* 115)

As usual, her interpolations are particularly revealing, and here they reveal a thinly veiled hostility to those refractory elements in Medford. The poem praises "unity and love":

> When no Contention Strife, or Fatal Jar,
> Disturb the Peace, and Raise the noisy War.

This is presumably what has been happening in Medford, and her addition of these lines has a note of rebuke, or even sarcasm, not present in the original psalm, reflecting the position of a minister's wife taking sides against those who opposed her husband. A few lines later, she adds another hint that those responsible for the town's contention are agents of ungodliness: "If *Sinners* wrangle, let the Saints agree; /The *Gospel* breathes out nought but *Unity.*" At the same time, however, it is also possible to read these lines as a lament over any disunity, one we might expect from a poet who had carefully paraphrased a vision of congregational harmony in Psalm 8. From that perspective, Turell's elaboration of verse 2 situates the religious leadership in a peculiar position:

> 'Tis like the *Oyntment,* which of old was pour'd
> On *Aaron's* Head, and down his Garments shower'd;
> Thro' all the Air perfuming Odour spreads,
> Diffusing Sweetness to the neighbouring Meads. (*RT,* 115)

The second couplet here implies, adding to the original psalm, that sacramental ordination, conveying special status on the priest, not only gives him authority but also is a source of sweetness and harmony for all that surrounds him, that is, the community. Harmony comes through a sacerdotal priesthood, and perhaps through the community's acceptance of it.

Her vision has a number of interesting implications. Certainly it assigns to the ordained minister a much more elevated role than did Psalm 8, for example—a role sacerdotal in nature, more in keeping with the emergent presbyterian order than with old-fashioned congregationalism. As such, the poem may plausibly be read as an endorsement for priestly—for Ebenezer Turell's—authority, and as a rebuke to those who "wrangle" with him. Or, most radically, it may express—though if it did, he evidently didn't see it— exasperation at Ebenezer, for not fulfilling the role of unifier, as an anointed priest should. In either case, this poem makes an interesting coda to the paraphrases of Psalm 8 and Psalm 137, both written before Jane Turell's marriage, and both of which, I have suggested, invoke a nonhierarchical *communitas*. While maintaining her commitment to a vision of congregational unity, she has moved to a more authoritarian concept of the relationship between minister and congregation. And, for better or for worse, she has abandoned her earlier exploration of the relation of mutuality between speaker-poet and community in favor of an identification with the priestly figure.

Even so, Jane Colman Turell's richest use of biblical language in this late period comes in her poems that employ the maternal, not marital imagery. Benjamin Colman noted that in addition to her illness and difficult pregnancies, Jane Turell suffered greatly from the death of her own mother. Her elegy for the elder Mrs. Colman uses interesting language that expresses that sense of loss, but also a hope for reunion that is best expressed in maternal language. She imagines, for example, her mother united with a distinctly maternal Christ: "Her Soul in Jesus arms remain." And, she hopes that she herself may be reunited in heaven with her mother, and prays for the "Quickening Spirit" that will allow her to do so—the language compares, again, spiritual animation to pregnancy (*RT*, 105).

And finally, the poem for which she is best known to present day readers, "Lines on Childbirth," employs that image of delivery to most expansive effect. This poem, written during her third pregnancy, is part consolatory elegy, part anticipatory expression of faith; it depicts the doubleness of the mother's experience. Like the paraphrase of Psalm 137, it intertwines the themes of fruitfulness and sterility, life and death, both intimately a part of pregnancy and of Colman Turell's religious experience.

> *Phoebus* has thrice his Yearly Circuit run,
> The Winter's over, and the Summer's done;
> Since the *bright Day* on which our Hands were join'd,
> And to *Philander* I my All resign'd.
>
> *Thrice* in my Womb I've found the pleasing Strife,
> In the first Struggles of my Infants Life:
> But O how soon by Heaven I'm call'd to mourn,
> While from my Womb a *lifeless Babe* is torn?
> Born to the Grave 'ere it had seen the Light,
> Or with one Smile had chear'd my longing Sight.
>
> Again in Travail Pains my Nerves are wreck'd.
> My Eye balls start, my Heart strings almost crack'd;
> Now I forget my Pains, and now I press

> *Philander's* Image to my panting Breast.
> Ten Days I hold him in my joyful Arms,
> And feast my Eyes upon his Infant Charms.
> But then the King of Terrors does advance
> To pierce it's Bosom with his Iron Lance.
> It's Soul releas'd, upward it takes it's Flight,
> Oh never more below to bless my Sight!
> Farewell sweet *Babes* I hope to meet above,
> And there with you Sing the Redeemer's Love.
>
> And now O gracious Saviour lend thine Ear,
> To this my earnest Cry and humbler Prayer,
> That when the Hour arrives with Painful Throes,
> Which shall my Burden to the World disclose,
> I may Deliverance have, and joy to see
> A living Child, to Dedicate to Thee. (*RT,* 103–4)

The poem contains a personal history, telling in the first three stanzas of Turell's marriage, the stillbirth of her first child, and the death, at eleven days old, of her second. Ebenezer tells us that the first pregnancy apparently was dangerous to the mother as well: "she knew nothing of her Delivery till two Days after it." About this stillbirth, Turell wrote in her diary that "My Womb became as it were a Tomb to my *Infant*" (*RT,* 101), the rhymes calling attention to the coincidence in pregnancy of the promise of life together with the threat of death. The poem also calls attention to the double edge to the mother's experience: both anticipation and pain ("pleasing strife"), joy and loss ("chear'd my longing Sight"/"call'd to mourn"), and death in life ("Born to the Grave"). It describes the stillbirth as having been unnaturally violent: "From my Womb a lifeless babe is torn." As in Psalm 137, the themes of fruitfulness and sterility come together in paradoxical juxtaposition. The second birth, for which she was awake, is described here in memorable language. Her intimacy with her child develops through her own bodily experience, including pain, of his birthing ("Again in Travail Pains my Nerves are wreck'd./My Eye balls start, my Heart strings almost crack'd"). That experience is the basis of their relationship, which involves not judgment but simple intimacy ("I hold him"). As in the first instance, the death of this infant is violent, an invasion from an outside power, the "King of Terrors."

The fourth stanza, in which the speaker prays that this current pregnancy will have a more successful result, contains the most subtle, fluid use of the delivery figure. The previous stanza had ended with a conventional resolution, in which the grieving mother accepts the loss ("Farewell sweet *Babes* I hope to meet above"). It thus puts the speaking mother, as well as her reader, in mind of her own death. It therefore broadens the context of the poem, suggesting that the language of delivery resonates beyond the immediate occasion of childbirth. The speaker's "painful Throes" could describe a time of spiritual struggle, much like Turell's wrestling with the problem of the Supper. More important, the stanza describes the moment at which that private travail must of necessity be made painfully public, "the Hour . . . /which shall my Burden to the World disclose." The moment of childbirth, the moment of publicly declaring oneself in communion with one's new church, the moment of death—all these are moments of trial, of risk and uncertainty, when inner experiences are presented to a surrounding community. The speaker prays for "Deliverance," to come through each experience safe and rid of a burden; the "living child" that she prays will result is both a vindication, a sign of God's approbation, and a continuation in the world of the graciousness that marked the delivery. This last stanza, then, movingly expresses a pregnant mother's hopes for herself and her child in language resonant with the most profound concerns of her culture, and resonant with her own preferred idiom for describing her spiritual experience.

The figures of pregnancy and childbirth seem to have been particularly rich for Jane Turell—not just because those experiences were also literal, biographical facts but also because they resonate with her spiritual experiences, which she also described in terms of her own body possessing a "good work" that nonetheless meant suffering and perseverance. Unlike the marriage poems, which rigidly limit the applications of their marriage image, this poem allows the figure of pregnancy to ramify, to point beyond its literal subject toward broader spiritual concerns.

The special fluidity that Turell found in this metaphor, its ability to suggest a profound and subtle spiritual meaning, is underscored by the contrast between this poem and two consolatory poems that Benjamin Colman wrote for her at approximately the same time, after the death of the second child.[64] The poems anticipate the two funeral sermons Benjamin Colman would preach for Jane Turell at her own death, for they provide models for grieving. In the first of those funeral sermons, Aaron "held his peace" after his two sons were suddenly struck down, maintaining an "adoring Silence and profound Submission" (*RT*, 3); David, on the other hand, accepted the death of his son with decorous words: "I shall go to him, but he shall not return to me." For Colman, these models provide two biblically sanctioned alternative postures, held in a neat balance: "There was a perfect Harmony in both together" (*RT*,

13). His consolatory poems for Jane similarly provide biblical models for grieving. Colman's main message in both poems is that she should grieve decorously, using both silence and speech. The first poem, echoing the biblical consolation offered to Patience Boston on the impending loss of her child at her own execution, compares the stoicism the grieving mother should feel to that of Abraham, who, commanded by God, "grasped the knife" and sacrificed his own son. Addressing his daughter as Urania, he writes that she should accept the death, like Abraham, with "Silence under Discipline": "Learn hence, *Urania*, to be dumb." In the second poem, he relates the story of the Shunnamite woman whose son dies suddenly, but who accepts the will of God with decorous speech: "*All's well*, my Lord," "Mild in her Anguish, in her Plaints discreet." His poems of consolation tell his daughter how to behave, providing biblical models—Abraham, the Shunnamite—like the model of Aaron and David that he would adopt for himself in the funeral sermons he would preach upon her own death in 1735. Jane Turell's poem, on the other hand, describes her inward experience. As we saw in the pastoral exchange on the Supper, Colman is interested in establishing the proper outward posture she should take with respect to God or the world; Jane Turell, in contrast, focuses on introspection. His interest here is in control, as it was in his discussions of the marriage figure; hers is in meditative expansiveness.

It was finally the images of pregnancy and delivery that for Jane Colman Turell were the richest and most expressive language her culture had to offer. The writings in which she employed that biblical figure are the ones in which she achieved the greatest spiritual insight and the greatest poetic subtlety. They were evidently sufficient unto the last. Ebenezer records her dying words, a prayer that expresses, in this most supple of figures, confidence in God even in a time of distress and irresolution: "*Thou hast deliver'd, thou dost deliver, and I trust in Thee that thou wilt still deliver*" (*RT*, 120).

Chapter 3

Flowing and Reflowing

Dialogic Emanations

In the winter of 1742, western Massachusetts was in the midst of a religious revival. People throughout the commonwealth—and in other colonies as well—were reporting extraordinary experiences of the Holy Spirit. Seven years previously, the towns of the Connecticut Valley had provided a preview of the current revival, and Northampton's minister, Jonathan Edwards, had published a widely read account, called *A Faithful Narrative of Surprising Conversions*, of the way in which the Spirit swept through the region, affecting all manner of people with religious renewal, causing many to join the church, and to have hopeful thoughts that they were saved. In 1740, the Spirit had returned to a more widespread area, and Northampton was again the center of attention: the most famous analyst of religious psychology still ministered there.[1] As the revival continued for several years, ministers came visiting, with many people stopping in at the Edwards house, and Jonathan Edwards was invited to preach in various places throughout the Valley. In January 1742, he left for a two-week trip to Leicester.

It was in some ways a bad time for him to leave. Sarah, his wife, kept the household together in Jonathan's absence, as people continued to gather at the Edwards house to pray together, to talk, and to exchange their own spiritual experiences and to remark on the spectacular way in which the Spirit had returned to Northampton. In the midst of all this activity, Sarah had an extraordinary experience herself, one that lasted for about ten days. Even as people were passing in and out of her house, she would lose strength, overwhelmed by the sense of the Spirit, and have to lie down for hours at a time. Possessed by a supernatural energy, she would leap up, only to sink down. She would grow cold and faint, and have to be carried off to bed. For two full nights,

151

Thursday and Friday, January 28th and 29th, she lay in bed in a state of half-wakefulness, having the nearest thing to a vision that Puritan orthodoxy would allow: "All night I continued in a constant, clear and lively sense of the heavenly sweetness of Christ's excellent and transcendent love, of his nearness to me, and of my dearness to him. . . . I seemed to myself to perceive a glow of divine love come down from the heart of Christ in heaven, into my heart, in a constant stream, like a stream or pencil of sweet light. . . . It seemed to be all that my feeble frame could sustain, of that fullness of joy, which is felt by those, who behold the face of Christ, and share his love in the heavenly world." "It was," she would say of it, "the sweetest night I ever had in my life."[2] So remarkable was Sarah Edwards's experience of enspiritedness, in fact, that upon learning of it after his return home, Jonathan asked her to write an account of all she had felt while he was gone.

She sat down to write that account, however, laboring under the burden of what was already the formidable reputation of her husband. Shepherd of the religious awakenings that were currently sweeping through most of New England and beyond, and their most prominent defender against skeptics, Jonathan Edwards had started his pastoral career in Northampton as heir apparent to the great divine Solomon Stoddard, dubbed "Pope" of the Connecticut River Valley for his dominance there; by the time of these current awakenings, Edwards had already influenced numerous students at Yale. Most immediate on Sarah's mind as she wrote, though, must have been the fact that in these heady days of what would come to be called the Great Awakening, her husband had asked her for this narrative, intending, she might have suspected, to use it in his next defense of those religious revivals. She was about to enter, in other words, the very public and vitriolic world of print. And indeed, in Jonathan's next published work, *Some Thoughts Concerning the Revival of Religion*, Sarah Edwards's experience is featured prominently, albeit disguised and reshaped, to epitomize the current awakenings.

This textual interchange epitomizes the tensions and collaborations of the pastoral relationship. Jonathan Edwards would use Sarah's narrative to his own ends, hiding her identity and even her gender by referring to her only as "the person," removing all identifying narrative details and social context, reshaping her experience to fit his own theory of religious psychology. Sarah, who stood in relation to Jonathan not only as a wife but as a congregant for all of her adult life, thus entered the public conversation about the phenomenon of the revival, but only at a cost. In using her text as he does, stripping it of its specificity and much of its character, Jonathan respects Sarah's privacy and dignity. He protects her from the public ridicule of writers like Charles

Chauncy who had discredited the awakenings as the undisciplined outpour-ings of women, children, and servants, disguising her so successfully, in fact, that some eighteenth-century readers were convinced that "the person" must have been Jonathan himself.[3] He protected her privacy, but he also appropri-ated her experience. Her original manuscript has now been lost, and the only reason we have something resembling it is that Sereno Dwight, her great-grandson, printed it in his nineteenth-century biography of Jonathan Edwards, part of an attempt to extend his legacy further.[4] That text is itself justly sus-pect, as are all nineteenth-century printings of colonial works, which tended to modernize and otherwise simplify the language. The story of Sarah Edwards's narrative, therefore, encapsulates the ambivalent power relations that we have seen working in one way or another with respect to all the womens' texts we have looked at. Our access to the original text is compromised, made to serve a clerical agenda.

There is a legend among Edwards biographers that the marriage of Jonathan and Sarah was an extraordinarily loving and intimate one. Samuel Hopkins reported that Jonathan on his deathbed spoke of the "uncommon union" he had with Sarah; Perry Miller began his biography with the anec-dote that a minister once told Jonathan that his wife was going to heaven "by a shorter road than himself," to which he nodded silently; and most dramati-cally, Jonathan Edwards's own apostrophe to Sarah Pierrepont, written in his notebook four years before their marriage, has provided fodder for its roman-ticization by biographers. Modern readers of Sarah Edwards's narrative, how-ever, have been skeptical of this portrait, believing that her narrative exposes significant tensions between them. Her experience of that January, some have argued, constituted a rebellion against ministerial authority; it was a perfor-mance before the people of Northampton betraying the conflicts that existed between the Edwards family and the town; it represented her appropriation of clerical teaching power.[5] One scholar has even argued that it had a long-term effect of distancing them from each other, and contributing, together with his general disappointment in the revivals, to Jonathan's growing disillu-sionment with community life, so that his later writings "disparag[e] the moral value of natural human love."[6] Birth records show that during their married life, Sarah conceived a child every two years, but 1742 is an excep-tion; and a December 1742 note from the town doctor to Jonathan Edwards, preserved because in an age of scarce paper he used the back of it for sermon notes, offers a remedy for a condition the doctor called "Hysterickall Orig-inall," implying that Sarah had some sort of gynecological problem that year that might have interrupted her childbearing.[7] This evidence reminds us that for Sarah Edwards, as for other colonial women, the reproductive cycle was a constant and present feature of life. Whether we read it as signalling a temporary emotional estrangement between her and her husband or a physical consequence of her unusual spiritual experience (or perhaps just a random medical occurrence), it is clear that that event was disruptive to the Edwards household, the Edwards marriage, and the Edwards pastoral relationhip, in more ways than one.

The pastoral/marital relationship is indeed one of the problematic issues in Sarah Edwards's narrative. At the very beginning, she reports that the trigger for her spiritual experience is her unease at a rebuke from her husband for her having "failed in some measure in point of prudence" in her dealings with another minister (Dwight, 172). Her concern for losing "the good opinion of my husband" testifies that the marital relation in Puritan theory and practice was one in which the husband's role was to instruct and rebuke his wife. Jonathan Edwards himself wrote as much in his "Miscellanies": "When a woman is married to an husband she receives him as a guide, as a protector, a safeguard, and defense. . . . God has so designed it, and therefore has made man of a more robust [nature] . . . with more wisdom, strength and courage, fit to protect and defend."[8] A stable union, however uncommon it may have been, depended on that hierarchy. The husbandly role Jonathan describes here sounds very much like a clerical one.

Sarah reports that Jonathan's rebuke to her behavior pushes her, as any husband or minister might, to even further depths of self-examination, with results that have both pastoral and marital implications. She imagines, for example, as an exercise in self-abnegation, "the feelings and conduct of my husband . . . chang[ing] from tenderness and affection, to extreme hatred and cruelty" (Dwight, 183). On the other hand, one of the themes of her narrative is her struggles with professional jealousy on her husband's behalf: she steels herself to accept the possibility that Samuel Buell, who was substituting for him in his absence, and others might have more success in stimulating a revival than Jonathan himself. It is either profoundly ironic, then, or evidence of a passive kind of rebellion, that Sarah's own experience took place in the absence of her husband and usual clerical supervisor.

One of the primary features of the Great Awakening itself was its disruption of normal pastoral relationships. The Awakening was noteworthy for both its assertion of lay experience over and against clerical authority and for the phenomenon of itinerancy: unattached celebrity ministers, like the British Methodist George Whitefield, who made a grand tour of the colonies, and, more infamously, New England's own James Davenport, who in his travels in

New England stirred up all manner of disorderly behavior, including a book burning, before finally recanting in 1744.[9] Exciting things could happen, the people of New England were realizing, when church routines were broken, or more precisely, when the institutional relationship between congregation and minister, mutually defining roles in the congregational tradition, were disrupted.[10] Jonathan Edwards himself had preached his sermon *Sinners in the Hands of an Angry God* to a much greater effect as a visitor in neighboring Enfield than he had in his own Northampton.

Was Sarah struggling with her subordination to her husband, and to the clerical class generally? Was she breaking free of his influence by having this spectacular experience independent of him, using it, finally, to detach herself from his influence?[11] Given the pertinence of these questions, it is important to look more deeply into the meaning of Jonathan Edwards's solicitation of Sarah Edwards's written narrative. Was it, and his subsequent editing and disguising of it, an attempt to reassert control over his wife and congregant? Or was it, more broadly, an attempt to reassert his clerical mastery over lay experience? In some ways, the two versions we have—Dwight's printing of Sarah's manuscript and Jonathan's summary of it in *Some Thoughts*—vie for authority. But to say that Jonathan revised Sarah Edwards's narrative is also to say that he was a reader. His revision reflects their pastoral relationship, constituting, in a sense, a dialogue, and showing both how he controlled her and what he valued in and learned from her. I will argue, in fact, that his revision both fits and challenges his own theological agenda.

The Danger of Narrative

It certainly was not, generally speaking, Jonathan Edwards's practice to slip others' words into his writings. His own powerful mind had to make everything its own. In the case of his revisions of Sarah's narrative, he leaves out details that we find most interesting—Sarah's struggles with professional jealousy on his behalf, and her interest in psalms. He attributes a sense of sinfulness to "the person" stronger than what comes through in her own writing. And, most notably, he takes out the narrative element of her account, reducing her experiences to a list of symptoms. It is for this last that Edwards has been most roundly criticized by modern readers.[12] Formally speaking, this revision expresses his deep suspicion of the narrative form.

Jonathan, of course, wrote his own spiritual autobiography, known as the "Personal Narrative." He also included the famous stories of Phoebe

Bartlet and Abigail Hutchinson in the earlier *A Faithful Narrative of Surprising Conversions* (the account of the 1735 Northampton revival); and he was later to edit and publish the *Diary of David Brainerd*. All these personal narratives, like his retelling of Sarah's, were to be exempla of some sort. And yet it is also the case that the personal narrative could hardly be said to be Edwards's genre of choice.

After being dismissed from Northampton in 1750, Edwards wrote from Stockbridge to a Scottish colleague that he regretted his handling of the awakenings there, especially his tolerance of the people's interest in relating their conversion experiences. That practice, he said at that time, led to spiritual pride and encouraged too much interest in "the particular steps and method" of the first conversion at the expense of attention to "the abiding sense of temper of their hearts."[13] Narrative itself was the problem. He regretted even the publication of his own *Faithful Narrative*, which, in telling the story of Northampton's awakening, had the effect of creating a spiritual smugness and carelessness about the rest of the life.

While it is understandable that Edwards would have felt this way in 1751, it is also the case that all his writings on the Awakening, including *A Faithful Narrative*, sustain a tension between narrative of the type he describes here and analysis of the phenomenon in the aggregate. Most often, he is less interested in telling individual stories than in describing the work of the Spirit. His argument is always that the Spirit is a historical force that cannot be limited to any pattern: "The Wind bloweth where it listeth."[14] This is why narrative, though seductive, is so problematic. Although the particulars of religious experience must be attended to and judged carefully, there is no pattern that can be pointed to; individual conversions are "surprising" in their unpredictability.

Even as Edwards continues to write more and more defensively in *The Distinguishing Marks, Some Thoughts Concerning the Revivals*, and *Religious Affections*, what distinguishes these analyses most is that they refuse to codify, even as they seem to claim to do so. What are the distinguishing marks of the Spirit? There are none that are conclusive. Any particular outward manifestation is not infallible proof of the work of God; neither is it proof that the Spirit is not working. His is a very different kind of analysis, from, say, William James's typology of the sick soul and the healthy-minded soul and also, in another way, from both the Puritan morphologists who preceeded Edwards, and the hagiographical impulse found in Cotton Mather's *Magnalia Christi Americana*, both of which establish a master-narrative for the saint's life.[15] It should follow, then, that the experience of individuals might be of little use to Edwards in his polemic. Even in his earliest writings, he anticipates what he would cite in that 1751 letter as the danger: that any narrative might suggest that there are limits to the way the Spirit works. People fall into the trap of spiritual pride when they think that any one story of conversion should provide a pattern. Despite the conspicuous exceptions to his normal procedure, despite his primary interest in the psychology of spiritual experiences, Edwards then approaches the writing of biography only very gingerly. Given his wariness about publishing specific accounts of the work of the Spirit that might take away from the historical force of the event, it is remarkable that Sarah Edwards's narrative appears to have been one in whose validity he had the utmost confidence. If he muted the specifically narrative aspects of her texts, his focus on "the person" in that section of *Some Thoughts* is nevertheless a kind of homage to his wife.

The Body Enspirited

Moreover, in revising her narrative he chooses to highlight what is perhaps its most potentially disruptive—and, for his audience, the most controversial— element: her location of spirituality in bodily experience. He meticulously lists all the bodily effects she reports: "the strength of the body taken away, so as to deprive of all ability to stand or speak; sometimes the hands clinched, and the flesh cold, but senses still remaining; animal nature often in a great emotion and agitation, and the soul very often, of late, so overcome with great admiration, and a kind of omnipotent joy, as to cause the person (wholly unavoidably) to leap with all the might, with joy and mighty exultation of soul; the soul at the same time being so strongly drawn towards God and Christ in heaven, that it seemed to the person as though soul and body would, as it were of themselves, of necessity mount up, leave the earth and ascend thither."[16] He tells his readers, using language similar to hers, that Sarah was reporting bodily states involving excess energy (forceful leaping), energy drain, or dissociative states similar to possession or trance.

We cannot overestimate the importance of this feature of Sarah's—and Jonathan's—report, for such bodily experiences had come to symbolize a collection of central issues surrounding the Awakening. Charles Chauncy, an Awakening opponent and Edwards's most immediate polemical adversary, had ridiculed precisely this feature, in his latest salvo, *Letter to Wishart*. His sarcastic words read almost as a caricature of Sarah Edwards's experience: "Mr *Whitefield's* Doctrine of *inward Feelings* began to discover itself in Multitudes, whose *sensible Perceptions* arose to such a Height, as that they *cried out, fell down, swooned away,* and, to all Appearance, were like Persons in Fits; and this, when the Preaching (if it may be so called) had in it as little well digested and connected good Sense, as you can well suppose."[17] For Chauncy, revivalists' contempt for the usual ministerial credentials, their valuing of inward feelings over outward conformity to church discipline, found an apt physical enactment in the bodies of those multitudes, who cried out, fell down, swooned away: an image of disorder so profoundly alien as to signal at best false experiences and imposter preaching, and at worst a dangerous and widespread social breakdown. Other reports of devilish dancing, burning books, and even illicit pregnancies were similarly given in horrified tones by Awakening critics, for whom again and again disorderly bodies embodied all the challenges to established authorities that they feared in the awakenings.[18]

Mary Douglas has written helpfully about the way in which the particular variations of bodily symbolism found in a given culture may signal its social patterning, or, in her words, "attitudes to bodily control [match] attitudes to social control."[19] Specifically, societies in which trance states are looked upon as benign spiritual experiences, she predicts, should be societies in which social controls are relatively relaxed; conversely, highly structured societies adopt religious symbols that emphasize bodily control and would look upon trance states with suspicion and fear.

Although Douglas's comments are meant to suggest a typology of societies, they may also provide a key to understanding the sociology of religious controversy. The Awakening converts, and Sarah Edwards, did not experience trance states exactly. But they did report—and others, friend and foe alike, observed—bodily manifestations of various kinds. Viewed with respect to Douglas's model, Chauncy's reaction to the fits and swoons he heard about is clear enough: he finds in them an image—an unnatural image—of social disorder. His attitude testifies to his own investment in an ordered society with complex and intricate structures—or better, his belief that society is so structured. The experience of bodily abandonment testified to by Sarah and others, on the other hand, was interpreted by them not as a sign of disorder but as a sign of the Spirit, signaling their perception of society as less structured.[20] For them, rather than signaling the dangerous dissolution of order, the bodily experience of spirituality connects them to the sacred.[21]

The meaning of Jonathan Edwards's reaction to Sarah's experience is less clear. Reporting her experience as a work of the Spirit, he nevertheless takes great pains to show that Sarah's enspiritedness does not lead to the disorderliness caricatured by the Awakening opponents. He stresses that "the person," despite her unusual and remarked upon experience, was not inclined to sweep aside pedestrian responsibities and civilities, attending to "worldly business . . . with great alacrity"—the business, we know, of running a large household and attending to her absent husband's many guests. Nor did she succumb to spiritual pride, even at the height of her experience, or pridefully inveigh, as others did, against "the danger of an unconverted ministry," but remained remarkably nonjudgmental and charitable toward others. In the notable passage that for Edwards can only be described as an outburst, he cries, "Now if such things are enthusiasm, and the fruits of a distempered brain, let my brain be evermore possessed by that happy distemper! If this be distraction, I pray God that the world of mankind may be all seized with this benign, meek, beneficent, beatifical, glorious distraction!"[22] Using the very words that commonly denigrated the revivals—"enthusiasm," "possessed," "distemper," "seized," "distraction"—he counterbalances these words with his own list of adjectives denoting beauty and orderliness.

The language he uses here is familiar from the Edwards lexicon, for it is always important to Edwards, despite his expansive generosity and openness to different types of experience, to claim that the work of the Spirit is productive of order, not disorder.[23] At least for his present controversialist purposes, then, he is just as eager to resist any evidence of relaxed social controls as Chauncy seems to be, rejecting Chauncy's intuitive sense that such bodily experience as Sarah Edwards's, which after all did keep her in bed and away from those guests for hours at a time, may suggest a less densely organized society with less firmly established roles for all its members. As such, Sarah's experience provided Jonathan with an example useful to his project of refuting Chauncy's and others' objections to bodily effects.

However, it is noteworthy that in his own "Personal Narrative," he himself does not report such experience. This well-known text, written in 1739 but not published, was intended as a careful illustration of awakening spirituality, to be used in much the same way that he would eventually use his wife's narrative. It is characterized by an extreme caution about locating spiritual experience in bodily perceptions, evincing, therefore, a method of describing conversion very different from that chosen by his wife.

To be sure, as a theorist of the religious affections, Jonathan Edwards commonly used sensory language to describe saving spiritual experience. He always made clear, however, that it was an inadequate metaphor for the "senses" of a saint. The "Personal Narrative" enacts the religious psychology he had analyzed more systematically elsewhere, dramatizing the difference between truly regenerate affections, a sign of saving grace, and mere intellectual knowledge:

"I have often since not only had a conviction, but a *delightful* conviction."[24] If he employs the language of bodily sensation throughout to illustrate that distinction, it is used always somewhat diffidently, calling attention to the purely figurative nature of the language he has chosen. "The sense I had of divine things, would often of a sudden as it were, kindle up a sweet burning in my heart; an ardor of soul, that I know not how to express" (*JER*, 284). Indeed, that sensate body, a necessary vehicle to hint, however imperfectly, at the nature of spiritual experience, consistently appears in an attitude of humility. Echoing his own *God Glorified in Man's Dependence* and the Bible, for example, he writes, "My heart as it were panted after this, to lie low before God, and in the dust; that I might be nothing, and that God might be all; that I might become as a little child" (*JER*, 288). This sentence, at once an amalgam of scriptural figures and an assertion of Edwards's Calvinist theology, points to an inherent tension: the self has substance and desires (a panting heart) and yet desires annihilation. Or, as Edwards himself puts it elsewhere in the "Personal Narrative," "I felt withal, an ardency of soul to be, what I know not otherwise how to express, than to be emptied and annihilated; to lie in the dust, and to be full of Christ alone" (*JER*, 293).

The highest kind of spiritual achievement, he believes, is a kind of self-forgetting, induced by being "filled up" or "swallowed" by God. God crowds out all other sensations. As Edwards indicates in another passage, "The sweetest joys and delights I have experienced, have not been those that have arisen from a hope of my own good estate; but in a direct view of the glorious things of the gospel. When I enjoy this sweetness, it seems to carry me above the thoughts of my own estate: It seems at such times a loss that I cannot bear, to take off my eye from the glorious, pleasant object I behold without me, to turn my eye in upon myself, and my own good estate" (*JER*, 292). All of these passages express the desire, paradoxical though it might be, for the desiring self to be annihilated, or, as the force of the metaphors points, to be made (or understood to be) small. While the "Personal Narrative", like *Religious Affections, Freedom of the Will* and the entire Edwards corpus, teaches that true religion consists in regenerate affections (i.e., the enspirited self), that narrative also testifies that those affections derive at least from the desire for concentration of the self into a point in order to magnify God's greatness.

Most often, in fact, the spiritual experiences that overwhelm Jonathan are perceptions of God's greatness coupled with the self's smallness—of extremities, or vast distances or vast disparities in size or quantity. God is awesome not only because of these notions conjured up of loudness or largeness (the thunder contains "the majestic and awful voice of [God]," Jonathan has his best spiritual experiences when "being alone in the mountains"—*JER,* 285), but because God himself encompasses extremes. Edwards describes that breadth with mesmerizing chiasmic oxymorons: "I seemed to see them both in a sweet conjunction: majesty and meekness joined together: it was a sweet and gentle, and holy majesty; and also a majestic meekness; an awful sweetness; a high, and great, and holy gentleness" (*JER,* 285).

The self also contains vast quantities—of sin—so vast as to be similarly evocative of sublime polarity. "My wickedness, as I am in myself, has long appeared to me perfectly ineffable, and swallowing up all thought and imagination; like an infinite deluge, or infinite mountains over my head." It "swallow[s] up all thought and imagination"; it is "an abyss infinitely deeper than hell," "bottomless" (*JER,* 294, 295). In a spiritual habit similar to the devotional gesture of ejaculatory prayer, Jonathan describes his sense of sin as a "heaping infinite upon infinite, and multiplying infinite by infinite." "I go about very often, for this many years, with these expressions in my mind, and in my mouth—'Infinite upon Infinite! Infinite upon Infinite!'" (*JER,* 294). Even as he experiences "vehement longings" for God and "delights" in the things of religion, Edwards simultaneously seems most moved by his perception not of beauty but of sublimity, and especially sublimity that comes of the combination of the vast and the tiny, the majestic and the meek, the mind-crowding sense of disparity.[25] The "Personal Narrative," then, partakes of the same aesthetic as that most memorably dramatized in *Sinners in the Hands of an Angry God*. The image of the "small and loathsome insect" hanging by a slender thread in a vast cosmos derives its power from that polarity, or disparity in size.

All this is familiar enough Edwardsean theology. It is hardly surprising to find a Calvinist of Jonathan Edwards's stature preaching the all-sufficiency of God and the entire inadequacy of the sinful soul. But we need only turn to Sarah Edwards's narrative (as printed in Dwight) to see what is essentially the same theological idea articulated with a much different inflection. For Sarah reports that her ejaculatory prayer—an expression that comes out of her repeatedly without prompting and without control—is not "infinite upon infinite!" but rather "My God my all, my God my all" (Dwight, 173). Her prayer testifies to the same sense that Jonathan reported, that God is overwhelming. But while his language referred to his own sin, infinite in quantity and distancing him infinitely from God, hers suggests God's intimacy: "*my* God, *my* all." The experience she reports of God is not Jonathan's sense of majesty but her own of God's proximity: "a continued view of God as *near* and as *my God*" (Dwight, 181). "Who shall separate us from the love of

Christ?" she reads in Romans, thinking "with undoubted certainty . . . as words which God did pronounce concerning *me*" (Dwight, 173, emphasis added). In contrast, Jonathan's favored scripture texts suggest a remote God: "My soul breaketh for the longing it hath" (Ps. 119, 28; *JER*, 286), "Not unto us, O Lord, not unto us, but unto thy name give glory" (Ps. 115.1; *JER*, 292). Even his quotation from Ct. 2.1, "I am the Rose of Sharon, the lily of the Valleys," (*JER*, 284) "represent[s]," he says, "the loveliness and beauty of Jesus Christ," and does not testify to nearness. While he longs to "lie low before God, and in the dust . . . that I might become as a little child," (*JER*, 288), he means to emphasize his lowness and distance from God; when Sarah writes, "Can I now at this time, with the confidence of a child, and without the least misgiving of heart, call God my Father?" (Dwight, 172), she means by the figure that she hopes not for distance and smallness, for polarity between herself and God, but rather for a familial intimacy, one that she reports she does feel: "he then sweetly smiled upon me, with the look of forgiveness and love" (Dwight, 172), as a close and caring, rather than remote and judgmental, parent might.

These contrasts between Sarah's and Jonathan's narratives reflect a difference not in theology but in affect. For both, God overwhelms the creature. In quoting Sarah in *Some Thoughts*, Jonathan need have no qualms about that central theological tenet. But each explains that idea with reference to a peculiar cosmic geography, and disposition of the enspirited body within that cosmos. As we've seen in previous examples, the precise logic of bodily imagery is important because it may suggest underlying understandings both of community structures and of the individual's relationship with God. Therefore, even images that seem to belong to the same "family" (as, in the Colman-Turell exchange, sexuality and childbirth) may have widely divergent meaning attached to them. It is significant, therefore, that Jonathan both recognizes Sarah's peculiar idiom—locating spiritual experience within an overwhelmed body (as opposed to desiring the annihilation of that body)—so different from his own, and takes care to preserve and highlight it in his appropriation of her narrative in *Some Thoughts*.

The best illustration of his openness to her preferred language comes early in his discussion of "the person," when he departs from his more frequent procedure of summarizing and listing Sarah's experiences, quoting from what I agree is her most striking passage: "(to use the person's own expressions) the soul remained in a kind of heavenly Elysium, and did as it were swim in the rays of Christ's love, like a little mote swimming in the beams of the sun, or streams of his life that come in at a window; and the heart was swallowed up in a kind of glow of Christ's love, coming down from Christ's heart in heaven, as a constant stream of sweet light, at the same time the soul all flowing out in love to him, so that there seemed to be a constant flowing and reflowing from heart to heart."[26] This is a near direct quotation from what could probably be called the peak moment of the experience she recounts in the Dwight edition:

> [A]ll night I continued in a constant, clear and lively sense of the heavenly sweetness of Christ's excellent and transcendent love, or his nearness to me, and of my dearness to him; with an inexpressibly sweet calmness of soul in an entire rest in him. I seemed to myself to perceive a glow of divine love come down from the heart of Christ in heaven, into my heart, in a constant stream, like a stream or pencil of sweet light. At the same time, my heart and soul all flowed out in love to Christ; so that there seemed to be a constant flowing and reflowing of heavenly and divine love, from Christ's heart to mine; and I appeared to myself to float or swim, in these bright, sweet beams of the love of Christ, like the motes swimming in the beams of the sun, or the streams of his light which came in at the window. My soul remained in a kind of heavenly elysium. (Dwight, 178)

Perhaps Jonathan was interested in this passage because he recognized his own mark on it. The light metaphor, while not unusual in any Christian context, was of course one of his particular signatures, expounded most prominently in the 1734 sermon *A Divine and Supernatural Light*, perhaps the best example among Jonathan's early printed works of his exploitation of the language of sensory perception to explain grace. Indeed, if we recall that Sarah was his congregant and student as well as his wife, it is not surprising that she should avail herself of the language and imagery she heard him use in the pulpit. But the inflection she gives the image of sunlight here, for all it shares with her husband's chosen language, is peculiar to her own style of spirituality and, ultimately, quite dissimilar to his. The paragraph I—and Jonathan—quote recalls a passage in his own "Personal Narrative" that makes extensive and dramatic use of the image and yet sounds so different. I refer to the well-known "little white flower" passage:

> The soul of a true Christian, as I then wrote my meditations, appeared like such a little white flower, as we see in the spring of the year; low and humble on the ground, opening its bosom, to

receive the pleasant beams of the sun's glory; rejoicing as it were, in a calm rapture; diffusing around a sweet fragrancy; standing peacefully and lovingly, in the midst of other flowers round about; all in like manner opening their bosoms, to drink in the light of the sun. (*JER*, 288).

The two passages share a basic metaphor. For both Jonathan and Sarah, God is represented by the sun, infinitely large, life-giving, and yet self-sufficient, emanating rays of light that connect the creature to it. Jonathan's passage, however, enacts distance and disparity, while Sarah, using the same principle, enacts communion. Jonathan's "little white flower," an emblem for the individual soul, is not that different from the much more terrifying image of the noxious insect in *Sinners in the Hands of an Angry God*: discrete, infinitely small bodies, outsized by the cosmos around them. God—or the sun—is infinitely large and powerful, but remote; in theologically orthodox manner, the great gap between God and creature, is crossed by the sun's rays—God's gracious doing—that hit the receptive soul ("opening its bosom"). Edwards completes his image with a vision of an elect community, in which all individual small flowers, similarly receptive, are struck by the sun's rays, or grace, and give up a beautiful refulgence, creating a harmonious and beautiful community. Like the "Personal Narrative" as a whole, though, this theological vision depends on a cosmos bounded by polarities, in which that little white flower remains small, finite, bounded. Edwards finishes his meditation by reemphasizing this idea: "my heart panted after this, to lie low before God, as in the dust, that I might be nothing, and that God might be all" (*JER*, 288).

We don't know if Sarah Edwards read Jonathan's narrative. She certainly would have been familiar with the image of light for the workings of grace on the creature, and Jonathan had developed it at length in his sermons, most notably in *A Divine and Supernatural Light*. When Sarah turns herself to that metaphor to help her explain her spiritual experiences, though, she locates her own created body not at the polar opposite of the sun, passively receiving the rays it sends down, but as motes swimming in the rays. Jonathan, or a little white flower, stays on the receiving end; Sarah climbs into the rays themselves. Jonathan's sunrays represent grace: they move in one direction and have one author, one impetus, God, leaving the little white flower only the option of receiving the sun's effects, and possibly creating more refulgence here on earth. Sarah's sunrays, she says, represent not grace but love. She receives the love of Christ and returns her own to him. Sarah thus blurs the boundaries between Creator and created that Jonathan's passage—and indeed, his whole narrative—carefully keeps distinct. Replacing grace with love, she shows that the creature shares a capacity with the creator. In the terms of the sunray metaphors, she allows the created body's boundaries to dissolve into that pathway, while her husband and pastor at all times depicts a very discretely bounded creature. Simply put, his vision of spirituality, illustrated here and enacted by his narrative as a whole, is resolutely dualistic, hers is dramatically not. Theologically speaking, she describes a much more intimate relationship with God than he does.

The contrast in their respective narratives reveals the essentially fluid nature of any religious symbolism, and illustrates how a shared language can contain significant variations in meanings and have multivalent effects, allowing equally supple uses by different members of the community to different ends. Although Sarah Edwards does not use explicitly maternal language in this passage, the language she does use, which is both body-centered and dissolving of bodily boundaries, functions similarly to the way Jane Colman Turell's maternal imagery does. As in the Colman-Turell letters, that language tends to be associated as well with a vision of congregational unity; moreover, its nondualistic character is the more evident in comparison to the language used by her main clerical advisor. The usefulness of Mary Douglas's insight, that images of bodily experience correlate with certain visions of community, is that it helps us clarify the implications of the differences between conversion narratives. Two important studies of conversion narratives from the Great Awakening, Susan Juster's and Barbara Epstein's, disagree about the gendering of community. Epstein remarks that women "expressed a particularly sharp pleasure in the sense of community created by a revival"; Juster, on the contrary, finds that men were more likely to concentrate on such communal ties in their narratives, while "women turned their energies inward in search of perfect physical subsumption into the body of Christ."[27] I will argue, on the contrary, that, as Douglas predicts, in Sarah Edwards's narrative, at least, the sense of overcoming boundaries both bodily and communal are associated, not competing features.

Jonathan Edwards quotes and approves his wife's metaphor, in spite of the fact that it centers on bodily experiences in a way that he himself was not comfortable with in shaping his own narrative. But what Jonathan Edwards did not see in his wife's preferred idiom, what he did not choose to excerpt, was precisely this connection between the blurring of bodily boundaries and the articulation of communal oneness: Sarah Edwards's narrative describes not only a body-centered spirituality, but also a vision of *communitas*, a communal experience of the Spirit, much better than did the language in his own

"Personal Narrative." To see that connection, we must reinsert the social into Sarah's narrative, and thereby reestablish the narrative context that Jonathan has edited out.

Sarah Edwards in Northampton

Sarah's own narrative conveys, of course, much more of a sense of social embeddedness than does Jonathan's analysis, providing, in fact, an interesting portrait of the complexities of life in a New England town during these revivals. As a minister's wife, Sarah would have felt the effects of this great excitement in very practical ways, including pressure on her household. During the week she describes, not only was she hosting Mr. Buell, Jonathan's replacement, but she seems to have had numerous other ministers and neighbors, some named, some not, visiting at the parsonage. Although the most spectacular aspects of her enspirited experience of these two weeks take place when she is alone—and it is these experiences that most interest Jonathan— her reconstructed narrative testifies as well to the important place community relations had in her experiences and to the spiritual style she exhibits.

The experience of community reported in Sarah's narrative reflects, to some degree, the fact that Jonathan Edwards's tenure as Northampton's minister was hardly a model of harmonious pastoral relations. After his prominent involvement in the awakenings, both the more widespread ones in the early '40s and the earlier local "frontier awakening" chronicled by him in *A Faithful Narrative*, Jonathan had a series of important conflicts with his congregation, culminating in his ignominious firing in 1750. Like other New England congregational ministers, Edwards frequently clashed with his congregation, which was responsible for fixing and paying his salary, over money. Within a year after Sarah's remarkable religious experience, both Edwardses wrote letters to the town begging that Jonathan be paid his overdue salary.[28] The townspeople, conscious that they were footing the bill, lodged complaints about the Edwardses' spending habits on luxurious manufactured goods, including Sarah's own dresses. Against this backdrop of financial tension, common enough in a congregational system,[29] there were additional sources of tension: Jonathan came in conflict with the prominent Hawley family; he offended the parents of Northampton by publicly chastising young people who had been mischievously reading a midwives' manual; and finally, reversing longstanding Northampton practice instituted by his grandfather, he set off a firestorm by declaring that those who wanted to take the Lord's Supper would now have to give a convincing relation of their saving experiences. Even the most sympathetic of Jonathan Edwards's biographers have attributed these clashes at least in part to his authoritarianism—what Perry Miller labeled his "hubris."[30] Sarah Edwards no doubt experienced these conflicts painfully, and it seems poignantly apt that in her narrative she reports that her great spiritual achievement seems to be her "holy indifference" to the world, especially "the opinions, the representations, and conduct of mankind respecting me" (Dwight, 177–78).[31]

This historical record describing a problematic relationship between the Edwards family and the community gives context to many otherwise odd remarks in their respective accounts. As evidence of "the person's" weanedness from the world, for example, Jonathan Edwards notes briefly in his summary that she "expressed a willingness to live and die in darkness and horror if God's honor should require it."[32] Sarah's account of what generated her statement is rather more dramatic. Noting the physically debilitating effects she was experiencing, she says that a neighbor, Mrs. P——, "had expressed her fears least I should die before Mr. Edwards' return, and he should think the people had killed his wife" (Dwight, 181). Indeed, throughout the narrative, Sarah puts herself through various mental tests, to see if she has truly achieved "indifference" to the world, and these tests invariably take the form of social ostracism, prefiguring, perhaps with a little more melodrama, the Edwardses' eventual banishment from Northampton. "There was then a deep snow on the ground," she writes, "and I could think of being driven from my home into the cold and snow, of being chased from the town with the utmost contempt and malice, and of being left to perish with the cold, as cast out by all the world, with perfect calmness and serenity" (Dwight, 174). Similarly, she could continue her spiritual equanimity, she finds, "if our house and all our property in it should be burnt up, and we should that night be turned out naked" (Dwight, 185); or "If I were surrounded by enemies, who were venting their malice and cruelty upon me, in tormenting me" (Dwight, 183).

When we imagine these tensions resulting from chronic community antagonisms combining with the busyness of the Edwards household during the time of the Awakening in particular, we can sympathetically picture Sarah chafing under the expectations of her role as Jonathan Edwards's wife and hostess. "When I came home," for instance, on a Wednesday, "found Mr. Buell, Mr. Christophers, Mr. Hopkins, Mrs. Eleanor Dwight, the wife of Mr. Joseph Allen, and Mr. Job Strong, at the house. . . . The intenseness of my feelings again took away my bodily strength" (Dwight, 176)—not surprising to anyone who has had to entertain unexpected guests. We can also imagine that the mystical bodily connection she finds with God suggests a desire to escape from those tensions: "No possible suffering appeared to be worth regarding: all persecutions and torments were a mere nothing. I seemed to dwell on high, and the place of defence to be the munition of rocks" (Dwight, 174). For Sarah's two-week-long spiritual experience demands at times that she be alone, "withdraw[ing] to my chamber"; she reports, despite Jonathan's insistence that her enspiritedness did not interfere with her attending to her worldly duties, that on several occasions during the week she spent much of the day in bed, neglecting all those houseguests. On the day of her peak experience, Thursday, January 28, she "accidently went into the room where Mr. Buell was conversing with some of the people"; so moved by the interchange, she eventually "sunk down" and had to be carried up to bed (Dwight, 177). She lay there between twelve and four in the afternoon, surely peak entertaining and dinner-serving hours. Finally, "a little while before I arose, Mr. Buell and the people went to meeting" (Dwight, 178), leaving the house at long last.

Is her enspirited body, drained of its energy and "sinking down" under the pressures of the demands of a very public hospitality, rebelling against the wifely role, and, more specifically the obligation of ministering to the needs of ministers?[33] In a sense, this is Chauncy's reading of the "doctrine of inward feelings" associated with the Awakening: that it is nothing more than an expression of disorderliness and therefore rebellion that he finds so distasteful but that present-day historians might champion.

This is only a partial reading of Sarah Edwards's narrative, however, for by her own testimony, what moves her so much as to lose her bodily strength— or alternatively, to leap up—is not an antisocial, anarchic antinomianism, but a most intense vision of congregational unity. The sight of so many people at the house fills her, she says, with "an intense desire that we might all arise, and, with an active, flowing, and fervent heart, give glory to God" (Dwight, 176). In this light, her habit of defining her self-abnegation in terms of social ostracism is merely another way of expressing the centrality of the corporate. Whether positively or negatively, shared enspiritedness looms largest in defining Sarah Edwards's spirituality. All her daylight experiences during those two days are characterized by a heightened sense of corporate enspiritedness. Often that sense of incorporation into the larger body is expressed through the experience of conversation. Even as she lay in bed between twelve and four on that Thursday, she was not alone, but "converse[d] very earnestly, with one or another of the pious women, who were present" (Dwight, 178). Likewise, she reports being exceedingly moved by a sight—either real or visionary—of a group of saints. Even before her peak experience of the motes, she says, "especially was I, while I remained in the meeting-house, from time to time overcome, and my strength taken away, by the sight of one and another, whom I regarded as the children of God" (Dwight, 176).[34] It is important that this passage has the same intensity of language that she uses for her private experiences and that while the image of the motes suggests a bridging of separation, a breaking down of boundaries and an achievement of oneness, this passage enacts all those ideas on the communal level.

Indeed, even that night's private vision of motes in the sunbeam doesn't remain only in her bedchamber but "continued during the morning" (Dwight, 179) and indeed beyond, into a communal context. All that following day, in fact, Sarah has numerous experiences of a heightened sense of corporate identity, in which the social implications of that private vision are worked out, in a theology of church. All day long, she says, "I could not refrain from conversing with those around me" (Dwight, 180). She begins the day with an exchange with a Mr. Sheldon, that incorporates the light metaphor that had been so central to her nighttime experience, and distantly echoes the Magnificat, Mary's testimony to Elizabeth of her angelic visitation: "That Sun has not set upon my soul all this night; I have dwelt on high in the heavenly mansions; the light of divine love has surrounded me; my soul has been lost in God, and has almost left the body" (Dwight, 179). Later in the day, someone reads from Watts's *Penitential Cries* the hymn that begins with Mary's words, "My soul doth magnify the Lord," sending Sarah into "transports of joy." The transmuting of the theme of Sarah's vision through her own words of testimony to Mr. Sheldon, and finally into the hymn is important, for the hymn, while apparently read aloud, is intended for congregational singing and is a focus for congregational worship. What begins as a private insight thus moves outward from the enspirited self to become a corporate statement, a corporate experience.

Indeed, soon after the reading of this hymn, the people who have assembled at the Edwards house go to a service, during which the experience of congregational worship is made concrete. There are sermons by the visiting Mr. Williams and Mr. Buell, Sarah tells us; but although she comments appreciatively about both clerical performances, it is the congregational experience that she finds more important. In the style of a Quaker meeting, the most significant spiritual experience she reports occurs between the two sermons, when apparently no minister is even present in the church: after the first sermon, "the congregation waited while Mr. Buell went home, to prepare to give them a Lecture. It was almost dark before he came, and in the mean time, I conversed in a very earnest and joyful manner, with those who were with me in the pew" (Dwight, 181). This detail of the workings of the Spirit in Northampton is consistent with an important Awakening theme, that the experience and testimony of regenerate lay people overshadows the teaching function of the credentialed ministry. Equally important to Sarah's report of the lay experience, however, is the phenomenon of laypersons not becoming individually elevated and authoritative, but sitting together in the pew in a conversational exchange. It is not only, then, that Sarah has a strong sense during this day of wanting to share her spiritual insights with others in a conversational way or through an act of corporate worship. The important theological insight of her experience and of her narrative is precisely the spiritual centrality of congregational unity and enspiritedness.

Her description of this corporate spirituality merits just as lengthy a quotation as her description of her more private mystical experience. The embodied spirituality that had been so prominent in that private vision remains in force in this passage, which also supplies an articulated theology of that vision of motes in the sunbeam.

> As I sat there, I had a most affecting sense of the mighty power of Christ, which had been exerted in what he had done for my soul, and in sustaining and keeping down the native corruptions of my heart, and of the glorious and wonderful grace of God in causing the ark to return to Northampton. So intense were my feelings, when speaking of these things, that I could not forbear rising up and leaping with joy and exultation. I felt at the same time an exceedingly strong and tender affection for the children of God, and realized, in a manner exceedingly sweet and ravishing, the meaning of Christ's prayer, in John xvii.21. "That they all may be one, as thou Father art in me, and I in thee, that they also may be one in us." This union appeared to me an inconceivable, excellent and sweet oneness; and at the same time I felt that oneness in my soul, with the children of God who were present. (Dwight, 180)

The theological insight that Sarah takes at this moment from the text of John's gospel is that the union expressed between the Father and the Son, that is, in a binary relationship of the two parts of the godhead, becomes, in Christ's prayer, a broader union, figured, perhaps, by that union of Father and Son but going out in many more directions and entailing many more people. What she understands is that a binary relationship of union can be enlarged into a multifaceted, corporate vision of union. So important is the text from John that Sarah returns to it that evening in her private reading. This passage, "Christ's dying discourse with his disciples, and his prayer with them," is an interesting choice for her. The "dying discourse" is the words of Jesus to the apostles at the Last Supper, when he instituted the ritual of communion. It is the moment, that is, when Church begins. In addition, the "dying discourse" includes not only the prayer for union (of which the sacrament of the Lord's Supper, so soon to become newly controversial in Northampton, is a sign) but also Jesus's promise that the Comforter, or Holy Spirit, will be with the disciples after his own imminent death. It is the moment in Johannine theology, that is, of a shift in focus from Christology to pneumatology, from incarnational revelation to Church. The promise that the Spirit will abide is a promise that the Church will abide, that the people will be enspirited. Jonathan, in his summary in *Some Thoughts*, would note that "only mentioning the word, 'the Comforter,' [would] immediately take away all [the person's] strength."[35] Sarah's own narrative gives ample testimony to the importance of this term, and therefore, I would argue, of the centrality of Church in her experience. The "transports" that Sarah had felt earlier in the day when the hymn had been read were induced by this idea of the "joyful presence of the Holy Spirit"—the Comforter—for the hymn beginning with the words of the Magnificat ends this way:

> My sighs at length are turn'd to songs,
> The Comforter is come.

Even several days later, she uses that Johannine vocabulary to express the spiritual sense of the nearness of God, so integral to her whole narrative: "So great and holy a God was so remarkably present. . . . [T]hese words, in the Penitential Cries—'THE COMFORTER IS COME!'—were accompanied to my soul with such conscious certainty . . . that I was falling to the floor" (Dwight, 184).

Sarah's spiritual experience, so thoroughly permeated with the theme of the corporate union, as constitutive of it, is repeated that Friday night in her bedroom, when she has a continuation of the spectacular vision she had had the previous evening, using much the same language. "I had an idea of a shining way, or path of light, between heaven and my soul, somewhat as on Thursday night, except that God seemed nearer to me, and as it were close by, and the way seemed more open, and the communication more immediate and more free" (Dwight, 181). She uses similar language to describe her feeling a few days later: "The road between heaven and my soul seemed open and wide" (Dwight, 183).

Significantly, on that Friday night as she meditates on the Johannine passage, she has another insight: "It seemed to me infinitely better to die to go to Christ, yet I felt an entire willingness to continue in this world as long as God pleased" (Dwight, 181). That is, she expresses the conviction that intimacy with God is possible not only on a one-to-one basis (dying to go to Christ) but on earth in community. Indeed, she had felt while in the congregational meeting that afternoon that "it appeared to me that he was going to set up a Reign of Love on the earth and that heaven and earth were, as it were, coming together" (Dwight, 181). Although she continues to test herself with the question of whether she can accept ostracism and bodily torments, and finds herself "made willing to die on the rack or at the stake" (Dwight, 182) or "surrounded by enemies, who were venting their malice and cruelty upon me" (Dwight, 183), her ties to the texture of earthly relationships, even if they cause suffering, are integral to her spiritual being. For better or worse, she is implicated in community, not alienated from it.

She even feels "in an unusual, and very lively manner, how great a part of Christianity lies in the performance of our social and relative duties to one another" (Dwight, 183). In *Some Thoughts*, Jonathan Edwards quotes her approvingly, hoping no doubt to answer critics like Chauncy who associated such experiences with a descent into anarchy. Sarah's own narrative, though, gives consistent emphasis to this idea of corporate harmony, expressed through the "relative duties" she fulfills, through conversation, and in almost a liturgical way, through singing.[36] Jonathan reports on these "symptoms" as more vocally exhibiting "A great delight in singing praises to God and Jesus Christ, and longing that this present life may be, as it were, one continued song of praise to God; longing, as the person expressed it, to sit and sing this life away; and an overcoming pleasure in the thoughts of spending an eternity in that exercise."[37] Appropriately enough, Dwight's printing of Sarah's narrative closes with a hymn. When a roomful of people has gathered at the Edwards house, Sarah has another vision of unity, prompting her—in an unusually dramatic sign of social levelling—to think "I should rejoice to follow the negro servants in the town to heaven."

> After this, they sang an hymn, which greatly moved me, especially the latter part of it, which speaks of the ungratefulness of not having the praises of Christ always in our tongues. Those last words of the hymn seemed to fasten on my mind, and as I repeated them over, I felt such intense love to Christ, and so much delight in praising him, I could hardly forbear leaping from my chair, and

singing aloud for joy and exultation. I continued thus extraordinarily moved until about one o'clock, when the people went away." (Dwight, 185–86)

Whatever tensions existed in Northampton, Sarah Edwards's report of spiritual experience, in which boundaries between herself and God are overcome as "motes swimming in the beam of the sun," thus issues not only in an indifference to the world, a dwelling above it, but also in a "lively sense" of an incorporation into a congregational identity that loses the boundaries or sense of separateness. However spectacular her private experience is, however regenerating it is, it also produces a sense of community. And however strange her behavior might seem, it is consistent with a textured sense of community, not "otherworldliness."

It is instructive that this emphasis, this connection between individual spiritual experience of merging with God and a congregational experience of wholeness is largely absent from Jonathan Edwards's own personal narrative. To be sure, in other works he characteristically pushed his analysis of spiritual psychology in the direction of the social. In his *Faithful Narrative*, which described the revivals at Northampton in the 1730s, he noted that the people of Northampton, as they went through their individual spiritual experiences of regenerating grace, achieved a harmony of discourse, making up with each other over earlier wrongs. His ambitious project *The History of the Work of Redemption* argues that revivals taking place in various parts of the world are part of redemption history, a world-historical phenomenon that is larger than the saving of any one individual, and might issue in a new kind of history. And of course, he concluded his *Religious Affections*, the 1746 work in which he codified the observations he had made over the previous ten years of the ways the Spirit works on human beings, with the climactic, Twelfth Sign: the work of the Spirit is often visible in good works in the world, and has, therefore, a social component.[38]

But in the "Personal Narrative" itself, he does not develop this idea. He cherishes, for example, his friendship with Mr. John Smith in New York, and keenly feels the loss of his company when they must part. But his consolation comes only from imagining heavenly reunion, not, as for Sarah, from joy in the experience of union now. "It was sweet to me to think of meeting dear Christians in heaven, where we should never part more" (*JER*, 289). Lying ill for three months in Windsor, he notes of his caretakers not the "relative duties" that they fulfill, which Sarah realizes is an important component of spirituality, but only that they look longingly out the window, which he takes to be an emblem of waiting for God. And, when the narrative moves to a description of his life at Northampton, he focuses on his being infinitely sinful, employing much of the binary language we saw earlier. Throughout the narrative, that is, Jonathan focuses on private experiences of his relationship with a distant God—in the fields, in his chamber. It is appropriate to his style of spirituality that the metaphor for community that he develops in the "Personal Narrative" is a loosely organized collection of little white flowers, each of which separately receives the rays of the sun. Such a collection might be a source of beauty, "diffusing a sweet fragrance around," but it lacks the kind of textured congregational identity to which Sarah's narrative testifies. These two narratives, though they share so many features of theology and imagery, represent contrasting spiritual styles, and that Sarah's imagery makes it possible for her to develop a language for the experience of corporate spiritualty, or *communitas*, that was so much a part of the revival experience. Jonathan Edwards's use of her personal experience in *Some Thoughts*, represents a significant expansion of his theological vocabulary; but he did not excerpt the communal sections to make the connection between her vision of God and her vision of a united community.

It is true that in the latter part of Edwards's career, having been dismissed from the Northampton pulpit, he devoted himself less to an articulation of the possibilities for the coming of the Spirit in a whole community, and more with more abstractly reasoned theology. The great theological treatises for which he became known—*The Great Doctrine of Original Sin Defended, The Nature of True Virtue, Freedom of the Will*—were written during his stay at Stockbridge, where his primary (and apparently for him, not very taxing) responsibility was ministering to an Indian church. Although he continued to articulate a remarkably consistent Calvinist theology, this latter decade of his career was marked by a retreat from pastoral involvement, never the most comfortable role for him, into his study.

However, in one of his last treatises, *Dissertation Concerning the End for Which God Created the World*, he returns to an idea he had come across before in the most eventful days of the Awakening. In the passage perhaps most frequently excerpted from that treatise, he writes:

> The great and last end of God's works . . . is indeed but *one*; and this *one* end is most properly and comprehensively called, THE GLORY OF GOD . . . and is fitly compared to an effulgence or emanation of light from a luminary. . . . Light is the external expression, exhibition and manifestation of the excellency of the

luminary, of the sun for instance: it is the abundant, extensive emanation and communication of the fulness of the sun to innumerable beings that partake of it. . . . The emanation or communication of the divine fulness, consisting in the knowledge of God, love to him, and joy in him, has relation indeed both to God and to the *creature*; but it has relation to God as its *fountain*, as the thing communicated, is something of his internal fulness. The water in the stream is something of the fountain; and the beams of the sun are something of the sun. And again they have relation to God as their *object*; for the knowledge communicated is the knowledge of God; and the love communicated, is the love of God; and the happiness communicated, is joy in God. In the creature's knowing, esteeming, loving, rejoicing in, and praising God, and the love communicated, is joy in God. The glory of God is both *exhibited* and *acknowledged*; his fulness is *received* and *returned*. Here is both an *emanation* and *remanation*. The refulgence shines upon and into the creature, and is reflected back to the luminary. The beams of glory come from God, are something of God, and are refunded back to their original. So that the whole is of God, and in God, and to God, and he is the beginning, and the middle, and the end.[39]

William Scheick has written of the *Dissertation* as a whole, that it represents a change in theology for Jonathan Edwards, "succeed[ing] in bridging the gap between man and God" that was so evident in his earlier works.[40] This change is most dramatically shown in this passage, where the image of the sunbeams reaching the creature and then being reflected back, has more in common with Sarah Edwards's narrative of spiritual experience than with his own. She had written "flowing and reflowing"; he writes "emanation and remanation." In both cases, the theology implies a God who is at least partially reconstructed by the regenerate creature's own remanation. In other words, in some way the creature becomes part of God, much as the motes climb up the sunbeam to God in Sarah Edwards's passage. Not only is the rhetoric more fluid, as Scheick observes, but the theology itself is less dualistic, less dependent on oppositions, striving for a vision of union with God. Jonathan's imagery then echoes Sarah's conception of an intimate relationship with God, one that ameliorates the abyss that had been so prominent in his "Personal Narrative," achieving intimacy by dissolving the boundaries between Creator and creature.[41]

Was this Sarah's mark on the Edwards corpus? Ten years earlier, in *Some Thoughts*, Jonathan had quoted her freely, knowing, though, that her idiom was different from his own. Here, he incorporates her conception into his own language, yearning for her "open road with God," and qualifying the severe binarism of his earlier works. The *Dissertation Concerning the End for Which God Created the World* is a fitting endpoint, then, of a two-way marital and pastoral conversation, in which lay testimony—and its variations in figuration and indeed theology—has worked its way into a treatise by a giant in American theology.

Epilogue

This study has highlighted the ways in which early eighteenth-century women used language that is centered on the body, language that seems connected to the experience of pregnancy and childbearing. Rather than attribute such language only to their common biological experience, however, I believe as well that all these cases suggest that for these women working out their own salvation meant not just understanding their relationship to God but testifying to their membership in a dense communion. To greater or lesser degrees, they discard the more dualistic idioms suggested to them by their clerical counselors, showing a preference for an idiom that, if it is not always specifically maternal, does suggest the permeability of bodily boundaries. Sarah Edwards's motes climb up the rays of the sun, Jane Turell chooses birthing imagery rather than the marriage binary, and even Esther Rogers, whose language is so self-protective, adapts an idiom that is essentially about communal wholeness, fashioning a spiritual self-identity to which community is inherently crucial.

The appearance of such language represents a challenge to traditional theology that goes far beyond its meaning as a way to flatter a female audience. Superficially, women may identify with childbirth language because of their biological experience. But theologically speaking, such language may have the more profound attraction of getting beyond dualistic models of subjection and dominance that they (and other fringe groups) may not find congenial. The identification of patriarchy with dualism is a basic feminist insight, shared by critical theorists as well as liberation theologians who claim that the rehabilitation and remembrancing of mother images of God is a critique, in a very fundamental way, of patriarchal religion and exegesis as they have developed through history.[1] That mother image, though it has gender,

177

functions differently, I have argued, from the more binary language of gendered sexuality. It is closely associated, moreover, with an ideal of communal interconnection. However much "modesty and reserve" are attributed to Sarah Edwards and Jane Colman Turell by their clerical admirers, their own writings insist on the primacy of the communal spiritual life. And the tragic stories of Esther Rogers and the other women hanged for killing their babies testify, along with their language, to a breakdown in that texture, such that a community strives to camouflage its own failed response to maternity with a flurry of talk about sex and lying.

It is important to my argument that these idioms emerge in homiletic dialogues, dialogues that reveal not only the linguistic practices of laywomen but also differences among those of the ministerial class. Benjamin Colman and Ebenezer Turell, John Rogers and his older contemporaries, although members of the same professional class who have privileged access to the dominant religious discourse, evince variations both in idiom and in pastoral style. These dialogues show not only that lay people had a variety of ministerial idioms from which to choose, but that they could even influence clerical discourse. So, Jonathan Edwards adopts Sarah's idiom, finally; Benjamin Colman is reminded of his own best language by his daughter; John Rogers, though off in Ipswich, becomes a published celebrity, because he lights upon a language that Esther Rogers has found congenial enough that she could credibly report a spectacular conversion: his success as a pastor gives him entry into public discourse. Many of our sources for early New England religious life are perforce works of the clergy; these rare dialogues allow us to develop the habit of reading such minister-authored texts as pastoral documents, that is, as documents inflected, even if silently, by lay people.

The project of recovering and elucidating lay testimony is one that I share with others, many of whom have tried as well to identify differences not just between clerical and lay but also between male and female voices.[2] This is a delicate business, for these respective languages are different not in kind but in nuance. To be sure, these variations are deployed along power vectors: by speaking in their own different voices, these women may resist or subvert the formulations of the dominant culture. But in another sense, to identify the multivocality of discourse is also simply to describe the inherent conditions of living in any group. It may describe ways in which women resist or subvert clerical domination of religious culture; clearly, it describes the ways in which they participate in that culture. The variations I describe here, however minute, are culturally important precisely because they are not overtly oppositional, but rather adapted to the language of the dominant group, heard by ministers as conformist, or conformist enough to be written into the public discourse. Understanding the complexities of such a symbology is crucial to the historian because it provides the tools with which to understand change, change that is gradual, drawing on the varied linguistic resources already developed through the dialogic process that is culture.

Notes

Introduction

1. David D. Hall, *Witch-Hunting in Seventeenth-Century New England: A Documentary History, 1638–1692* (Boston: Northeastern University Press, 1991), p. 302.

2. The work of the *annalistes* on the history of spirituality is usefully discussed by Caroline Walker Bynum in *Jesus as Mother: Studies in the Spirituality of the High Middle Ages* (Berkeley: University of California Press, 1982), p. 3ff. Other historians working in Europe and the United States on collective mentalities include Natalie Zemon Davis, Robert Darnton, Carlo Ginzburg, and Peter Burke. David D. Hall, "Toward a History of Popular Religion in Early New England," *WMQ* 41 (1984):49–55, has discussed the relevance of this work to early American studies, and his own *Worlds of Wonder, Days of Judgment: Popular Religious Belief in Early New England* (New York: Alfred A. Knopf, 1989), exemplifies its methods.

3. See *Worlds of Wonder, Days of Judgment*, especially pp. 3–70.

4. Mitchell Breitwieser, *American Puritanism and the Defense of Mourning: Religion, Grief, and Ethnology in Mary White Rowlandson's Captivity Narrative* (Madison: University of Wisconsin Press, 1990); William J. Scheick, "Authority and Witchery: Cotton Mather's *Ornaments* and Mary English's Acrostic," *Arizona Quarterly* 51 (1995):1–32. For important works of scholarship that have developed the approaches mentioned here, see Emory Elliott, *Power and the Pulpit in Puritan New England* (Princeton: Princeton University Press, 1975); Teresa Toulouse, *The Art of Prophesying: New England Sermons and the Shaping of Belief* (Athens: University of Georgia Press, 1987); Charles E. Hambrick-Stowe, *The Practice of Piety: Puritan Devotional Discipline in Seventeenth-Century New England* (Chapel Hill:

University of North Carolina Press, 1982); Patricia Caldwell, *The Puritan Conversion Narrative: The Beginnings of American Expression* (New York: Cambridge University Press, 1983).

5. Perry Miller, *The New England Mind: From Colony to Province* (Cambridge, Mass.: Harvard University Press, 1953), p. 213.

6. Kenneth K. Shipton, "The New England Clergy of the 'Glacial Age'," Colonial Society of Massachusetts, *Publications* 32 (1937):24–54.

7. Miller, p. 209; John Putnam Demos, *Entertaining Satan: Witchcraft and the Culture of Early New England* (New York: Oxford University Press, 1982), p. 372; Paul Boyer and Stephen Nissenbaum, *Salem Possessed: The Social Origins of Witchcraft* (Cambridge, Mass.: Harvard University Press, 1974).

8. For these ecclesiastical developments, see, among others, Richard F. Lovelace, *The American Pietism of Cotton Mather: Origins of American Evangelicalism* (Grand Rapids, Mich.: William B. Eerdman's, 1979); J. William T. Youngs Jr., *God's Messengers: Religious Leadership in Colonial New England, 1700–1750* (Baltimore: The Johns Hopkins University Press, 1976); Paul R. Lucas, *Valley of Discord: Church and Society along the Connecticut River, 1636–1725* (Hanover, N.H.: University Press of New England, 1976).

9. Edwin Ardener has developed the very useful idea of "dominant" and "muted" groups. A "muted" or disempowered group, such as women, develops its own idiom for giving voice to their experiences and perceptions, but this idiom takes a form acceptable to the dominant group (men). That is, a seeming absence of theological conflict or heterogeneity in a cultural discourse may mask the presence of diverse idioms whose variations are slight but significant; or, in Shirley Ardener's words, "It is the small deviations from any norm which may be crucial." See *Perceiving Women*, ed. Shirley Ardener (London: Malaby Press, 1975), p. xix. Note that my argument departs significantly (or at least explores a different dynamic) from some important works in Puritan studies that describe how the community defines itself by exclusion or expulsion of the other. See Kai T. Erikson, *Wayward Puritans: A Study in the Sociology of Deviance* (New York: John Wiley & Sons, 1966), and Carol F. Karlsen, *The Devil in the Shape of a Woman: Witchcraft in Colonial New England* (New York: W. W. Norton & Company, 1987).

10. Daniel A. Cohen, *Pillars of Salt, Monuments of Grace: New England Crime Literature and the Origins of American Popular Culture, 1674–1860* (New York: Oxford University Press, 1993).

11. Cotton Mather, *Ornaments for the Daughters of Zion, or The Character and Happiness of a Vertuous Woman* (Boston, 1692), p. 48; Ann Douglas, *The Feminization of American Culture* (New York: Alfred Knopf, 1977); Mary

Maples Dunn, "'Saints and Sisters': Congregational and Quaker Women in the Early Colonial Period," in *Women in American Religion*, ed. Janet Wilson James (Philadelphia: University of Pennsylvania Press, 1980), 27-46; Amanda Porterfield, *Female Piety in Puritan New England: The Emergence of Humanism* (New York: Oxford University Press, 1992); Margaret W. Masson, "The Typology of the Female as a Model for the Regenerate: Puritan Preaching, 1690–1730," *Signs: Journal of Women in Culture and Society* 2 (1976):304–15; Laurel Thatcher Ulrich, "Vertuous Woman Found: New England Ministerial Literature, 1688–1735," *Women in American Religion*, ed. James, 67–87.

12. Most major works by Jonathan Edwards, including *Some Thoughts Concerning the Revival*, appear in the ongoing Yale University Press edition, *Works of Jonathan Edwards*; his defenses of the Awakening, including *Some Thoughts*, are conveniently collected in Volume 4, ed. C. C. Goen. Edwards works to which I will refer may be found either in the Yale edition of *Works* or more conveniently in the *Jonathan Edwards Reader*, ed. Smith, Stout, and Minkema (New Haven: Yale University Press, 1995).

13. Susan Juster, *Disorderly Women: Sexual Politics and Evangelicalism in Revolutionary New England* (Ithaca, N.Y.: Cornell University Press, 1994), p. 10.

14. Richard L. Bushman, *From Puritan to Yankee: Character and the Social Order in Connecticut, 1690–1765* (Cambridge, Mass.: Harvard University Press, 1967); Natalie Zemon Davis, *Women on the Margins: Three Seventeenth-Century Lives* (Cambridge, Mass.: Harvard University Press, 1995).

15. The concept of liminality is most familiar from Victor Turner's *The Ritual Process: Structure and Anti-Structure* (Chicago: Aldine Publishing Company, 1969). See Erik R. Seeman, "'She Died like Good Old Jacob': Deathbed Scenes and Inversions of Power in New England, 1675–1775," *Publications of the American Antiquarian Society* 104(1994):285–314 for an interesting treatment of women's deathbed scenes as liminal events.

16. Nathaniel Ward, *The Simple Cobler of Aggawam in America* (1647), ed. Paul M. Zall (Lincoln: University of Nebraska Press, 1969), p. 9.

17. *The Poems of Edward Taylor*, ed. Donald F. Stanford (New Haven: Yale University Press, 1960), p. 437.

18. Taylor, p. 438.

19. David Warren Sabean, *Power in the Blood: Popular Culture and Village Discourse in Early Modern Germany* (Cambridge: Cambridge University Press, 1984), pp. 28–30.

20. Important recent readings of first-generation Puritan discourse have suggested that two alternative strains existed within Puritanism. See Andrew Delbanco, *The Puritan Ordeal* (Cambridge, Mass.: Harvard University Press,

1989), and Janice Knight, *Orthodoxies in Massachusetts: Rereading American Puritanism* (Cambridge, Mass.: Harvard University Press, 1994).

21. Victor W. Turner, *The Ritual Process: Structure and Anti-Structure* (Chicago: Aldine Publishing Company, 1969), pp. 94–165.

22. Turner has been cogently criticized for painting these social processes with too broad a brush, being insufficiently attendant to diverse experiences within society. Caroline Walker Bynum has argued that liminality means something different for women than for men; Ardener (who identifies "dominant" and "muted" groups) faults Turner for ignoring the multiplicity of symbolizations within a society: "individuals of all ages and both sexes contribute to that totality of symbolism—which merely appears a 'forest' when one fails to look at the trees" (Ardener, p. 15). See Caroline Walker Bynum, "Women's Stories, Women's Symbols: A Critique of Victor Turner's Theory of Liminality," in *Fragmentation and Redemption: Essays on Gender and the Human Body in Medieval Religion* (New York: Zone Books, 1992), pp. 27–51.

23. Mary Douglas, *Natural Symbols: Explorations in Cosmology* (New York: Pantheon Books, 1982), pp. 18, 65–81.

1. To Love and Make a Lie

1. *Journal of the Rev. John Pike*, Massachusetts Historical Society, *Proceedings* 14 (September 1875), 134.

2. *SCJ* 3 (1700–1714):49–50.

3. *The Diary of Samuel Sewall*, 1674–1729, ed. M. Halsey Thomas (New York: Farrar, Straus & Giroux, 1973), vol. 1, p. 465; John Rogers, *Death the Certain Wages of Sin* (Boston, 1701).

4. For discussions of execution publications, including sermons, see Ronald A. Bosco, "Early American Gallows Literature: An Annotated Check List," *RALS* 8 (1978):81–107; Bosco, "Lectures at the Pillory: The Early American Execution Sermon," *AQ* 30 (1978):156–76; Daniel E. Williams, "Rogues, Rascals, and Scoundrels: The Underworld Literature of Early America," *American Studies* (1983):5–19; Lawrence W. Towner, "True Confessions and Dying Warnings in Colonial New England," *Publications of the Colonial Society of Massachusetts*, vol. 59, *Collectors: Sibley's Heirs* (1982): 523–39; Wayne C. Minnick, "The New England Execution Sermon," *Speech Monographs* 35 (1968):77–89; Walter Lazenby, "Exhortations as Exorcism: Cotton Mather's Sermons to Murderers," *QJS* 57 (1971):50–56. For discussion of Esther Rogers and *Death the Certain Wages of Sin* specifically, see

Daniel E. Williams, "'Behold a Tragick Scene, Strangely Changed into a Theater of Mercy': The Structure and Significance of Criminal Conversion Narratives in Early New England," *AQ* 38 (1986):327–47. Daniel A. Cohen, *Pillars of Salt, Monuments of Grace: New England Crime Literature and the Origins of American Popular Culture* (New York: Oxford University Press, 1993) also includes a discussion of Esther Rogers's case, pp. 59–66.

5. These follow, of course, on Michel Foucault, *Discipline and Punish: The Birth of the Prison*, tr. Alan Sheridan (New York: Vintage, 1979). There is a particularly well-developed scholarly literature on crime in early modern England: see Hay et al., *Albion's Fatal Tree: Crime and Society in Eighteenth Century England* (New York: Pantheon Books, 1975), J. A. Sharpe, *Crime in Seventeenth-Century England* (Cambridge: Cambridge University Press, 1983), and John Langbein, *The London Hanged: Crime and Civil Society in the Eighteenth Century* (New York: Cambridge University Press, 1992). See also Pieter Spierenburg, *The Spectacle of Suffering* (New York: Cambridge University Press, 1984).

6. Daniel A. Cohen, *Pillars of Salt and Monuments of Grace: New England Crime Literature and the Origins of American Popular Culture, 1674–1860* (New York: Oxford University Press, 1993), p. 79.

7. Cotton Mather, *The Call of the Gospel* (Boston, 1686); Cotton Mather, *Pillars of Salt* (Boston, 1699).

8. David D. Hall, *Worlds of Wonder, Days of Judgment: Popular Religious Belief in Early New England* (New York: Alfred A. Knopf, 1989), pp. 178-84.

9. John Rogers, *Death the Certain Wages of Sin*, p. 143. Subsequent quotations from *Death the Certain Wages of Sin* will be identified within the text with a page number.

10. See Cohen, *Pillars of Salt, Monuments of Grace*, pp. 59–66, for another discussion of the relationships between the ministers in this incident.

11. Cotton Mather, *A Sorrowful Spectacle* (Boston, 1715), p. 90.

12. John Demos, *Entertaining Satan: Witchcraft and the Culture of Early New England* (New York: Oxford University Press, 1982), pp. 368–86; Carol F. Karlsen, *The Devil in the Shape of a Woman: Witchcraft in Colonial New England* (New York: W.W. Norton, 1987), p. 296; Christine Leigh Heyrman, "Specters of Subversion, Societies of Friends: Dissent and the Devil in Provincial Essex County, Massachusetts," in *Saints and Revolutionaries: Essays on Early American History*, ed. David Hall, John M. Murrin, and Thad W. Tate (New York: W.W. Norton, 1984), pp. 38–74.

13. Karlsen asserts that the two crimes were associated in early New England, with infanticide accusations often made against suspected witches (p. 21).

14. Increase Mather, *The Folly of Sinning* (Boston, 1699), pp. 38–39.

15. Cotton Mather, *Warnings from the Dead* (Boston, 1693), p. 73.

16. Kathleen Verduin, "'Our Cursed Natures': Sexuality and the Puritan Conscience," *NEQ* 56 (1983):220–37, makes the observation that "the association of sexuality and idolatry in biblical examples . . . informed contemporary threats to the orthodox Puritan faith" (p. 230), citing the "association of heresy and sexuality" in the Ann Hutchinson case, and especially the biblical city of Sodom.

17. Mather, *Warnings from the Dead*, pp. 43–44; Samuel Danforth, *The Cry of Sodom Enquired Into* (Boston, 1674). N. E. H. Hull, *Female Felons: Women and Serious Crime in Colonial Massachusetts* (Urbana: University of Illinois Press, 1987), remarks on the frequency of the domino theory of crime in the Puritan sermon literature, p. 56.

18. *Pillars of Salt*, p. 105.

19. John Williams, *Warnings to the Unclean* (Boston, 1699), p. 51.

20. *A Sorrowful Spectacle*, 39, 11.

21. That even such a sensational event as a neonaticide should be recast as a language problem may seem strange but it is not unique. "Wragg is in custody," Matthew Arnold would write nearly two hundred years later, wincing at the debased language of the newspaper describing the arrest of a contemporary infanticide. Like "An Holy Rebuke to the Unclean Spirit," *The Function of Criticism at the Present Time* masks its social critique with an aesthetic one: is it really the girl's ugly name that so offends the ear, or the dingy circumstances of her life in the workhouse that the Victorian critic wants to call to the imaginations of otherwise complacent Britishers? Mather, too, prefers to define his culture in terms of the quality of its language, its vital conversation, and to attack its enemies as linguistic outlaws.

22. Samuel Willard, *Impenitent Sinners Warned* (Boston, 1698), p. 19.

23. *Warnings from the Dead*, p. 66.

24. *The Folly of Sinning*, p. 69.

25. *Warnings from the Dead*, p. 6.

26. *The Folly of Sinning*, p. 15.

27. Daniel E. Williams, "Puritans and Pirates: A Confrontation Between Cotton Mather and William Fly in 1726," *EAL* 22 (1987):233–51. See also Cohen, *Pillars of Salt, Monuments of Grace*, pp. 66–69, for a discussion of pirate execution sermons.

28. Cotton Mather, *Faithful Warnings to Prevent Fearful Judgments* (Boston, 1704), p. 16.

29. *Faithful Warnings*, pp. 40–41.

30. *Faithful Warnings*, pp. 37–38.

31. *Faithful Warnings*, p. 46.

32. Willard, *Impenitent Sinners Warned*, "To The Reader," n.p.

33. See Roger Thompson, "Adolescent Culture in Colonial Massachusetts," *Journal of Family History* 9 (1984):127–44, for a convenient review of the debate about the concept of adolescence and the significance of youth culture in early modern culture. See also Thompson's *Sex in Middlesex: Popular Mores in a Massachusetts County, 1649–1699* (Amherst: University of Massachusetts Press, 1986); Ross W. Beales Jr., "In Search of the Historical Child: Miniature Adulthood and Youth in Colonial New England," *AQ* 27 (1975): 379–98; and N. Ray Hiner, "Adolescence in Eighteenth-Century America," in *History of Childhood Quarterly: A Journal of Psychohistory* 3 (1975):253–80 for New England materials; see also Natalie Davis, *Society and Culture in Early Modern France* (Stanford, Calif.: Stanford University Press, 1975).

34. *Warnings to the Unclean* 62, 68, 59. See Patricia Tracy, *Jonathan Edwards, Pastor: Religion and Society in Eighteenth-Century Northampton* (New York: Hill and Wang, 1980), pp. 106–7, for a discussion of "night walking" and youth culture.

35. Williams, *Warnings to the Unclean*, pp. 29–30, Mather, *Warnings from the Dead*, p. 34.

36. For example, they do not use these verses: "In the twilight, in the evening, in the black and dark night, And behold, there met him a woman with the attire of an harlot, and subtil of heart (She is loud and stubborn, her feet abide not in her house; Now is she without, now in the streets, and lieth in wait at every corner). . . . With her much fair speech she caused him to yield, with the flatterings of her lips she forced him" (Proverbs 7).

37. Willard, *Impenitent Sinners Warned*, "To The Reader," n.p.; Williams, *Warnings to the Unclean*, pp. 9–10; Mather, *Warnings from the Dead*, p. 52, 53.

38. Karlsen, p. 198.

39. Sewall, *Diary*, I.445.

40. Andrew Delbanco's *The Puritan Ordeal* argues that two strains of thought run through Puritan theology and indeed through nineteenth-century American culture: one based on a theory of positive sin, and one on privative sin. The contrast I develop here between John Rogers and his colleagues is analagous to Delbanco's.

41. Sewall, *Diary*, I.451.

42. Or, "the cosmos is seen through the medium of the body." Mary Douglas, *Natural Symbols: Explorations in Cosmology* (New York: Pantheon Books, 1982), pp. 18, 70.

43. Heyrman, "Specters of Subversion, Societies of Friends," has been most influential on my thinking here.

44. Cohen remarks on Rogers's Great Awakening support, p.66.

45. Turner's vocabulary (*communitas*) here helps clarify the fact that differences between pro- and anti-Awakening spiritual styles can be found even decades in advance of that revival.

46. There have, of course, been many studies of Hawthorne's use of New England history, from Marion L. Kesselring's *Hawthorne's Reading, 1828–1850* to Charles Ryskamp, "The New England Sources of *The Scarlet Letter*," *American Literature* 31 (1959):257–72, to Michael Colacurcio, "Footsteps of Ann Hutchinson: The Context of *The Scarlet Letter*," *ELH* 39 (1972). While many of these studies focus on Hawthorne's knowledge of New England history through nineteenth-century sources, it is possible that he may have read *Death the Certain Wages of Sin* as well. Belcher's opening comment in his section of that text recalls not only the color of Hester's "A" but also the opening scene describing her stepping over the threshold of the prison: "a poor Wretch, entering into Prison a Bloody Malefactor, her Conscience laden with Sins of a Scarlet Die, but . . . [in] the Space of Eight Months she came forth, Sprinkled, Changed, Comforted, a Candidate of Heaven" (*DCWS*, 118).

47. Some students of sermon literature bring a high degree of skepticism about the authenticity of the lay voices represented in these publications. Daniel E. Williams, for example, remarks in "Rogues, Rascals, and Scoundrels" that "it is highly unlikely that the words actually came from the condemned, and highly likely that they came from the minister" (8). My own view accords more closely with Daniel A. Cohen's: see note 6.

48. Joshua Coffin, *A Sketch of the History of Newbury, Newburyport, and West Newbury* (Boston: Samuel G. Drake, 1845), pp. 68–69.

49. John Owen King, *The Iron of Melancholy: Structures of Spiritual Conversion in America from the Puritan Conscience to Victorian Neurosis* (Middletown: Wesleyan University Press, 1983), p. 74.

50. John Pike, "Journal of the Rev. John Pike, 1678–1709," *Proceedings of the Massachusetts Historical Society*, first series, 14 (1875), p. 134; John Marshall, "Diary, 1697–1709," *Proceedings of the Massachusetts Historical Society*, second series, 1 (1884), 148–61.

51. William D. Piersen, *Black Yankees: The Development of an Afro-American Subculture in Eighteenth-Century New England* (Amherst: University of Massachusetts Press, 1988) pp. 26–36.

52. Joshua Coffin, *A Sketch of the History of Newbury, Newburyport, and West Newbury* (Boston: Samuel G. Drake, 1845), pp. 68–69.

53. Carol F. Karlsen, *The Devil in the Shape of a Woman: Witchcraft in Colonial New England* (New York: W.W. Norton, 1987), p. 198.

54. See, for example, Karlsen, pp. 194–202; Roger Thompson, *Sex in Middlesex: Popular Mores in a Massachusetts County, 1649–1699* (Amherst: University of Massachusetts Press, 1986), pp. 19–33; 54–70; Robert V. Wells, "Illegitimacy and Bridal Pregnancy in Colonial America," in *Bastardy and its Comparative History,* ed. Peter Laslett, Karla Oosterveen, and Richard M. Smith (Cambridge: Harvard University Press, 1980), pp. 349–61.

55. *A Sorrowful Spectacle,* p. 91.

56. *Acts and Resolves,* I.55. The law is also reprinted in Thomas Foxcroft, *Lessons of Caution to Young Sinners* (Boston, 1733). The Bastard Neonaticide Act was an important context for New England infanticides; for cases of infanticide from other regions, see, for example, Lou Rose, "A Memorable Trial in Seventeenth-Century Maryland," *Maryland Historical Magazine* 83 (1988):365–68, and Sharon Ann Burnston, "Babies in the Well: An Underground Insight into Deviant Behavior in Eighteenth-Century Philadelphia," *The Pennsylvania Magazine* 106 (1982):151–86.

57. Mark Jackson, *New-born Child Murder: Women, Illegitimacy and the Courts in Eighteenth-Century England* (Manchester, U.K.: Manchester University Press, 1996), pp. 37–47; Karlsen, pp. 198–202.

58. Jackson, pp. 60–78.

59. Helena M. Wall, *Fierce Communion: Family and Community in Early America* (Cambridge, Mass.: Harvard University Press, 1990), p. 147; see also David H. Flaherty, *Privacy in Colonial New England* (Charlottesville: University Press of Virginia, 1967), Robert St. George, "'Heated' Speech and Literacy in Seventeenth-Century New England," in *Seventeenth-Century New England,* ed. David D. Hall and David Grayson Allen (Boston, 1984), pp. 275–321; Roger Thompson, "'Holy Watchfulness' and Communal Conformism: The Functions of Defamation in Early New England Communities," *NEQ* 56 (1983):504–22. For statistics about bastard neonaticide prosecutions, see Peter C. Hoffer and N. E. H. Hull, *Murdering Mothers: Infanticide in England and New England, 1558–1803* (New York: New York University Press, 1984) pp. 56–57, 74–75. For reprint of the Bastard Neonaticide Act, see Foxcroft, *Lessons of Caution,* n.p.

60. Thomas Laqueur, "Bodies, Details, and the Humanitarian Narrative," in Lynn Hunt, ed., *The New Critical History* (Berkeley: University of California Press, 1989), 176-204; Jackson, pp. 113–23.

61. Hoffer and Hull, 65–78; Jackson, 140–45.

62. Wall, p. 95.

63. Sewall, *Diary*, I.451.

64. *SCJ* 3:49 (July 15, 1701).

65. Jackson discusses the issue of violence, pp. 100–102, but only in terms of cases in which concealment could not be proved. Presumably, concealment made the question of violence moot.

66. See Mary Beth Norton, *Founding Mothers and Fathers: Gendered Power and the Forming of American Society* (New York: Alfred A. Knopf, 1996), pp. 222–39, for a discussion of women's communities, including midwife networks: Norton shows how such women's communities may at times operate separately from men's, but nonetheless have their own mechanisms for controlling their members.

67. *SCJ* 68 (1715–21), May 3, 1715.

68. *A Sorrowful Spectacle*, p. ii.

69. Suffolk Files, v. 99, No. 10355.

70. Richard W. Wertz and Dorothy C. Wertz, *Lying-In: A History of Childbirth in America* (New York: The Free Press, 1977), p. 4.; see also Adrian Wilson, "The Ceremony of Childbirth and Its Interpretation," *Women as Mothers in Pre-Industrial England*, ed. Valerie Fildes (New York: Routledge, 1990), pp. 68–107; Judith Walzer Leavitt, *Brought to Bed: Childbearing in America, 1750 to 1950* (New York, 1986); Catherine M. Scholten, "'On the Importance of the Obstetrick Art': Changing Customs of Childbirth in America, 1760 to 1825," *WMQ*, third series, 34 (1977) 429–31; Scholten, *Childbearing in American Society, 1650–1850* (New York, 1985); Laurel Thatcher Ulrich, *Good Wives: Image and Reality in the Lives of Women in Northern New England 1650–1750* (New York: Oxford University Press, 1983); Ulrich, *A Midwife's Tale: The Life of Martha Ballard, Based on Her Diary, 1783–1812* (New York: Random House, 1990).

71. Ulrich, *Good Wives*, p. 127.

72. Hoffer and Hull, p. 10. On the other hand, Hoffer and Hull also note that in later decades convictions fell off when juries looked for reasons to find an absence of premeditation: prior arrangements with the midwife, for example, or evidence that the expectant mother had prepared linens for the child; see *Murdering Mothers*, pp. 68–69.

73. We frequently see in our own time, of course, instances of young pregnant women not seeking out obstetrical services. The phenomenon of "denial of pregnancy," either consciously to avoid social consequences or unconsciously, as part of a stress-related reaction to a crisis pregnancy, has been reported in current medical literature. The explanations in that literature for this phenomenon are various. See, for example, Steven E. Pitt and Erin M.

Bale, "Neonaticide, Infanticide, and Filicide: A Review of the Literature," *Bulletin of American Academy of Psychiatry and the Law* 23 (1991): 375–86; C. M. Green and S. V. Manohar, "Neonaticide and Hysterical Denial of Pregnancy," *British Journal of Psychiatry* 156 (1990):121–23; P. J. Resnick, "Murder of the Newborn: A Psychiatric Review of Neonaticide," *American Journal of Psychiatry* 126 (1970):1414–20; V. J. Hirschmann and E. Schwartz, "Structural Analysis of Female Infanticide," *Psychotherapy* 8 (1958):1–20.

74. Roger Thompson, *Sex in Middlesex*, pp. 23–24, Wertz and Wertz, pp. 7–8, Hoffer and Hull, p. 15. See also James C. Oldham, "On Pleading the Belly: A History of the Jury of Matrons," *Criminal Justice History* 6 (1984): 1–64.

75. Thompson, p. 22.

76. Wall, *Fierce Communion*, notes that the process of childbirth would be a realm for which an ideal of neighborly obligation persisted beyond the seventeenth century, even as, in her argument, that communal ethos was gradually shaken. Citing a New York law that mandated that midwives not discriminate against economically disadvantaged women, she comments, "Towns were larger, neighbors were less intimate, and midwifery was a business—but the community still owed something to women in childbed," p. 95.

77. This case has been discussed extensively by Ulrich, *Good Wives*, pp. 197–201.

78. Suffolk Court Files, vol. 31, no. 2636.

79. Jackson notes the presence of this detail in a number of English cases, pp. 102, 121.

80. Ulrich was the first to discover that Elizabeth Emerson was the sister of Hannah Dustin, the woman who four years later was praised by Cotton Mather for having escaped from her Indian captors by killing them, in his sermon, *Humiliations Follow'd with Deliverances* (Boston, 1697); see *Good Wives*, pp. 184–85. Hannah, who had just given birth, had been taken captive together with Mary Neff, the midwife, whose continuing relationship with the family may be related to her scrupulousness here.

81. Suffolk Court Files, vol. 216 (papers not dated, July 1649–February 1728–29), no. 28850.

82. Karlsen, pp. 198–202; Jackson, pp. 30–36.

83. *The Folly of Sinning*, p. 46.

84. *Pillars of Salt*, p. 43.

85. Suffolk Court Files, no. 3718.

86. *Warnings to the Unclean* (Boston, 1699), p. 57.

87. *Warnings to the Unclean*, pp. 56, 57.

88. *Warnings to the Unclean*, p. 21.

89. Increase Mather had used this term in his execution sermon for the murderer James Morgan, who killed someone while drunk. "Oh how many," Mather says, "have by means of this Sin, been guilty of *Interpretative Murder!* They have caused others to die by making them drunk." In the same passage, Mather comments particularly on the problem of English settlers providing liquor to Indians, reflecting the widely held belief that Native Americans were particularly vulnerable to alcohol and holding the English community therefore indirectly responsible for providing them with liquor. See Increase Mather, *Sermon Occasioned by the Execution of a Man Found Guilty of Murder* (Boston, 1686), p. 29–30.

90. Suffolk County Files, no. 3718.

91. *Pillars of Salt*, p. 104.

92. Hoffer and Hull note that as infanticide convictions became less frequent, women could avoid conviction by invoking a "want-of-help" defense of the type I am suggesting here (Hoffer and Hull, *Murdering Mothers*, p. 68). Cotton Mather's account in *Pillars of Salt* gives the story a much more damning spin, adding details that appear neither in Williams's sermon nor in the court documents: Smith was "attended with a *Conception*, which tho' she endeavored to render it an Abortive, the Holy providence of God would not suffer it to be so. She did, with much Obstinacy, Deny and Conceal her being with *Child*: and when the *Child* was Born, she smothered it, but the Neighbours found it out immediately" (*Pillars of Salt*, p. 104). If the story he repeats is to be believed, then Sarah may have consulted Mary Lyes about an abortifacient. See Ulrich, *A Midwife's Tale*, p. 56, and Thompson, *Sex in Middlesex*, p. 25. 46, 157, 183.

93. Suffolk Court Files, no. 3718.

94. Jackson, pp. 113–23.

95. *Warnings to the Unclean*, p. 57.

96. Hoffer and Hull call this sermon "a moving last echo of this genre," p. 58.

97. Thomas Foxcroft, *Lessons of Caution to Young Sinners* (Boston, 1733), p. 70. Subsequent references to *Lessons of Caution* will be identified within the text with a page number.

98. Suffolk County Files, vol. 251 (July–August 1733), no. 35693.

99. The argument of Perry Miller's *The New England Mind* is of course that the Harvard-trained ministry lost their influence as Puritanism declined over the course of the first century of Massachusetts settlement, so that the

"fourth generation," Foxcroft's, had become quite marginalized. See J. William T. Youngs Jr., *God's Messengers: Religious Leadership in Colonial New England, 1700–1750* (Baltimore and London: The Johns Hopkins University Press, 1976), for a discussion of the various strategies used by the ministries to respond to this cultural change.

100. Cornelia Dayton's study of New Haven court cases notes an *increase* in prosecutions for infanticide after 1740, all involving individuals of marginal status, including African or Indian servants like Katherine Garret, and suggests that this newly selective prosecution points to a "heightened anxiety at mid-century over what was evidently a growing population of unmarried women for whom domestic service threatened to become a permanent rather than a temporary way of life"; she notes, however, that these cases usually resulted in acquittal. See Cornelia Hughes Dayton, *Women Before the Bar: Gender, Law, and Society in Connecticut, 1639–1789* (Chapel Hill: University of North Carolina Press, 1995), pp. 210–13. See also Kathleen Joan Bragdon, "Crime and Punishment Among the Indians of Massachusetts, 1675–1750," *Ethnohistory* 28 (1981):23–32.

101. William B. Sprague, *Annals of the American Pulpit*, vol. 1, notes that Eliphalet Adams had comparatively extensive contacts with Native American groups, and knowledge of Native American language. Cohen, pp. 75–76, notes the participation of the Moodys in the revivals that came to be known as the Great Awakening (see also Sibley, IV.362–63).

102. Eliphalet Adams, *A Sermon, Preached on the Occasion of the Execution of Katherine Garret* (New London, 1738), p. 38. Subsequent quotations from this sermon will be identified within the text with a page number.

103. Cohen, pp. 75–76.

104. *A Faithful Narrative of the Wicked Life and the Remarkable Conversion of Patience Boston* (Boston, 1738), p. 12. Subsequent citations of *A Faithful Narrative* will be identified within the text with a page number.

105. See Cohen, pp. 71–80, for a discussion of this text and its connections to the revival movement.

106. *SCJ*, 1730–1733, pp. 122–23.

2. On Wedlock and the Birth of Children

1. Benjamin Colman, *Reliquiae Turellae et Lachrymae Paternae* (Boston, 1735), p. 219. Subsequent citations of *Reliquiae Turellae* will be identified within the text with "*RT*" and page numbers.

2. For important assessments of Turell's poetry, see Emily Stipes Watts, *The Poetry of American Women from 1633 to 1945* (Austin: University of Texas Press, 1977), pp. 30–35; Pattie Cowell, "Puritan Women Poets of America," in *Puritan Poets and Poetics: Seventeenth-Century American Poetry in Theory and Practice*, ed. Peter White (University Park: Pennsylvania State University Press, 1975), pp. 21–32; David S. Shields, "The Religious Sublime and New England Poets of the 1720s," *EAL* 15.3 (Winter 1984/85): 231–48.

3. Laurel Thatcher Ulrich, *Good Wives: Image and Reality in Northern New England, 1650–1750* (New York: Oxford University Press, 1982), p. 3. For a discussion of ministerial presentations of ideal womanhood, see Ulrich, "Vertuous Women Found: New England Ministerial Literature, 1688–1735," in *Women in American Religion*, ed. Janet Wilson James (Philadelphia: University of Pennsylvania Press, 1980), pp. 67–87.

4. David S. Shields, *Civil Tongues and Polite Letters in British America* (Chapel Hill: University of North Carolina Press, 1997); 232n. See also Elaine Hobby, *Virtue of Necessity: English Women's Writing, 1649–1688* (London: Virago Press, 1988), and Margaret J. M. Ezell, *Writing Women's Literary History* (Baltimore: The Johns Hopkins University Press, 1993).

5. *Winthrop's Journal: History of New England, 1630–1645*, ed. James Kendall Hosmer (New York, 1908), 2.225.

6. Ivy Schweitzer, *The Work of Self-Representation: Lyric Poetry in Colonial New England* (Chapel Hill: University of North Carolina Press, 1991), p. 173.

7. Schweitzer, p. 131.

8. Phyllis Mack, *Visionary Women: Ecstatic Prophecy in Seventeenth-Century England* (Los Angeles: University of California Press, 1992), especially pp. 165–221; Hobby, pp. 26–53; Ezell, p. 65.

9. The Revelation passage as a whole is an important source of iconography for the Virgin Mary ("a woman clothed with the Sun, and the moon under her feet, and upon her head a crown of twelve stars," v.1). Some Catholic iconography reintroduces the female actor in the struggle against Satan, showing Mary with a serpent under her foot, as suggested by Genesis. See Marina Warner, *Alone of All Her Sex: The Myth and Cult of the Virgin Mary* (1976; New York: Vintage Books, 1983), chaps. 16 and 18, esp. pp. 244–45, for discussion of imagery associated with these passages. Warner notes that Jerome's Vulgate reads "she shall crush thy head"; this mistranslation, although corrected in the Authorized Version, may have been the source of the female antagonist in popular iconography.

10. Madeline Forell Marshall, *The Poetry of Elizabeth Singer Rowe (1674–1688)* (Lewiston, N.Y.: Edwin Mellon Press, 1987), pp. 3–4, 42, and passim. See also Beth Wynn Fisken, "Mary Sidney's *Psalmes*: Education and Wisdom" in *Silent but for the Word: Tudor Women as Patrons, Translators, and Writers of Religious Works*, ed. Margaret Patterson Hannay (Kent, Ohio: Kent State University Press, 1985), pp. 166–83, for another woman poet's use of the psalms to establish her own poetic voice.

11. Natalie Zemon Davis, *Society and Culture in Early Modern France* (Stanford, Calif.: Stanford University Press, 1975), pp. 86–88, 171–72.

12. "Preface to *The Bay Psalm Book*," in Perry Miller and Thomas H. Johnson, *The Puritans: A Sourcebook of Their Writings*, rev. ed. (New York: Harper & Row, 1963), p. 672.

13. See Laura L. Becker, "Ministers vs. Laymen: The Singing Controversy in Puritan New England, 1720–1740," *NEQ* 55 (1982):79–96, on disputed date.

14. *The Accomplished Singer* (Boston, 1721), pp. 22–23.

15. Modern-day musicologists see the Old Way–New Way controversy as an attempt by a people to preserve their traditional folk ways against learned intervention. See Gilbert Chase, *American Music from the Pilgrims to the Present*, rev. 2nd ed. (Urbana and Chicago: University of Chicago Press, 1987), pp. 19–37.

16. Patricia J. Tracy, *Jonathan Edwards, Pastor: Religion and Society in Eighteenth-Century Northampton* (New York: Hill and Wang, 1980), p. 112.

17. Eldon R. Turner makes this point in his provocative article, "Earwitnesses to Resonance in Space: An Interpretation of Puritan Psalmody in Early Eighteenth-Century New England," *AmerS* 25 (1984):25–47. In his schema, the clergy opposed the patriarchal customs of what he calls lay peasant culture, and promoted the interests of women against them. Although the New Way appears to have empowered women, Turner regrets the suppression by clerical interests of "country style" epistemology, to which spatial relations were more important than temporal. In his view, the "enspirited space" of the New England peasantry was eventually "tamed" by temporal ways of perception. The singing quarrel, styles of architecture and carpentry all enacted this cultural conflict.

18. Ola Elizabeth Winslow, *Meetinghouse Hill: 1630–1783* (1952; New York: W. W. Norton, 1972), pp. 150–70.

19. For further discussions of the singing controversy, see Joyce Irwin, "The Theology of 'Regular Singing'" *NEQ* 51 (1978):176–92; Becker, "Ministers vs. Laymen"; Turner, "Earwitnesses to Resonance in Space." For New

England psalm-singing in general, see David W. Music, "The Diary of Samuel Sewall and Congregational Singing in Colonial New England," *The Hymn* 41 (1990):7–15, and David W. Music, "Cotton Mather and Congregational Singing in Puritan New England," *SPAS* 2 (1991):1–30.

20. J. William T. Youngs Jr., *God's Messengers: Religious Leadership in Colonial New England, 1700–1750* (Baltimore and London: The Johns Hopkins University Press, 1976).

21. George W. Harper, "Clericalism and Revival: The Great Awakening in Boston as a Pastoral Phenomenon," *NEQ* 57 (1984):554–66.

22. *The Declaration of a Number of the Associated Pastors of Boston and Charles-Town* (Boston, 1742).

23. *The New England Mind: From Colony to Province* (Cambridge, Mass.: Harvard University Press, 1953), p. 271. For a related discussion, see Bruce C. Daniels, "Sober Mirth and Pleasant Poisons: Puritan Ambivalence toward Leisure," *American Studies* 34 (1993):121–37.

24. Teresa Toulouse, *The Art of Prophesying: New England Sermons and the Shaping of Belief* (Athens: University of Georgia Press, 1987), pp. 56–63; see also Clayton Harding Chapman, "Benjamin Colman and Philomela," *NEQ* 42 (1969):214–31, and David Morris, *The Religious Sublime, Christian Poetry, and Critical Tradition in Eighteenth-Century England* (Lexington: University Press of Kentucky, 1972).

25. Boston, 1707, p. 7. Subsequent citations from *The Government and Improvement of Mirth* will be identified within the text with "*M*" and a page number.

26. Robert Alter notes that the Hebrew in verse 2 is unclear (*The Art of Biblical Poetry* [New York: Basic Books, 1985], p. 118). It is interesting that Colman Turell would have felt free to interpolate extensively in the very verse that needs interpretation even to make comprehensible. We are not told that Jane Colman studied Hebrew with her father (and it is very unlikely); but this coincidence could reflect her having absorbed some of his biblical learning.

27. Note that her emphasis may diminish clerical power, but it also rejects the peasant patriarchy that Eldon Turner associates with the Old Way. See note 17.

28. Hobby notes the significance of images of barrenness in English women's poetry: Mary Cary's use of the image is a "direct challenge to an orthodoxy which would see her only significant products as those of her body" (*Virtue of Necessity*, p. 31).

29. See E. Brooks Holifield, *The Covenant Sealed: The Development of Puritan Sacramental Theology in Old and New England, 1570–1720* (New

Haven: Yale University Press, 1974); and Robert G. Pope, "New England vs. the New England Mind: The Myth of Declension," in *Puritan New England: Essays on Religion, Society, and Culture*, ed. Alden T. Vaughan and Francis J. Bremer (New York: St. Martin's Press, 1977), pp. 314–25.

30. Kathleen M. Swaim, "Come and Hear: Women's Puritan Evidences," in *American Women's Autobiography: Fea(s)ts of Memory*, ed. Margo Culley (Madison: University of Wisconsin Press, 1992), 32-56; Susan Juster, *Disorderly Women: Sexual Politics and Evangelicalism in Revolutionary New England* (Ithaca, N.Y.: Cornell University Press, 1994).

31. For arguments of intimidation and control, see Schweitzer, *The Work of Self-Representation* and Ann Kibbey, *The Interpretation of Material Shapes in Puritanism: A Study of Rhetoric, Prejudice, and Violence* (Cambridge: Cambridge University Press, 1986); for arguments about enabling women's experiences, see Amanda Porterfield, *Feminine Spirituality in America: From Sarah Edwards to Martha Graham* (Philadelphia: Temple University Press, 1980); Gerald Moran, "'Sisters' in Christ: Women and the Church in Seventeenth-Century New England," in *Women in American Religion*, ed. Janet Wilson James (Philadelphia: University of Pennsylvania Press, 1980), pp. 47–65; Moran, "'The Hidden Ones': Women and Religion in Puritan New England," in *Triumph Over Silence: Women in Protestant History*, ed. Richard L. Greaves (Westport, Conn.: Greenwood Press, 1985), 125–149; and Lonna M. Malmsheimer, "Daughters of Zion: New England Roots of American Feminism" *NEQ* 50 (1977): 484–504. Some writers argue that female imagery does not imply a specifically female model for sainthood: see Laurel Thatcher Ulrich, "Vertuous Woman Found"; and Margaret Masson, "The Typology of the Female as a Model for the Regenerate: Puritan Preaching, 1690–1730," *Signs: Journal of Women in Culture and Society* 2 (1976):304–15. There is also a group of writers who interpret the presence of such language as pointing only to the "playful flexibility of roles available to the faithful" (David Leverenz, *The Language of Puritan Feeling: An Exploration in Literature, Psychology, and Social History* [New Brunswick, N.J.: Rutgers University Press, 1980, p. 143]), or "a wide range of usage and . . . a graphic expression of sensuality and gender polymorphousness" (Michael P. Winship, "Behold the Bridegroom Cometh: Marital Imagery in Massachusetts Preaching, 1630–1730," *EAL* 27 [1992]: 170–84).

32. For demographic analysis, see Mary Maples Dunn, "'Saints and Sisters': Congregational and Quaker Women in the Early Colonial Period," in *Women in American Religion, ed.* Janet Wilson James (Philadelphia: University of Pennsylvania Press, 1984), pp. 27-46; Richard D. Shiels, "The Feminization of American Congregationalism, 1730–1835," *AQ* 20 (1968):

624–44; Richard L. Bushman, *From Puritan to Yankee: Character and the Social Order in Connecticut, 1690–1765* (Cambridge, Mass: Harvard University Press, 1967), especially pp. 183–95; Patricia U. Bonomi, *Under the Cope of Heaven: Religion, Society, and Politics in Colonial America* (New York: Oxford University Press, 1986), especially pp. 87–127.

33. See Ulrich, Malmsheimer, Masson.

34. Amanda Porterfield, *Female Piety in Puritan New England: The Emergence of Humanism* (New York: Oxford University Press, 1992), pp. 154–56.

35. Masson, p. 315.

36. "Introduction: The Complexity of Symbols," in *Gender and Religion: On the Complexity of Symbols*, ed. Caroline Walker Bynum, Stevan Harrell, and Paula Richman (Boston: Beacon Press, 1986), p. 2. In this introduction to a collection of essays on gendered metaphors in various religious traditions, Bynum compares the theories about religious metaphor that have been advanced by Clifford Geertz, Victor Turner, and Paul Ricoeur, explaining that the contributors to the volume find Ricoeur most useful. Geertz, Bynum says, tends to see religious symbols as more or less direct models for social reality. For Ricoeur, in contrast, religious symbols are "opaque, oblique, analogical" (p. 9). Given the current indebtedness of early American studies to Geertz, Bynum's remarks should be of great interest to students of early American religion. The relevant works by Ricoeur are *The Symbolism of Evil*, trans. E. Buchanan (Boston: Beacon Press, 1967), "The Symbol Gives Rise to the Thought," in *Ways of Understanding Religion*, ed. Walter H. Capps (New York: Macmillan, 1972), pp. 309–17; and "The Specificity of Religious Language," *Semeia* 4 (1975):1–145.

37. Bynum notes, for example, that medieval historians have assumed that medieval women internalized misogynist theologies and other gender-marked religious formulations articulated by their male teachers. Bynum's own work on medieval Christianity suggests, however, that women's spiritualities were much less dependent on articulations of the nature of gender roles than their male counterparts—and some historians—assumed. She does find, however, that the men she studies, when they use gender-marked language that requires them to take on female personae or "feminine" traits (nurturance or weakness), tend to make much of that reversal, using it as an image of conversion. Women mystics, on the other hand, while they do recognize divergent biological roles for the sexes (male as begetter, female as conceiver), are less impressed by the dichotomous vision common to the men, and do not assign distinctive moral qualities to the genders; "women themselves did

not, by and large, see woman as a marked category." Bynum, "'. . . And Woman His Humanity': Female Imagery in the Religious Writing of the Later Middle Ages," in *Gender and Religion*, p. 269.

38. Bynum, "Introduction," p. 2.

39. Linda A. Mercadente, *Gender, Doctrine, and God: The Shakers and Contemporary Theology* (Nashville: Abingdon Press, 1990), pp. 157, 15.

40. These two commonplaces of Puritan religious language were described long ago by Edmund S. Morgan, the first in "The Puritans' Marriage with God," *South Atlantic Quarterly* 48 (1949):107–12, and the second in *The Puritan Family: Religion and Domestic Relations in Seventeenth-Century New England*, rev. ed. (New York: Harper & Row, 1966). The argument here, that there are two strains of spirituality coexisting within Puritanism, shares something with such recent works as Andrew Delbanco's *The Puritan Ordeal* (Cambridge, Mass.: Harvard University Press, 1989) and Janice Knight's *Orthodoxies in Massachusetts: Rereading American Puritanism* (Cambridge, Mass.: Harvard University Press, 1994). Although I am not using Victor Turner's terms in this discussion, it should be evident that there is a connection between the interpretation of marriage that stresses orderly social relationships and "structure," and the interpretation that obviates those structures with "*communitas.*"

41. See Michael P. Winship, "Behold the Bridegroom Cometh! Marital Imagery in Massachusetts Preaching, 1630–1730," *EAL* 27 (1992):170–84, who argues that Colman's muting of the erotic potential of the marital metaphor, typical of his generation, is related to a change in eighteenth-century society from a hierarchical model to a contractual one. Winship thus associates marital language exclusively with such hierarchicalism.

42. Schweitzer remarks that Edward Taylor routinely brings together these two images (pp. 88–89).

43. Caroline Bynum's study of Cistercian language notes the opposite development in the twelfth century, when discussions of the marriage of Christ to the Church are replaced by references to the marriage of Christ to the individual soul. She ties this development to the "feminization" of religious language in the twelfth century (*Jesus as Mother*, p. 138). I will argue that Colman's work reverses that process: the individual bride/soul is replaced by the corporate church as bride, and language is "de-feminized."

44. Benjamin Colman, *Practical Discourses Upon the Parable of the Ten Virgins* (Boston, 1747), p. 12. This work was originally published in London in 1707, but I have relied for pagination on the later, more accessible, Boston

edition. Subsequent citations of this work will be identified within the text with "*PV*" and page numbers.

45. It is consistent as well with the language and sacramental theology Colman declaims in later works that deal more specifically with the Supper. When in *A Discourse of the Pleasure of Religious Worship* (1717), for example, Colman associates marital imagery with the Supper, it is largely divested of its erotic tone. Rather than describing the desire of the bride for her bridegroom on her wedding day, he adopts the perspective of the wedding guests (Mt. 22.1–14), describing the satisfaction of the guests at the wedding feast, wearing appropriate wedding garments and eating under Christ's banner of love. The marriage is not an erotic affair but a convivial one. We sociably memorialize Christ in the meal, just as "we are glad sometimes when our friends ask us to eat with them at their Tables, or when they come to eat with us at ours." Or, we keep the memorial "as some happy People keep with Joy the *day of their Espousals*," memorializing in calm equanimity the anniversary of a day, rather than reenacting the anticipatory excitement and overpowering ecstasy associated with a first conversion, or union with the bridegroom. We look, we do not take part. See *Four Sermons Preached at the Lecture in Boston, to Which Is Added a Discourse on Psalm 122 (A Discourse of the Pleasure of Religious Worship, in Our Publick Assemblies* (Boston, 1717), pp. 158, 157.

46. Benjamin Colman, *Some of the Glories of our Lord and Saviour Jesus Christ, Exhibited in Twenty Sacramental Discourses, Preached at Boston in New England* (London, 1728). Citations of this work will be identified within the text with "SG" and page numbers.

47. Holifield, *The Covenant Sealed*, p. 13.

48. Toulouse, p. 67.

49. Toulouse, pp. 56–57.

50. Edmund S. Morgan, *The Puritan Family: Religion and Domestic Relations in Seventeenth-Century New England*, rev. ed. (New York: Harper & Row, 1966).

51. In sermon nine, after he has scrupulously avoided the notion of marriage as couple in favor of the notion of marriage as group celebration, he does include one paragraph in the "uses" section that returns to the binary idea, reiterating the standard call for husbands to love their wives and wives to obey their husbands: "Let us take care that our Houses resemble Heaven; *i.e.* Let the Carriage of Husbands and Wives shadow out something of the Love and Union which there is between Christ and his Church. . . . The Love of Christ is the Pattern and Law to Husbands, and the Church's dutiful Subjection to him the Rule and Measure of the Wives Behaviour. And what a

Paradise would every House be, and what a Heaven should we have on Earth, if we could always eye, and in any good Measure come up to, these heavenly Patterns!" (*PV,* 286). This paragraph, with its emphasis on binary marriage, seems to me to be a mechanical afterthought, quite disjointed from the rest of the text. Even here, though, heavenly marriage provides a model for social marriage not so much because of the inherent good of binary power relations (as in Perkins, for example), but for the sake of peace and concord.

52. See, for example, *Four Sermons Preached at the Lecture in Boston . . . to Which Is Added a Discourse of the Pleasure of Religious Worship* (Boston, 1717), p. 80; *Some of the Glories,* pp. 83–84.

53. Specifically, Bynum's finding that in some contexts "commentaries on the Song of Songs [i.e., erotic language] competed with a theology of motherhood" (*Jesus as Mother,* p. 141) well describes the patterns of that imagery in Benjamin Colman's writings, and is consistent with my sense of the difference in the Christian tradition of images of maternity: they do not participate in dualistic theologies. On the presence of maternal imagery in twelfth-century Cistercian writings, Bynum has remarked that maternal symbols could be significant "for a theology that maintained—over against Cathar dualism—the goodness of creation in all its physicality" (*Jesus as Mother,* p. 134).

54. Carol Ochs, *Beyond the Sex of God: Toward a New Consciousness— Transcending Matriarchy and Patriarchy* (Boston: Beacon Press, 1977); Rosemary Radford Ruether, *New Woman/New Earth: Sexist Ideologies and Human Liberation* (San Francisco: Harper and Row, 1975).

55. For biography and bibliography on Ebenezer Turell, see Clifford F. Shipton, *Sibley's Harvard Graduates, vol. 6 (1713–1721)* (Boston: Massachusetts Historical Society, 1942), pp. 574–82. In explaining Turell's opposition to the New Lights, Medford's nineteenth-century historian, Charles Brooks, wrote, "We do not suppose that Mr. Turell was one of those men who can make ice perform the offices of fire; nor was such a man then needed in Medford. In his intercourse with his people, he was kind-hearted, social, and dignified. There was about him a morning freshness which was very agreeable." Charles Brooks, *History of the Town of Medford, from Its First Settlement, in 1630, to the Present Time, 1855* (Boston: James M. Usher, 1855), p. 235.

56. Ebenezer Turell's account of this incident, left in manuscript among his papers, was published as "Detection of Witchcraft" in *Collections of the Massachusetts Historical Society,* second series, 10 (1823):6–22.

57. Turell, "Detection of Witchcraft," p. 17. This printed account names the individuals involved only by their initials. John Demos has identified the

family as the Blanchards (*Entertaining Satan: Witchcraft and the Culture of Early New England* [New York: Oxford University Press, 1982], p. 393). Demos also misidentifies Turell as having been the pastor involved in the Blanchard children's original deception.

58. Turell, "Detection of Witchcraft," pp. 7, 19, 12, 16.

59. Quoted in Marshall, p. 128.

60. Jonathan Edwards, "Sinners in the Hands of an Angry God," in *A Jonathan Edwards Reader*, ed. John E. Smith, Harry S. Stout, and Kenneth P. Minkema (New Haven: Yale University Press, 1995), pp. 97–98.

61. Mary Douglas, *Natural Symbols: Explorations in Cosmology* (New York: Pantheon Books, 1982), p. 70.

62. By the end of her life she had had four pregnancies: two resulted in stillbirths; the child conceived at about the time of this letter died eleven days after its birth; and a final son outlived his mother by only a year, dying at age six. Turell herself, if we grant Benjamin Colman's medical diagnosis ("hysteric distemper") any validity, may have died of some complication of gynecological or obstetrical origin. Although death in childbirth as well as death of the infant were certainly possibilities, birth-related mortality rates in early New England were rather low, especially compared to rates in England. See Richard A. Wertz and Dorothy C. Wertz, *Lying-In: A History of Childbirth in America* (New York: The Free Press, 1977). Both Wertz and Wertz and David E. Stannard, *The Puritan Way of Death: A Study in Religion, Culture, and Social Change* (New York: Oxford University Press, 1977), agree that the Puritans, in Stannard's words, "greatly *over*estimated the presence of mortality in their own society" (57). Jane Colman Turell's experience of losing three infants at birth may have been unusually harsh, though not unheard of; but her perception of the real possibility of death was typical of contemporary women.

63. See Clayton Harding Chapman, "Benjamin Colman's Daughters," *NEQ* 26 (1953):169–92, for biographical details; and Pattie Cowell, ed., *Women Poets in Pre-Revolutionary America*, "Abigail Colman Dennie," pp. 241–43, for a distillation and Abigail's one surviving poem, addressed to Jane. See also Cowell's remarks in "Puritan Women Poets in America," in *Puritan Poets and Poetics: Seventeenth-Century American Poetry in Theory and Practice*, ed. Peter White (University Park: Pennsylvania State University Press, 1985), pp. 21–32.

64. They are printed in Ebenezer Turell, *The Life and Character of the Reverend Benjamin Colman* (Boston, 1749), pp. 188–91.

3. Flowing and Reflowing

1. For basic and helpful treatments of the Great Awakening, see Edwin Gaustad, *The Great Awakening in New England* (New York, 1957); C. C. Goen, *Revivalism and Separatism in New England, 1740–1800* (New Haven: Yale University Press, 1962); and Patricia U. Bonomi, *Under the Cope of Heaven: Religion, Society, and Politics in Colonial America* (New York: Oxford University Press, 1986). Some recent work has made us aware of the constructedness of the very phenomenon known as the Great Awakening. See Jon Butler, "Enthusiasm Described and Decried: The Great Awakening as Interpretive Fiction," *Journal of American History* 69 (1982):305–25; Butler, *Awash in a Sea of Faith: Christianizing the American People* (Cambridge, Mass.: Harvard University Press, 1990); and Joseph Conforti, "The Invention of the Great Awakening, 1795–1842," *EAL* 26 (1991):99–118.

2. Sereno Dwight, *The Life of President Edwards* (New York: G. & C. & H. Carvill, 1830), pp. 178–79. All subsequent citations of Sarah Edwards's narrative will be identified within the text.

3. See, for example, Isaac Watts's 14 September 1743 letter to Benjamin Colman, quoted in C. C. Goen, ed., *The Works of Jonathan Edwards*, vol. 4: *The Great Awakening* (New Haven: Yale University Press, 1972), p. 70.

4. Sereno Dwight, *The Life of President Edwards*; Perry Miller, *Jonathan Edwards* (1949; Amherst: University of Massachusetts Press, 1981); Patricia Tracy, *Jonathan Edwards, Pastor: Religion and Society in Eighteenth-Century Northampton* (New York: Hill and Wang, 1980).

5. Julie Ellison, "The Sociology of 'Holy Indifference': Sarah Edwards' Narrative," *American Literature* 56 (1984):479–95; Sandra Gustafson, "Jonathan Edwards and the Reconstruction of 'Feminine' Speech," *American Literary History* 6 (1994):185–212.

6. Ruth Bloch, "Women, Love, and Virtue in the Thought of Edwards and Franklin," in *Benjamin Franklin, Jonathan Edwards, and the Representation of American Culture*, ed. Barbara B. Oberg and Harry S. Stout (New York: Oxford University Press, 1993), p. 140.

7. Dr. Samuel Mather's note is on the back of sermon notes, Box 8, No. 567, Beinecke MS collection. On interruption of the birth cycle, Patricia Bonomi's research is cited in Bloch, p. 140.

8. *Miscellanies*, in *A Jonathan Edwards Reader*, ed. John E. Smith, Harry S. Stout, and Kenneth P. Minkema (New Haven: Yale University Press, 1995), p. 38.

9. Harry S. Stout and Peter Onuf, "James Davenport and the Great Awakening in New London," *The Journal of American History* 71 (1983): 556-78.

10. See David Hall, *The Faithful Shepherd: A History of the New England Ministry in the Seventeenth Century* (Middletown, Conn.: Wesleyan University Press, 1968), for a discussion of the traditions of the Puritan ministry; see Timothy Hall, *Contested Boundaries: Itineracy and the Reshaping of the Colonial American Religious World* (Durham, N.C.: Duke University Press, 1994) for a discussion of the implications of itineracy.

11. This is Ruth Bloch's argument.

12. See, for example, Ellison, "The Sociology of 'Holy Indifference'."

13. Letter to Thomas Gillespie, 1 July 1751, in C. C. Goen, ed., *The Works of Jonathan Edwards*, vol. 4: *The Great Awakening* (New Haven: Yale University Press, 1972), p. 564.

14. *Some Thoughts Concerning the Revival*, in C. C. Goen, *The Works of Jonathan Edwards*, vol. 4: *The Great Awakening* (New Haven: Yale University Press, 1972), p. 294.

15. See Sacvan Bercovitch, *The Puritan Origins of the American Self* (New Haven: Yale University Press, 1975), for a discussion of the traditions of biography to which the *Magnalia* belongs; see also Wayne Proudfoot, "From Theology to a Science of Religions: Jonathan Edwards and William James on Religious Affections," *Harvard Theological Review* 82 (1989):149–65.

16. *Some Thoughts*, in *Works*, 4:332–33.

17. Charles Chauncy, *A Letter from a Gentleman in Boston, to Mr. George Wishart, One of the Ministers of Edinburgh, Concerning the State of Religion in New-England* (Edinburgh, 1745). Rpt. in Richard L. Bushman, ed., *The Great Awakening: Documents on the Revival of Religion, 1740–1743* (Chapel Hill: University of North Carolina Press, 1969), p. 118.

18. The most well-known critique of the Awakening is Chauncy's *Seasonable Thought on the Revivals* (Boston, 1743), which was written to answer Edwards's *Some Thoughts*. See Amy Schrager Lang, *Prophetic Woman: Anne Hutchinson and the Problem of Dissent in the Literature of New England* (Berkeley: University of California Press, 1987), pp. 72–106. See also Cedric B. Cowing, "Sex and Preaching in the Great Awakening," *AQ* 20 (1968): 624–44; and Harry S. Stout and Peter Onuf, "James Davenport and the Great Awakening in New London," *Journal of American Literature* 71 (1983):556–78.

19. Mary Douglas, *Natural Symbols: Explorations in Cosmology* (1970; New York: Pantheon Books, 1982), p. xxiii.

20. Douglas, pp. 64–81.

21. The important point here is that both Sarah Edwards and Charles Chauncy live in the same society but perceive that society's degree of structuring differently. Again, Douglas's words are helpful in explaining how this disparity may reflect gender and class differences. "The social division of labour involves women less deeply than their menfolk in the central institutions—political, legal, administrative, etc.—of their society. They are indeed subject to control. But the range of controls they experience is simpler, less varied. Mediated through fewer human contacts, their social responsibilities are more confined to the domestic range . . . the web of their social life, though it may tie them down effectively enough, is of a looser texture" (Douglas, p. 84).

22. *Some Thoughts,* in *Works of Jonathan Edwards,* 4:341.

23. In describing the 1735 revival in *A Faithful Narrative of Surprising Conversions,* for example, he had written, "Our converts then remarkably appeared united in dear affection to one another, and many have expressed much of that spirit of love which they felt toward all mankind; and particularly to those that had been least friendly to them. Never, I believe, was so much done in confessing injuries, and making up differences as the last year" (*The Works of Jonathan Edwards,* 4:184).

24. "Personal Narrative," in *A Jonathan Edwards Reader,* ed. John E. Smith, Harry S. Stout, and Kenneth P. Minkema (New Haven: Yale University Press, 1995), p. 283. Subsequent citations of Jonathan Edwards's "Personal Narrative" will be identified within the text with "*JER*" and a page number.

25. Roland André Delattre, *Beauty and Sensibility in the Thought of Jonathan Edwards: An Essay on Aesthetics and Theological Ethics* (New Haven: Yale University Press, 1968).

26. *Some Thoughts,* in *Works of Jonathan Edwards,* 4:332.

27. Barbara Leslie Epstein, *The Politics of Domesticity: Women, Evangelicalism, and Temperance in Nineteenth-Century America* (Middletown, Conn.: Wesleyan University Press, 1981), p. 43; Susan Juster, *Disorderly Women: Sexual Politics and Evangelicalism in Revolutionary New England* (Ithaca: Cornell University Press, 1994), p. 72.

28. Tracy, p. 157.

29. Kenneth Shipton, "The New England Clergy of the Glacial Age" (Colonial Society of Massachusetts, *Publications* 32 [1937]:24–54); James W. Schmotter, "Ministerial Careers in Eighteenth-Century New England: The Social Context, 1700–1760," *Journal of Social History* 9 (1975–76).

30. See Miller, *Jonathan Edwards*, and Tracy, *Jonathan Edwards, Pastor.*

31. Julie Ellison, "The Sociology of 'Holy Indifference': Sarah Edwards's Narrative," *American Literature* 56 (1984):479–95, highlights this aspect of the narrative.

32. *Some Thoughts*, in *The Works of Jonathan Edwards*, 4:337.

33. Sandra Gustafson, "Jonathan Edwards and the Reconstruction of 'Feminine' Speech," *American Literary History* 6 (1994):185–212, makes this suggestion. Recall Douglas's observation, though, that religious insights are not compensations for a lack of cultural power but rather positive explanations of the subject's world model.

34. Ellison also stresses the public nature of Sarah Edwards's experiences, to say that it "has the character of a performance given by her for the people" (486). Although Ellison does not discuss Sarah's 'motes in the sunbeam' image, her comment, "The whole distinction between inner and outer, private and social, breaks down in her case" (417) is quite consistent with my analysis here.

35. *Some Thoughts*, in *The Works of Jonathan Edwards*, 4:337.

36. See Stout and Onuf, "James Davenport and the Great Awakening in New London," p. 567, for a much more disorderly example of singing among New Light adherents; and see chapter 2, above, for a discussion of the connection between congregational singing and specifically lay piety.

37. *Some Thoughts*, in *The Works of Jonathan Edwards*, 4:337–38.

38. The Edwards literature is, of course, vast. But see Alan Heimert, *Religion and the American Mind* (Cambridge, Mass.: Harvard University Press, 1966); Harry S. Stout, "The Puritans and Edwards," in *Jonathan Edwards and the American Experience*, ed. Nathan O. Hatch and Harry S. Stout (New York: Oxford University Press, 1988); and Gerald R. McDermott, *One Holy and Happy Society: The Public Theology of Jonathan Edwards* (University Park: Pennsylvania State University Press, 1992).

39. *The Works of Jonathan Edwards*, vol. 8, *Ethical Writings*, ed. Paul Ramsey (New Haven: Yale University Press, 1989).

40. William J. Scheick, *The Writings of Jonathan Edwards: Theme, Motif, and Style* (College Station: Texas A&M Press, 1975), p. 137.

41. Janice Knight, "Learning the Language of God: Jonathan Edwards and the Typology of Nature," *WMQ* 48 (1991):531–51, demonstrates the centrality of such emanation or refulgence to Edwards's theology, as illustrated particularly in *Dissertation Concerning the End for Which God Created the World.*

Epilogue

1. See Phyllis Trible, *God and the Rhetoric of Sexuality* (Philadelphia: Fortress Press, 1978); Carol Ochs, *Behind the Sex of God: Toward a New Consciousness—Transcending Matriarchy and Patriarchy* (Boston: Beacon Press, 1977); Rosemary Radford Ruether, *New Woman/New Earth: Sexist Ideologies and Human Liberation* (San Francisco: Harper & Row, 1975).

2. See Patricia Caldwell, *The Puritan Conversion Narrative: The Beginnings of America Expression* (New York: Cambridge University Press, 1983); Kathleen M. Swain, "Come and Hear: Women's Puritan Evidences," in *American Women's Autobiography: Fea(s)ts of Memory*, ed. Margo Culley (Madison: University of Wisconsin Press, 1992), pp. 32–56; Susan Juster, "'In a Different Voice': Male and Female Narratives of Religious Conversion in Post-Revolutionary America," *AQ* 41 (1989):34–62; Barbara Leslie Epstein, *The Politics of Domesticity: Women, Evangelicalism, and Temperance in Nineteenth-Century America* (Middletown, Conn.: Wesleyan University Press, 1991).

Works Cited and Consulted

A Note on Court Records

The court records consulted here are those of the Superior Court of Judicature, which are housed in the Massachusetts Archives, Boston, Massachusetts. I have referred to the record book of indictments and convictions as *SCJ*; further documents kept by the clerk are preserved as the Suffolk County Files, also housed in the Massachusetts Archives.

Abbreviations

AmerS	*American Studies*
AQ	*American Quarterly*
EAL	*Early American Literature*
EIHC	*Essex Institute Historical Collections*
ELH	*Journal of English Literary History*
NEQ	*New England Quarterly*
QJS	*Quarterly Journal of Speech*
RALS	*Resources for American Literary Study*
SCJ	Record book of indictments, Supreme Court of Judicature, housed in Massachusetts Archives, Boston, Massachusetts
SPAS	*Studies in Puritan American Spirituality*
WMQ	*William and Mary Quarterly*

Primary Works

Adams, Eliphalet. *A Sermon, Preached on the Occasion of the Execution of Katherine Garret.* New London, 1738.

The Bay Psalm Book. "Preface." *The Puritans: A Sourcebook of Their Writings.* Ed. Perry Miller and Thomas H. Johnson. Rev. ed. New York: Harper & Row, 1963. 670–72.

Boston, Patience. *A Faithful Narrative of the Wicked Life and the Remarkable Conversion of Patience Boston.* Boston, 1738.

Bradstreet, Anne. *The Works of Anne Bradstreet.* Ed. Jeannine Hensley. Cambridge, Mass.: Harvard University Press, 1967.

Chauncy, Charles. A Letter . . . to Mr. George Wishart (1742). *The Great Awakening: Documents on The Revival of Religion, 1740–1745.* Ed. Richard L. Bushman. Chapel Hill: University of North Carolina Press, 1969. 116–21.

———. *Seasonable Thoughts on the Revivals.* Boston, 1743.

Colman, Benjamin. *An Argument for, and Persuasive Unto the Great and Important Duty of Family Worship.* Boston, 1728.

———. *Death and the Grave without Any Order. A Sermon Preached July 7, 1728. Being the Lord's Day after a Tragical Duel and Most Lamented Death.* Boston, 1728.

———. *Four Sermons Preached at the Lecture in Boston . . . to Which Is Added a Discourse on Ps. 122 [A Discourse on the Pleasure of Religious Worship, in Our Publick Assemblies].* Boston, 1717.

———. *The Friend of Christ, and of His People.* Boston, 1731.

———. *The Government and Improvement of Mirth, According to the Laws of Christianity.* Boston, 1707.

———. *The Hainous Nature of the Sin of Murder and the Great Happiness of Deliverance from it.* Boston, 1713.

———. *A Holy Walk with God. Funeral Sermon Preached upon the Death of the Truly Vertuous and Religious Grove Hirst.* Boston, 1717.

———. *The Honour and Happiness of the Vertuous Woman.* Boston, 1716.

———. *A Humble Discourse of the Incomprehensibleness of God.* Boston, 1715.

———. *It is a Fearful Thing to Fall into the Hands of the Living God. A Sermon Preached to Some Miserable Pirates On the Lord's Day before Their Execution.* Boston, 1726.

———. *The Judgment of Providence in the Hand of Christ: His Voice to Us in the Terrible Earthquake.* Boston, 1727.

————. *Parents and Children Should Be Together at the Lord's Table.* Boston, 1727.

————. *Practical Discourses upon the Parable of the Ten Virgins.* 1707; Boston, 1747.

————. *Reliquiae Turellae, et Lachrymae Paternae. The Father's Tears over His Daughter's Remains . . . To Which Are Added, Some large Memoirs of Her Life and Death.* Boston, 1735.

————. *Some of the Glories of Our Lord and Saviour Jesus Christ, Exhibited in Twenty Sacramental Discourses, Preached at Boston in New-England.* London, 1728.

Cotton, John. *Milk for Babes: Drawn From the Breasts of Both Testaments, Chiefly for the Spirituall Nourishment of Boston babes in either England.* London, 1646.

Danforth, Samuel. *The Call of Sodom Enquired Into.* Boston, 1674.

Dwight, Sereno. *The Life of President Edwards.* New York: G.&C.&H. Carvill, 1830.

Edwards, Jonathan. *Images and Shadows of Divine Things.* Ed. Perry Miller. New Haven: Yale University Press, 1948.

————. *A Jonathan Edwards Reader.* Ed. John E. Smith, Harry S. Stout, and Kenneth P. Minkema. New Haven: Yale University Press, 1995.

————. *The Works of Jonathan Edwards.* New Haven: Yale University Press, 1957–.

Eliot, John. *John Eliot's Indian Dialogues: A Study in Cultural Interaction* [Cambridge, Mass. 1671]. Ed. Henry W. Bowden and James P. Ronda. Westport, Conn.: Greenwood Press, 1980.

Foxcroft, Thomas. *Lessons of Caution to Young Sinners.* Boston, 1733.

Henry, Matthew. *The Communicant's Companion.* Eighth edition. Boston, 1723.

Hooker, Thomas. *The Application of Redemption.* London, 1656–7.

Hopkins, Samuel. *The Life and Character of the Late Reverend Mr. Jonathan Edwards.* Boston, 1765.

Mather, Cotton. *The Accomplished Singer.* Boston, 1724.

————. *The Call of the Gospel.* Boston, 1686.

————. *Faithful Warnings to Prevent Fearful Judgments.* Boston, 1704.

————. *Humiliations, Followd with Deliverances.* Boston, 1697.

————. *Magnalia Christi Americana; or, The Ecclisiastical History of New England* (London, 1702). Ed. Thomas Robbins. Hartford: Silas Andrus & Son, 1853. 2 vols.

————. *A Monitor for Communicants.* Boston, 1715.

———. *Ornaments for the Daughters of Zion, or The Character and Happiness of a Vertuous Woman.* Boston, 1692.

———. *Pillars of Salt.* Boston, 1699.

———. *A Sorrowful Spectacle.* Boston, 1715.

———. *Warnings from the Dead.* Boston, 1693.

Mather, Cotton, and others. *A Course of Sermons on Early Piety.* Boston, 1721.

Mather, Increase. *The Folly of Sinning.* Boston, 1699.

———. *A Sermon Occasioned by the Execution of a Man Found Guilty of Murder.* Boston, 1686.

Pike, John. *Journal of the Rev. John Pike,* Massachusetts Historical Society, *Proceedings* (14 September 1875), 134.

Rogers, John. *Death the Certain Wages of Sin.* Boston, 1701.

Sewall, Samuel. *The Diary of Samuel Sewall, 1674–1729.* Ed. Halsey Thomas. 2 vols. New York: Farrar, Straus, & Giroux, 1973.

Taylor, Edward. *The Poems of Edward Taylor.* Ed. Donald E. Stanford. New Haven: Yale University Press, 1960.

Turell, Ebenezer. "Detection of Witchcraft." *Collections of the Massachusetts Historical Society,* second series, 10 (1823):6–22.

———. *The Life and Character of the Reverend Benjamin Colman.* Boston, 1747.

Ward, Nathaniel. *The Simple Cobler of Aggawam in America* (1647). Ed. Paul M. Zall. Lincoln: University of Nebraska Press, 1969.

Willard, Samuel. *Impenitent Sinners Warned.* Boston, 1698.

Williams, John. *Warnings to the Unclean.* Boston, 1699.

Williams, Roger. *A Key into the Language of America* (1643). Ed. John J. Teunissen and Evelyn J. Hinz. Detroit: Wayne State University Press, 1973.

Winthrop, John. *Winthrop's Journal, "History of New England," 1630–1649.* Ed. James Kendall Hosmer. New York, 1908.

Secondary Works

Adams, Howard C. "Benjamin Colman: A Critical Biography." Diss., Pennsylvania State University, 1976.

Alter, Robert. *The Art of Biblical Poetry.* New York: Basic Books, 1985.

Ardener, Shirley, ed. *Perceiving Women.* London: Malaby Press, 1975.

Beales, Ross W., Jr. "In Search of the Historical Child: Miniature Adulthood and Youth in Colonial New England." *AQ* 27 (1979):379–98.

Becker, Laura L. "Ministers vs. Laymen: The Singing Controversy in Puritan New England, 1720–1740." *NEQ* 55 (1982):76–96.

Bercovitch, Sacvan. *The Puritan Origins of the American Self.* New Haven: Yale University Press, 1975.

Bloch, Ruth. "Women, Love, and Virtue in the Thought of Edwards and Franklin." *Benjamin Franklin, Jonathan Edwards, and the Representation of American Culture.* Ed. Barbara B. Oberg and Harry S. Stout. New York: Oxford University Press, 1993. 134–51.

Bonomi, Patricia U. *Under the Cope of Heaven: Religion, Society, and Politics in Colonial America.* New York: Oxford University Press, 1986.

Bosco, Ronald A. "Early American Gallows Literature: An Annotated Checklist." *RALS* 8 (1978):81–107.

———. "Lectures at the Pillory: The Early American Execution Sermon." *AQ* 30 (1978):156–76.

Boyer, Paul, and Stephen Nissenbaum. *Salem Possessed: The Social Origins of Witchcraft.* Cambridge, Mass.: Harvard University Press, 1974.

Bragdon, Kathleen Joan. "Crime and Punishment among the Indians of Massachusetts, 1675–1750." *Ethnohistory* 28 (1981):23–32.

Breitwieser, Mitchell. *American Puritanism and the Defense of Mourning: Religion, Grief, and Ethnology in Mary White Rowlandson's Captivity Narrative.* Madison: University of Wisconsin Press, 1990.

Brooks, Charles. *History of the Town of Medford, from Its First Settlement, in 1630, to the Present Time, 1855.* Boston: James M. Usher, 1855.

Brown, Anne S. "Visions of Community in Eighteenth-Century Essex County: Chebacco Parish and the Great Awakening," *EIHC* 125 (1989):237–62.

Burke, Peter. *Popular Culture in Early Modern Europe.* New York: Harper Torchbooks, 1978.

Burnston, Sharon Ann. "Babies in the Well: An Underground Insight into Deviant Behavior in Eighteenth-Century Philadelphia." *The Pennsylvania Magazine* 106 (1982):151–86.

Bushman, Richard L. *From Puritan to Yankee: Character and the Social Order in Connecticut, 1690–1765.* Cambridge, Mass.: Harvard University Press, 1967.

Butler, Jon. *Awash in a Sea of Faith: Christianizing the American People.* Cambridge, Mass.: Harvard University Press, 1990.

———. "Enthusiasm Described and Decried: The Great Awakening as Interpretive Fiction." *Journal of American History* 69 (1982):305–25.

Bynum, Caroline Walker. "'. . . And Woman His Humanity': Female Imagery in the Religious Writing of the Later Middle Ages." *Gender and*

Religion: On the Complexity of Symbols. Ed. Caroline Walker Bynum, Stevan Harrell, and Paula Richman. Boston: Beacon Press, 1986. 257–88.

———. "Introduction: The Complexity of Symbols." *Gender and Religion: On the Complexity of Symbols.* Ed. Caroline Walker Bynum, Stevan Harrell, and Paula Richman. Boston, Beacon Press, 1986. 1–20.

———. *Jesus as Mother: Studies in the Spirituality of the High Middle Ages.* Berkeley: University of California Press, 1982.

———. "Women's Stories, Women's Symbols: A Critique of Victor Turner's Theory of Liminality." *Fragmentation and Redemption: Essays on Gender and the Human Body in Medieval Religion.* New York: Zone Books, 1992. 27–51.

Caldwell, Patricia. *The Puritan Conversion Narrative: The Beginnings of American Expression.* New York: Cambridge University Press, 1983.

———. "The Silent Woman in Early American Literature." Center for American Culture Studies, Columbia University. Spring, 1988.

Chapman, Clayton Harding. "Benjamin Colman and His Daughters." *NEQ* 26 (1953):169–92.

———. "Benjamin Colman and Philomela." *NEQ* 42 (1969):214–31.

Chase, Gilbert. *American Music from the Pilgrims to the Present.* Rev. 2nd ed. Urbana and Chicago: University of Chicago Press, 1987.

Coffin, Joshua. *A Sketch of the History of Newbury, Newburyport, and West Newbury.* Boston: Samuel G. Drake, 1845.

Cohen, Daniel A. *Pillars of Salt, Monuments of Grace: New England Crime Literature and the Origins of American Popular Culture 1674–1860.* New York: Oxford University Press, 1993.

Colacurcio, Michael. "Footsteps of Ann Hutchinson: The Context of *The Scarlet Letter.*" *ELH* 39 (1972).

Conforti, Joseph. "The Invention of the Great Awakening, 1795–1842." *EAL* 26 (1991):99–118.

Cott, Nancy F. *The Bonds of Womanhood: "Women's Sphere" in New England, 1780–1835.* New Haven: Yale University Press, 1977.

Cowell, Pattie. "Puritan Women Poets in America." *Puritan Poets and Poetics: Seventeenth-Century American Poetry in Theory and Practice.* Ed. Peter White. University Park: Pennsylvania State University, 1985. 21–32.

———. *Women Poets in Pre-Revolutionary America 1650–1775: An Anthology.* Troy, N.Y.: The Whitston Publishing Company, 1981.

Cowing, Cedric B. "Sex and Preaching in the Great Awakening." *AQ* 20 (1968):624–44.

Davies, Horton. *Worship and Theology in England from Andrews to Baxter and Fox, 1673–1690.* Princeton, N.J.: Princeton University Press, 1975.

———. *Worship and Theology in England from Watts and Wesley to Maurice, 1690–1850.* Princeton, N.J.: Princeton University Press, 1961.

Davis, Natalie Zemon. *Society and Culture in Early Modern France.* Stanford, Calif.: Stanford University Press, 1975.

———. "Some Tasks and Themes in the Study of Popular Religion." *The Pursuit of Holiness in Late Medieval and Renaissance Religion.* Ed. Charles Trinkaus and Heiko A. Oberman. Leiden: E. J. Brill, 1974. 307–36.

———. *Women on the Margins: Three Seventeenth-Century Lives.* Cambridge, Mass.: Harvard University Press, 1995.

Dayton, Cornelia Hughes. *Women before the Bar: Gender, Law and Society in Connecticut, 1639–1789.* Chapel Hill: University of North Carolina Press, 1995.

Delattre, Roland André. *Beauty and Sensibility in the Thought of Jonathan Edwards: An Essay on Aesthetics and Theological Ethics.* New Haven: Yale University Press, 1968.

Delbanco, Andrew. *The Puritan Ordeal.* Cambridge. Mass.: Harvard University Press, 1989.

Demos, John Putnam. *Entertaining Satan: Witchcraft and the Culture of Early New England.* New York: Oxford University Press, 1982.

Dodds, Elisabeth D. *Marriage to a Difficult Man: The "Uncommon Union" of Jonathan and Sarah Edwards.* Philadelphia: The Westminster Press, 1971.

Douglas, Ann. *The Feminization of American Culture.* New York: Alfred A. Knopf, 1977.

Douglas [Wood], Ann. "'The Fashionable Diseases': Women's Complaints and Their Treatment in Nineteenth-Century America." *Journal of Interdisciplinary History* 4 (1973):25–52.

Douglas, Mary. *Natural Symbols: Explorations in Cosmology.* 1970. New York: Pantheon Books, 1982.

Dunn, Mary Maples. "'Saints and Sisters': Congregational and Quaker Women in the Early Colonial Period." *Women in American Religion.* Ed. Janet Wilson James. Philadelphia: University of Pennsylvania Press, 1980. 27–46.

Elliott, Emory. "The Development of the Puritan Funeral Sermon and Elegy: 1660–1750." *EAL* 15 (1980):151–64.

———. *Power and the Pulpit in Puritan New England.* Princeton: Princeton University Press, 1975.

Ellison, Julie. "The Sociology of 'Holy Indifference': Sarah Edwards' Narrative." *American Literature* 56 (1984):479–95.

Epstein, Barbara Leslie. *The Politics of Domesticity: Women, Evangelicalism, and Temperance in Nineteenth-Century America.* Middletown, Conn.: Wesleyan University Press, 1981.

Erikson, Kai T. *Wayward Puritans: A Study in the Sociology of Deviance.* New York: John Wiley & Sons, 1966.

Ezell, Margaret J. M. *Writing Women's Literary History.* Baltimore: Johns Hopkins University Press, 1993.

Fisken, Beth Wynne. "Mary Sydney's *Psalmes*: Education and Wisdom." *Silent But for the Word: Tudor Women as Patrons, Translators, and Writers of Religious Works.* Ed. Margaret Patterson Hannay. Kent, Ohio: Kent State University Press, 1985. 166–183.

Flaherty, David H. *Privacy in Colonial New England.* Charlottesville: University Press of Virginia, 1967.

Foucault, Michel. *Discipline and Punish: The Birth of the Prison.* Trans. Alan Sheridan. New York: Vintage, 1979.

Friedman, Susan Stanford. "Creativity and the Childbirth Metaphor: Gender Difference in Literary Discourse." *Speaking of Gender.* Ed. Elaine Showalter. New York: Routledge, 1989. 73–100.

Gaustad, Edwin. *The Great Awakening in New England* (New York, 1957). Goucester, Mass.: P. Smith, 1965.

Goen, C. C. *Revivalism and Separatism in New England, 1740–1800.* New Haven: Yale University Press, 1962.

Green, C. M., and S. V. Manohar. "Neonaticide and Hysterical Denial of Pregnancy." *British Journal of Psychiatry* 156 (1990):121–23.

Greven, Philip. *Four Generations: Population, Land, and Family in Colonial Andover, Massachusetts.* Ithaca, N.Y.: Cornell University Press, 1970.

Gustafson, Sandra. "Jonathan Edwards and the Reconstruction of 'Feminine' Speech." *American Literary History* (1994): 185–212.

Hall, David D. *The Antinomian Controversy, 1636–1638; A Documentary History.* Middletown, Conn.: Wesleyan University Press, 1968.

———. *The Faithful Shepherd: A History of the New England Ministry in the Seventeenth Century.* Chapel Hill: University of North Carolina Press, 1972.

———. "Toward a History of Popular Religion in Early New England." *WMQ* 41 (1984):49–55.

———. *Witch-hunting in Seventeenth-Century New England: A Documentary History, 1638–1692.* Boston: Northeastern University Press, 1991.

————. *Worlds of Wonder, Days of Judgment: Popular Religious Belief in Early New England.* New York: Alfred A. Knopf, 1989.

Hall, Timothy. *Contested Boundaries: Itineracy and the Reshaping of the Colonial American Religious World.* Durham, N.C.: Duke University Press, 1994.

Hambrick-Stowe, Charles E. *The Practice of Piety: Puritan Devotional Discipline in Seventeenth-Century New England.* Chapel Hill: University of North Carolina Press, 1982.

Hamm, Charles. *Music in the New World.* New York: W. W. Norton, 1983.

Harper, George W. "Clericalism and Revival: The Great Awakening in Boston as a Pastoral Phenomenon." *NEQ* 57 (1984): 554–66.

Hay, Douglas et al. *Albion's Fatal Tree: Crime and Society in Eighteenth Century England.* New York: Pantheon Books, 1978.

Heimert, Alan. *Religion and the American Mind.* Cambridge, Mass.: Harvard University Press, 1966.

Heyrman, Christine Leigh. *Commerce and Culture: The Maritime Communities of Colonial Massachusetts, 1690–1750.* New York: W. W. Norton, 1984.

————. "Specters of Subversion, Societies of Friends: Dissent and the Devil in Provincial Essex County, Massachusetts." *Saints and Revolutionaries: Essays on Early American History.* Ed. David Hall, John M. Murrin, Thad W. Tate. New York: W. W. Norton & Company, 1984. 38–74.

Hiner, N. Ray. "Adolescence in Eighteenth-Century America." *History of Childhood Quarterly: A Journal of Psychohistory* 3 (1975):251–80.

Hirschmann, V. J., and E. Schwartz. "Structural Analysis of Female Infanticide." *Psychotherapy* 8 (1958):1–20.

Hobby, Elaine. *Virtue of Necessity: English Women's Writing 1649–88.* London: Virago Press, 1988.

Hoffer, Peter C., and N. E. H. Hull. *Murdering Mothers: Infanticide in England and New England, 1558–1803.* New York: New York University Press, 1984.

Holifield, E. Brooks. *The Covenant Sealed: The Development of Puritan Sacramental Theology in Old and New England, 1570–1720.* New Haven: Yale University Press, 1974.

Hornberger, Theodore. "Benjamin Colman and the Enlightenment." *NEQ* 12 (1939):227–40.

Hull, N. E. H. *Female Felons: Women and Serious Crime in Colonial Massachusetts.* Urbana: University of Illinois Press, 1987.

Innes, Stephen. *Labor in a New Land: Economy and Society in Seventeenth-Century Springfield.* Princeton: Princeton University Press, 1983.

Irwin, Joyce. "The Theology of 'Regular Singing'" *NEQ* 51 (1978):176–92.

Jackson, Mark. *New-Born Child Murder: Women, Illegitimacy, and the Courts in Eighteenth-Century England.* Manchester, U.K.: Manchester University Press, 1996.

Johnson, Parker, "Jonathan Edwards's 'Personal Narrative' and the Northampton Controversy." *Cithara* 26 (1987):31–47.

Juster, Susan. *Disorderly Women: Sexual Politics and Evangelicalism in Revolutionary New England.* Ithaca, N.Y.: Cornell University Press, 1994.

———. "'In A Different Voice': Male and Female Narratives of Religious Conversion in Post-Revolutionary America." *AQ* 41 (1989):34–62.

Kamensky, Jane. "Words, Witches, and Woman Trouble: Witchcraft, Disorderly Speech, and Gender Boundaries in Puritan New England." *EIHC* 128 (1992):286-302.

Karlsen, Carol F. *The Devil in the Shape of a Woman: Witchcraft in Colonial New England.* New York: W. W. Norton, 1987.

Kesselring, Marion L. *Hawthorne's Reading, 1828–1850.* New York: New York Public Library, 1949.

Kibbey, Ann. *The Interpretation of Material Shapes in Puritanism: A Study of Rhetoric, Prejudice, and Violence.* Cambridge: Cambridge University Press, 1986.

King, John Owen. *The Iron of Melancholy: Structures of Spiritual Conversion in America from the Puritan Conscience to Victorial Neurosis.* Middletown: Wesleyan University Press, 1981.

Knight, Janice. "Learning the Language of God: Jonathan Edwards and the Typology of Nature." *WMQ,* third series, 48 (1991):531–51.

———. *Orthodoxies in Massachusetts: Rereading American Puritanism.* Cambridge, Mass.: Harvard University Press, 1994.

Lambert, Frank. "The Great Awakening as Artifact: George Whitefield and the Construction of Intercolonial Revival, 1739–1745." *Church History* 60 (1991):223–46.

Lang, Amy Schrager. *Prophetic Woman: Anne Hutchinson and the Problem of Dissent in the Literature of New England.* Berkeley: University of California Press, 1987.

Langbein, John. *The London Hanged: Crime and Civil Society in the Eighteenth Century.* New York: Cambridge University Press, 1992.

Laqueur, Thomas. "Bodies, Details, and the Humanitarian Narrative." *The New Cultural History.* Ed. Lynn Hunt. Berkeley: University of California Press, 1989. 176–204.

Lazenby, Walter. "Exhortations to Exorcism: Cotton Mather's Sermons to Murderers." *QJS* 57 (1971):50–56.

Leavitt, Judith Walzer. *Brought to Bed: Childbearing in America, 1750 to 1950.* New York: Oxford University Press, 1986.

Leverenz, David. *The Language of Puritan Feeling: An Exploration in Literature, Psychology, and Social History.* New Brunswick, N.J.: Rutgers University Press, 1980.

Lothrop, Samuel K. *A History of the Church in Brattle Street, Boston.* Boston: William Crosby and H. P. Nichols, 1851.

Lovelace, Richard F. *The American Pietism of Cotton Mather: The Origins of American Evangelicalism.* Grand Rapids, Mich.: William B. Eerdman's, 1979.

Lucas, Paul R. "'An Appeal to the Learned': The Mind of Solomon Stoddard." *Puritan New England: Essays on Religion, Society, and Culture.* Ed. Alden T. Vaughan and Francis J. Bremer. New York: St. Martin's Press, 1977. 326–45.

———. *Valley of Discord: Church and Society along the Connecticut River, 1636–1725.* Hanover, N.H.: University Press of New England, 1976.

Mack, Phyllis. *Visionary Women: Ecstatic Prophecy in Seventeeth-Century England.* Berkeley: University of California Press, 1992.

Malmsheimer, Lonna M. "Daughters of Zion: New England Roots of American Feminism." *NEQ* 50 (1977):484–504.

Marshall, Madeline Forell. *The Poetry of Elizabeth Singer Rowe (1674–1737).* Lewiston, New York: Edwin Mellon Press, 1987.

Masson, Margaret W. "The Typology of the Female as a Model for the Regenerate: Puritan Preaching, 1690–1730." *Signs: Journal of Women in Culture and Society* 2 (1976):304–15.

McDermott, Gerald R. *One Holy and Happy Society: The Public Theology of Jonathan Edwards.* University Park: Pennsylvania State University Press, 1992.

Mercadente, Linda. *Gender, Doctrine, and God: The Shakers and Contemporary Theology.* Nashville: Abingdon Press, 1990.

Miller, Perry. *Jonathan Edwards.* 1949: Amherst: University of Massachusetts Press, 1981.

———. "Jonathan Edwards' Sociology of the Great Awakening." *NEQ* 21 (1948):50–77.

———. *The New England Mind: From Colony to Province.* Cambridge, Mass.: Harvard University Press, 1953.

———. *The New England Mind: The Seventeenth Century.* Cambridge, Mass.: Harvard University Press, 1939.

Minnick, Wayne C. "The New England Execution Sermon." *Speech Monographs* 35 (1968):77–89.

Moran, Gerald F. "'Sisters' in Christ: Women and the Church in Seventeenth-Century New England." *Women in American Religion.* Ed. Janet Wilson James. Philadelphia: University of Pennsylvania Press, 1980. 47–65.

———. "'The Hidden Ones': Women and Religion in Puritan New England." *Triumph over Silence: Women in Protestant History.* Ed. Richard L. Greaves. Westport, Conn.: Greenwood Press, 1985. 125-149.

Morgan, Edmund S. *The Puritan Family: Religion and Domestic Relations in Seventeenth-Century New England.* Rev. ed. New York: Harper and Row, 1966.

———. "The Puritan's Marriage with God." *South Atlantic Quarterly* 48 (1949):107–12.

Morris, David. *The Religious Sublime, Christian Poetry, and Critical Tradition in Eighteenth-Century England.* Lexington: University Press of Kentucky, 1972.

Morss, Myra Brayton. "Mrs. Jane Turell." *Medford Historical Register* 5 (1902): 1–12.

"Mrs. Jane Turell." *North American Review* 93 (July, 1861):22–35.

Nash, Gary. *The Urban Crucible: The Northern Seaports and the Origins of the American Revolution.* Abridged version. Cambridge, Mass.: Harvard University Press, 1986.

Niehbuhr, H. Richard. *The Social Sources of Denominationalism.* 1929. New York: H. Holt and Co., 1957.

Norton, Mary Beth. *Founding Mothers and Fathers: Gendered Power and the Forming of American Society.* New York: Alfred A. Knopf, 1996.

———. "'My Resting Reaping Times': Sarah Osborn's Defense of her 'Unfeminine' Activities, 1767." *Signs* 2 (1976):515–29.

Ochs, Carol. *Behind the Sex of God: Toward a New Consciousness—Transcending Matriarchy and Patriarchy.* Boston: Beacon Press, 1977.

Oldham, James C. "On Pleading the Belly: A History of the Jury of Matrons." *Criminal Justice History* 5 (1984):1–64.

Piersen, William D. *Black Yankees: The Development of an Afro-American Subculture in Eighteenth-Century New England.* Amherst: University of Massachusetts Press, 1988.

Pitt, Steven E., and Erin M. Bale, "Neonaticide, Infanticide, and Filicide: A Review of the Literature." *Bulletin of American Academy of Psychiatry and the Law* 23 (1991): 375–86.

Pope, Robert G. *The Half-Way Covenant: Church Membership in Puritan New England.* Princeton: Princeton University Press, 1969.

————. "New England vs. the New England Mind: The Myth of Declension." *Puritan New England: Essays on Religion, Society, and Culture.* Ed. Alden T. Vaughan and Francis J. Bremer. New York: St. Martin's Press, 1977. 314–25.

Porterfield, Amanda. *Female Piety in Puritan New England: The Emergence of Humanism.* New York: Oxford University Press, 1992.

————. *Feminine Spirituality in America: From Sarah Edwards to Martha Graham.* Philadelphia: Temple University Press, 1980.

————. "The Mother in Eighteenth-Century American Conceptions of Man and God." *Journal of Psychohistory* 15 (1987):189–205.

Proudfoot, Wayne. "From Theology to a Science of Religions: Jonathan Edwards and William James on Religious Affections." *Harvard Theological Review* 82 (1989):159–62.

————. *Religious Experience.* Berkeley: University of California Press, 1985.

Resnick, P. J. "Murder of the Newborn: a Psychiatric Review of Neonaticide." *American Journal of Psychiatry* 126 (1970):1414–20.

Ricoeur, Paul. "The Specificity of Religious Language." *Semeia: An Experimental Journal for Biblical Criticism* 4 (1975):1–145.

————. "The Symbol Gives Rise to the Thought." *Ways of Understanding Religion.* Ed. Walter H. Capps. New York: Macmillan, 1972. 304–17.

Rose, Lou. "A Memorable Trial in Seventeenth-Century Maryland." *Maryland Historical Magazine* 83 (1988):365–68.

Ruether, Rosemary Radford. *New Woman/New Earth: Sexist Ideologies and Human Liberation.* San Francisco: Harper & Row, 1975.

Rutman, Darrett B. "New England as Idea and Society Revisited." *WMQ* 41 (1984):56–61.

Ryskamp, Charles. "The New England Sources of *The Scarlet Letter*." *American Literature* 31 (1959):257–72.

Sabean, David Warren. *Power in the Blood: Popular Culture and Village Discourse in Early Modern Germany.* Cambridge: Cambridge University Press, 1984.

Sadowy, Chester. "Benjamin Colman (1673–1747) as Literary Artist." Ph.D. diss. University of Pennsylvania, 1974.

Scheick, William J. "Authority and Witchery: Cotton Mather's *Ornaments* and Mary English's Acrostic." *Arizona Quarterly* 51 (1995):1–32.

————. *The Writings of Jonathan Edwards: Theme, Motif, and Style.* College Station: Texas A&M Press, 1975.

Schmotter, James W. "Ministerial Careers in Eighteenth-Century New England: The Social Context, 1700–1760." *Journal of Social History* 9 (1975–76):253–55.

Scholten, Catherine M. *Childbearing in American Society, 1650–1850.* New York, 1985.

———. "'On the Importance of the Obstetrick Art': Changing Customs of Childbirth in America, 1760 to 1825." *WMQ,* third series, 34 (1977): 429–31.

Schweitzer, Ivy. *The Work of Self-Representation: Lyric Poetry in Colonial New England.* Chapel Hill: University of North Carolina Press, 1991.

Seeman, Erik R. "'She Died Like Good Old Jacob': Deathbed Scenes and Inversions of Power in New England, 1675–1775," *Publications of the American Antiquarian Society* 104 (1994):285–314.

Selement, George. "The Meeting of Elite and Popular Minds at Cambridge, New England, 1630–1645." *WMQ* 41 (1984):32–48.

Sharpe, J. A. *Crime in Seventeenth-Century England.* Cambridge: Cambridge University Press, 1983.

Shields, David S. *Civil Tongues and Polite Letters in British America.* Chapel Hill: The University of North Carolina Press, 1997.

———. "The Religious Sublime and New England Poets of the 1720s." *EAL* 19.3 (Winter 1984/85):231–48.

Shiels, Richard D. "The Feminization of American Congregationalism, 1730–1835." *AQ* 33 (1981):46–62.

Shipton, Kenneth K. "Ebenezer Turell." *Sibley's Harvard Graduates, vol. 6, 1713–1721.* Boston: Massachusetts Historical Society, 1942. 574–82.

———. "The New England Clergy of the 'Glacial Age'." Colonial Society of Massachusetts, *Publications* 32 (1937):24–54.

Sibley, John Langdon, and Clifford K. Shipton, eds. *Biographical Sketches of Those Who Attended Harvard College.* 17 vols. Cambridge: Charles William Sever/Harvard University Press and Boston: Massachusetts Historical Society, 1873–1975.

Silverman, Kenneth. *The Life and Times of Cotton Mather.* New York: Harper & Row, 1984.

Smith-Rosenberg, Carroll. *Disorderly Conduct: Visions of Gender in Victorian America.* New York: Oxford University Press, 1985.

Spierenburg, Pieter. *The Spectacle of Suffering.* New York: Cambridge University Press, 1984.

Sprague, William B. *Annals of the American Pulpit.* 9 vols. New York: Robert Carter and Brothers, 1857–69.

St. George, Robert. "'Heated' Speech and Literacy in Seventeenth-Century New England." *Publications of the Colonial Society of Massachusetts,* vol. 63. *Collections: Seventeenth-Century New England.* Ed. David D.

Hall and David Grayson Allen. Boston: Colonial Society of Massachusetts, 1984. 275–321.

Stannard, David E. *The Puritan Way of Death: A Study in Religion, Culture, and Social Change.* New York: Oxford University Press, 1977.

Stout, Harry S. "The Puritans and Edwards." *Jonathan Edwards and the American Experience.* Ed. Nathan O. Hatch and Harry S. Stout. New York: Oxford University Press, 1988. 142-159.

Stout, Harry S., and Peter Onuf. "James Davenport and the Great Awakening in New London." *Journal of American History,* 71 (1983):556–78.

Swaim, Kathleen M. "Come and Hear: Women's Puritan Evidences." *American Women's Autobiography: Fea(s)ts of Memory.* Ed. Margo Culley. Madison: University of Wisconsin Press, 1992. 32–56.

Sweet, Leonard I. *The Minister's Wife: Her Role in Nineteenth-Century American Evangelicalism.* Philadelphia: Temple University Press, 1983.

Thickstun, Margaret Olofson. "Mothers in Israel: The Puritan Rhetoric of Child-Bearing." *Praise Disjoined: Changing Patterns of Salvation in Seventeenth-Century English Literature.* Ed. William P. Shaw. New York: Peter Lang, 1991. 71–87.

Thompson, Roger. "Adolescent Culture in Colonial Massachusetts." *Journal of Family History* (1984):127–144.

———. "'Holy Watchfulness' and Communal Conformism: The Functions of Defamation in Early New England Communities." *NEQ* 56 (1983):504–22.

———. *Sex in Middlesex: Popular Mores in a Massachusetts County, 1649–1699.* Amherst: University of Massachusetts Press, 1986.

Toulouse, Teresa. *The Art of Prophesying: New England Sermons and the Shaping of Belief.* Athens: University of Georgia Press, 1987.

Towner, Lawrence W. "True Confessions and Dying Warnings in Colonial New England." *Publications of the Colonial Society of Massachusetts,* vol. 59, *Collectors: Sibley's Heirs* (1982):523–39.

Tracy, Patricia J. *Jonathan Edwards, Pastor: Religion and Society in Eighteenth-Century Northampton.* New York: Hill and Wang, 1980.

Trible, Phyllis. *God and the Rhetoric of Sexuality.* Philadelphia: Fortress Press, 1978.

Turner, Eldon R. "Earwitnesses to Resonance in Space: An Interpretation of Puritan Psalmody in Early Eighteenth-Century New England," *AmerS* 25 (1984):25–47.

Turner, Victor. *A Forest of Symbols: Aspects of Ndembu Ritual.* Ithaca, N.Y.: Cornell University Press, 1967.

———. *The Ritual Process: Structure and Anti-Structure.* Chicago: Aldine, 1969.

Ulrich, Laurel Thatcher. *Good Wives: Image and Reality in the Lives of Women in Northern New England 1650–1750.* New York: Oxford University Press, 1983.

———. *A Midwife's Tale: The Life of Martha Ballard. Based on Her Diary, 1783–1812.* New York: Random House, 1990.

———. "Vertuous Woman Found: New England Ministerial Literature, 1668–1735." *Women in American Religion.* Ed. Janet Wilson James. Philadelphia: University of Pennsylvania Press, 1980. 67–87.

Verduin, Kathleen. "'Our Cursed Natures': Sexuality and the Puritan Conscience." *NEQ* 56 (1983):220–37.

Wall, Helena. *Fierce Communion: Family and Community in Early America.* Cambridge, Mass.: Harvard University Press, 1990.

Warner, Marina. *Alone of All Her Sex: The Myth and Cult of the Virgin Mary.* 1976. New York: Vintage Books, 1983.

Watts, Emily Stipes. *The Poetry of American Women from 1632 to 1945.* Austin: University of Texas, 1977.

Wells, Robert V. "Illegitimacy and Bridal Pregnancy in Colonial America." *Bastardy and its Comparative History.* Ed. Peter Laslett, Karla Oosterveen, and Richard M. Smith. Cambridge: Harvard University Press, 1980. 149–161.

Welter, Barbara. *Dimity Convictions: The American Woman in the Nineteenth Century.* Athens: Ohio University Press, 1976.

Wertz, Richard A., and Dorothy C. Wertz. *Lying-In: A History of Childbirth in America.* New York: The Free Press, 1977.

Wild, Helen T. "The Congregational Church in Medford." *The Medford Historical Register* 37.1 (March 1934):1–10.

Williams, Daniel E. "'Behold a Tragick Scene, Strangely Changed into a Theater of Mercy': The Structure and Significance of Criminal Conversion Narratives in Early New England." *AQ* 38 (1986):327–47.

———. "Puritans and Pirates: A Confrontation between Cotton Mather and William Fly in 1726." *EAL* 22 (1987):233–51.

———. "Rogues, Rascals, and Scoundrels: The Underworld Literature of Early America." *American Studies* (1983):5–19.

Wilson, Adrian. "The Ceremony of Childbirth and Its Interpretation." *Women as Mothers in Pre-Industrial England.* Ed. Valerie Fildes. New York: Routledge, 1990.

Winship, Michael P. "Behold the Bridegroom Cometh! Marital Imagery in Massachusetts Preaching, 1630–1730." *EAL* 27 (1992):170–84.

Winslow, Ola Elizabeth. *Meetinghouse Hill: 1630–1783.* 1952. New York: W. W. Norton, 1972.

Yarbrough, Steven R., and John C. Adams. *Delightful Convictions: Jonathan Edwards and the Rhetoric of Conversion.* Westport, Conn.: Greenwood Press, 1993.

Youngs, J. William T. Jr. *God's Messengers: Religious Leadership in Colonial New England, 1700–1750.* Baltimore and London: The Johns Hopkins University Press, 1976.

Zuckerman, Michael. *Peaceable Kingdoms: New England Towns in the Eighteenth Century.* New York: Alfred A. Knopf, 1970.

Index